INCULTURATION

Intercultural and Interreligious Studies

edited by

Arij A. Roest Crollius, S.J.

XIX

CENTRE "CULTURES & RELIGIONS" – PONTIFICAL GREGORIAN UNIVERSITY

UNITY IN DIVERSITY

A Philosophical and Ethical Study
of the Javanese Concept of *Keselarasan*

by
ANDREAS YUMARMA

ROME 1996

ISBN 88-7652-726-5

EDITRICE PONTIFICIA UNIVERSITÀ GREGORIANA
Piazza della Pilotta, 35 - 00187 Roma

TABLE OF CONTENTS

ACKNOWLEDGMENTS

I am very happy to express my deep gratitude to all those who have helped me towards the completion of this work. First of all, I am deeply indebted to Father Arij A. Roest Crollius, S.J., for his scholarly guidance, careful reading and positive criticism which have offered both constant encouragement and stimulating direction. I appreciate his spirit of dedication and availability. To the Faculty of Philosophy at the Gregorian University which has granted me the occasion to do this doctoral work, I offer my gratitude. My thanks are due to Fathers Richard Gleeson and Tom Michel, S.J., for their suggestions at the initial stage of this work. I would like to express my gratitude to Father Nico Sprokel S.J., for his inspiring discussions and valuable advice.

I am indebted to Dr. Bernard Arps, of the Faculty of Art, Department of Languages and Culture of Southeast Asia and Oceania at the University of Leiden and Dr. Nigel Philip, of the School of Oriental and African Studies at the University of London, for their interest and suggestions. Many thanks to the library of the School of Oriental and African Studies (S.O.A.S.) at the University of London, the Library at the University of Leiden and the library of Koninklijk Instituut voor Taal-, Land- en Volkenkunde (KITLV) in Leiden, for their facilities and services which were of great help to me, as well as to those of the libraries of ISMEO and the Pontificio Instituto di Studi Arabi e d'Islamistica in Rome. To

Father Huub Flohr, Mr. Supriyanto, L. Murbandono and Koert Meijer, I would like to express my gratitude, for their care and help. Many thanks are due to Sr. Audrey Marie Rothweil, F.C.J.M., for the English correction and sympathetic understanding.

In particular, I would like to express my sincere gratitude to my Bishop, His Eminence Julius Cardinal Darmaatmadja, S.J., who granted me the opportunity to do this research and to complete my studies. Personally, I wish to thank Father Joe Übelmesser, S.J., and Mr. Erwin Lang for the financial assistance given to me during my study.

I address my gratitude to the previous rector of the Collegio Olandese, Bishop M.P.M Muskens, and the present rector Reverend Rud Smit. This is the college where I lived and enjoyed hospitality during these years of study. My thanks are due to the Jesus, Mary and Joseph (JMJ) sisters, the students at the Collegio Olandese, my Indonesian friends and the many others by name not mentioned herein, whom I also wish to remember with a grateful word, for their support and help. Finally I turn to my beloved parents and my dearest sisters and brothers to whom I am indebted for their prayer, love, affection and support.

Andreas Yumarma

PREFACE

With this 19th volume of INCULTURATION the subtitle has changed into "Intercultural and Interreligious Studies." Three specific qualities of this series are thus more clearly put into evidence. On the first place, the word "studies," without taking away the provisory character of these publications (they are not "manuals"), underscores the academic standards they strive to live up to. Secondly, the word "intercultural" has been chosen in order to express in a more understandable way the conviction of the initiators of this series that inculturation takes place in situations of intercultural contact or of acculturation, without, however, it being reduced to these situations. Finally, with "interreligious" is better articulated the fact that culture always has a religious conviction at its origin, just as a religion cannot live without a culture.

From now on, this series will be more restrictive about the studies published in it. It is the aim of these publications, to bring to the attention and knowledge of pastors, researchers and teachers various situations of "interculturality" and "interreligiosity" and their relevance for the process of inculturation, as also the multiple tasks of interreligious dialogue, which is one aspect of the process of inculturation.

It is with joy and gratitude that has been welcomed as the first volume in this new perspective the present study on "Harmony in Diversity." Fr. Yumarma has done a frontier-breaking work of research on his own culture and the instruments it offers to live in situations of interculturality and interreligiosity. The lessons contained in the term *Keselarasan* reach far beyond Java and Indonesia. The author has, however, also dared to show some negative sides of this very same concept. His philosophical background lends a particular depth to this work.

One may hope that this study will stimulate persons in different cultures and religions to explore the potential of inherited wisdom that can help to cope with situations of diversity, cultural, social or religious, in order to live towards a harmony that has the unmistakable elements of justice and peace.

Arij A. Roest Crollius, S.J.

ABBREVIATIONS

BKI	Bijdragen tot de Taal-, Land- en Volkenkunde
De Trin.	De Trinitate
GBHN	Garis Besar Haluan Negara (Principle Guidelines of the State)
Gk.	Greek
I.	Indonesian
Jav.	Javanese
KGPAA	Kanjeng Gusti Pangeran Adipati Arya (A title of the king of Surakarta)
L.	Latin
LP3ES	Lembaga Penelitian, Pendidikan dan Penerangan, Ekonomi dan Sosial
MPRS	Majelis Permusyaratan Rakyat Sementara (Provisional Supreme Council People of Indonesian Republic)
P.	Pali
R. Ng.	Raden Ngabei (Javanese title or rank in Javanese society)
Rep.	Republic
Skr.	Sanskrit
V.O.C.	Vereenigde Oostindische Compagnie, Dutch East India Company

INTRODUCTION

The dialectical significance of unity in diversity in the Javanese idea of *Keselarasan* is important in her culture and society. Moreover, *Keselarasan* is central to Javanese philosophy in the sense that the notion of *Keselarasan* penetrates Javanese thought pattern, lifestyle, and it is profoundly collegated to philosophical questions such as human existence, ethics, time, identity and communication.

The Javanese live the concept of *Keselarasan*. It is the basic concept for maintaining harmony in personal life and inter-societal relationships. The concept of *Keselarasan* incorporates the principles of peace (*rukun*), respect for others (*hormat*), and consciousness of one's own place (*empan papan*). Accordingly, human beings are integrated in a world wherein the powers of the cosmos regulate all nature in a balanced manner. This is what the concept of *Keselarasan* signifies harmony and unity in and among people, nature and God, and it includes the recognition of each being as needful of the other, as well as an appeal for conscious interdependence and the understanding of one's own rightful place. With regard to its formation and origin, comprehension of the concept of *Keselarasan* implies a wider understanding than that which is restricted to its ethical significance. Consequently, we herein define *Keselarasan* as a quality of relationship to which one assigns the characteristics of balance, concordance, avoidance of public conflict and the unified composite of the whole of reality.

There are many "inner wisdom movements" whereby the Javanese live such a concept of *Keselarasan* in mind, feelings and culture. Being conscious of and practising the principles of *Keselarasan* enable a human

1

being to live contentedly with his neighbour and his God. *Keselarasan* expresses a philosophical view of reality that extends to the cosmos, human beings and Javanese ethics. Therefore, it is not insignificant that *Keselarasan* is the basis of the famous Javanese tolerance and openness. It has contributed to the historical, cultural and ethical unity of the more than 13,667 islands of Indonesia, in which many tribes, with their local, diverse languages, 5 major religions and more than 209 indigenous beliefs, can live without loss of their identity.

It is this reason that I speak of the people who live *Keselarasan*. They remain open to nature and accept the various religions and diversity. It could be that the concept of *Keselarasan* becomes a critique for the synthesis derived from thesis and antithesis, since the formal religions which sometimes become exclusive towards other religion groups bring out the division among peoples. The process of dialectical synthesis might hide a culture of violence. The formal religions historically also inherit seeds of conflict and hidden violence. It happens because of the limitations of human understanding of the revelation and the interests of individuals or groups. In other words, religions such as Hinduism, Buddhism, Islam, and Christianity sometimes put aside the importance of coexistence and mutual cooperation as they are found in the concept of *Keselarasan*.

This study make use of descriptive, philosophical and cultural analysis. The descriptive method is used to pinpoint the geographical and historical background of the concept of *Keselarasan*. Through philosophical analysis I intend to systematically expose how those philosophical questions such as space and time, identity and otherness, communication, Javanese ethics and virtues, and unity in diversity form intrinsic aspect of *Keselarasan*. This study takes into account by means of analysis of culture and ethics, their important roles in thought, lifestyle and the comprehension of reality in which the expressions of the concept of *Keselarasan* exist and develop.

In Chapter I, I speak about the geographical and historical description of Indonesia as a backdrop to the staging of *Keselarasan*. The place of Javanese culture in Indonesia and their reciprocal relationships also interwine in our investigation of the origins of

Keselarasan.

The formation of the concept of *Keselarasan* is discussed in Chapter II. There I discuss Javanese thought and external influences on *Keselarasan.* Javanese thought will be discussed with reference to *Wédhatama* and *Wayang*, as primary sources, since the literature and culture of Java reach their height in these works. Influences from outside are posited because of the openness of *Keselarasan* whose core has existed in the authentic Javanese thought since the beginning, and these will be discussed. Furthermore, religious influences such as Hinduism, Buddhism, Islam and Christianity are shown to leave their impacts on the concept of *Keselarasan.* In addition, a comprehensive overview of *Keselarasan* is offered at the end of the chapter.

In Chapter III, I make an in-depth analysis of the concept of *Keselarasan.* An examination of the concept itself leads us to the philosophical themata of unity in diversity, space and time, identity and otherness, ethical postulata, communication and so forth. This chapter comprises the sum and substanstance of this book.

In conclusion, I discuss some of the particular aspects and expressions of the concept of *Keselarasan* in the Indonesian motto *Bhinneka Tunggal Ika* and Pancasila in Chapter IV. Furthermore, this last part also deals with a critique of the philosophical basis of dialogue.

The concept of *Keselarasan* becomes a new point of departure for philosophical reflection on unity in diversity. For this reason, a systematic comprehension of Javanese philosophical views and the search for new tenets for a dialogue of coexistence are in answer to this author's expectant hope for a contribution, however small, to world unity.

Finally, this study certainly could stimulate further advancement of Javanese philosophy in this author's future works; as well as contribute to the enrichment of Indonesian philosophy, if not philosophy in general.

CHAPTER I

THE GEOGRAPHICAL AND HISTORICAL DESCRIPTION
OF INDONESIA
AS THE CONTEXT OF THE CONCEPT *KESELARASAN*

I. GEOGRAPHICAL DESCRIPTION OF INDONESIA

The etymology of *"Indonesia"* shows its derivation from the Greek words *"Indos"* and *"Nesos"* which mean "Indian Islands." Logan, an Englishman used the name "Indonesia" for the first time in 1850.[1] Adolph Bastian[2] used the term "Indonesia" in 1884.[3] This later made the term "Indonesia" known widely as the geographical name indicating all the islands between the continent of Australia and that of Asia proper (including the Philippines and Madagascar). Previously, Indonesia had other names, i.e. *"Nusantara"* and *"Dutch East Indies."* Nusantara is derived from the Sanskrit words *"Nusa"* meaning "island," and *"antara"* meaning "other, distant, inside or among." Ki Hajar Dewantara[4] used this term for the first time to indicate "the Empire of Islands," a group of islands or an archipelago. The Indonesian people generally use the name "Indonesia" to describe the series of islands from the city of Sabang to that of Merauke.[5] "Indonesia" became the name of the country on the

---

[1] A. Gunawan Setiardjo, *Hak-Hak Asasi Manusia Berdasarkan Ideologi Pancasila* (Human Rights Based on the Ideology of Pancasila), Yogyakarta, 1993, p. 32.

[2] Adolph Bastian is a German ethnologist and geographer who introduced the word of "Indonesia" in 1884. Cf. Hans Helfritz, *Indonesien. Ein Reisebegleiter Java, Sumatra, Bali und Sulawesi (Celebes)*, Köln, 1988, p. 9.

[3] Cf. A. Gunawan Setiardjo, *Hak-Hak Asasi Manusia Berdasarkan Ideologi Pancasila* (Human Rights Based on the Ideology of Pancasila), Yogyakarta, 1993, p. 32.

[4] Ki Hajar Dewantoro is the founder of the Taman Siswa's movement in Java (beginning 20th century). This movement is a national organisation which concerns with education.

[5] "Sabang" is a town on the Island of Sumatra. "Merauke" is a town on the island of Irian Jaya. The expression of *"Sabang to Merauke"* points out the perspective of unity and the territory of the Indonesian archipelago.

28th of October 1928, when Indonesian youths made a pledge of "one country," "one nation," and "one language," namely "Indonesia."[6] This geographical and historical description of Indonesia serves as a background sketch for the treatment of *"keselarasan"*.

Geographically, Indonesia lays across the main sea between Eastern and Southern Asia.[7] It consists of islands forming a crossroad of two oceans, the Pacific and Indian Oceans. These islands stretch from the tip of the Malay Peninsula eastward to the Philippines and Australia. They extend from eastern longitude 95° to 142° and from northern latitude 10° to southern latitude 10° in the equatorial zone.[8] Bernard Vlekke describes Indonesia as the second largest group of islands in the world, after Greenland which holds first rank.[9] Indonesia is the largest country in Southeast Asia.

The area of the Republic of Indonesia is estimated at 9.8 million km^2, which consists of a land mass of more than 1.9 million km^2 and sea territory of about 7.9 million km^2.[10] The main islands are Sumatra, Java and Madura, Kalimantan or Borneo, Sulawesi, and Irian Jaya.[11] Besides these, there are many other smaller islands; the total number of which is

---

[6] The Indonesia's National Anthem, the "Indonesia Raya" composed by Wage Rudolf Supratman, was also introduced at the Indonesian Youth Congress on 28th October 1928. Thus the name of Indonesia was mentioned in the Indonesian National's Anthem; later the text of the Indonesian Proclamation of the Independence also explicitly used the name of "Indonesia" as follows : "Kami bangsa Indonesia dengan ini menyatakan kemerdekaan Indonesia. ....." (Herewith we, the Indonesian nation, proclaimed the Independence of Indonesia. ..."). Cf. M.P. M. Muskens, *Partner in Nation Building. The Catholic Church in Indonesia*, Aachen, 1979, p. 146; H. Johardin, et al., (eds.), *Indonesia 1988, An Official Handbook*, Jakarta, 1988, p. 39.

[7] Cf. B.H.M. Vlekke, *Nusantara. A History of Indonesia*, Leiden, 1959, p. 5.

[8] J. Pujasumarta, *L'Indonesia: Una Società Pluralistica*, in: *La Spiritualità dei Laici Secondo Il Detto del Concilio Vaticano II*, (Dissertation), Rome, 1987, p. 261.

[9] Cf. B.H.M. Vlekke, *Nusantara. A History of Indonesia*, Leiden, 1959, p. Xi.

[10] Biro Pusat Stastistik, *Stastistik Indonesia 1992. Stastitical Yearbook of Indonesia 1992*, Jakarta, 1992, p. 3.

[11] H. Johardin, et al. (eds.), *Indonesia 1988. An Official Handbook*, Jakarta, 1988, p. 15.

more than 13,667.[12]

From the geological perspective, the Indonesian archipelago has a characteristically rugged and volcanic mountain terrain with its concomitant fertile soil. Dense tropical forests generally cover the land,[13] thick, alluvial swamps sometimes cover the coastal plains. An equatorial double rainy season characterizes the weather of Indonesia.[14] There are two factors that cause this seasonal situation. First, the earth's rotation accounts for territorial changes from the tropic of Cancer to the tropic of Capricorn. Second, there is the factor of Indonesia's location between the continents of Asia and Australia.[15] This climatic situation enabled the indigenous inhabitants to search for islands, mountains and peninsulas by means of sailboats. They used astronomy or the position of the stars to navigate and to determine exact locations.[16]

The geographic location of Indonesia gives it a strategic place in trade and nautical routes. Indonesia is the bridge which spans the Indian and Pacific Oceans, two continents of Asia and of Australia. Thus Indonesia has contact with the continent of Asia, i.e., the Malay

---

[12] Biro Pusat Stastistik, *Stastistik Indonesia 1992. Statistical Yearbook of Indonesia 1992*, Jakarta, 1992, p. 3.

[13] Cf. H. Johardin, et al., (eds.), *Indonesia 1988. An Official Handbook*, Jakarta, 1988, p. 15.

[14] Cf. T. S., Raffles, *The History of Java*, Singapore, 1978, pp. 115-115; H. Johardin, et al., (eds.), *Indonesia 1988. An Official Handbook*, Jakarta, 1988, p. 16.

[15] "...Ada dua faktor yang menyebabkan sistem angin di Indonesia menyimpang dari daerah tropik lainnya. Pertama, peredaran bumi mengitari matahari yang menyebabkan "daerah angin mati" itu berpindah-pindah dari lintang Mengkara (tropic of Cancer) ke lintang Jadayat (tropic of Capricorn). Faktor yang kedua ialah lokasi Indonesia di antara dua kontinen, Asia dan Australia." ("... There are two factors causing the differences of the Indonesian weather from other tropical zones. Firstly, the rotation of the earth going around the sun causes territorial changes from the topic of Cancer to the tropic Capricorn. Secondly, the location of Indonesia between the continent of Asia and Australia"). Uka Tjandrasasmita, (ed.), *Sejarah Nasional Indonesia III. Jaman Pertumbuhan dan Perkembangan Kerajaan-kerajaan Islam di Indonesia* (National Hystory of Indonesia III. The Periods of Growth and Development of Islamic Kingdoms in Indonesia), Jakarta, 1976, p. 2.

[16] Waluku star known by Javanese peasants implied the knowledge of astronomy in navigation.

7

Peninsula, the Philippines, Formosa, South China and India. The relationship between Indonesia and Australia came about by way of Nusa Tenggara or Irian Jaya.[17] This geographical fact brought in turn a relationship between these islands and these countries from the very beginning. This is evidenced by the coastal Malays, who are people of Malayan, Javanese and Makasarese origin. Encounters of the inhabitants have formed a rich Indonesian history and culture.

II.   HISTORICAL DESCRIPTION OF INDONESIA

One must view the Javanese culture, in which the concept of *Keselarasan* developed, in the contexts of the history of Indonesia, the reciprocal influences of Javanese thought, and the plurality of Indonesia. On the one hand, Javanese culture has a profound influence throughout Indonesia. On the other hand, a variety of lingual and cultural mores in Indonesia exert a strong influence on Javanese thought. Therefore, we can and should discuss in some detail Indonesian history and the place of the Javanese culture in it.

A.   Pre-History of Indonesia

To understand the pre-history of Indonesia, we need to retrace archaeological/ethnological discoveries. Archaeological and ethnological research has made an immense contribution to the reconstruction of the pre-history of Indonesia.

Some ethnographers and anthropologists[18] have advanced the

---

[17] R.P. Soejono, (ed.), *Sejarah Nasional Indonesia I. Jaman Prasejarah di Indonesia* (National History of Indonesia I. Prehistoric Age in Indonesia), Jakarta, 1975, p. 19.

[18] Dubois, E., Harrison, T., Hekeren H. R. van, Hooijer, D.A., Heine Geldern, R. von, and Jacob,T. had given great attention to the fossils found in the Indonesian archipelago.

proposition that different types of primates existed before the appearance of *Homo Sapiens* or recent man. In 1890 Eugène Dubois found some skeletal remains that could not be classified as that of either ape or man. G.H. von Koenigswald called it *Homo Modjokertensis* and assigned it to the Middle-Pleistocene Age. Some anthropologists have made the assumption that the origin of the Javanese dates from 1,800,000 years ago.[19] The discovery of a fossil at *Trinil* in Central Java in 1891, is the basis for this assumption. Dubois called that fossil *Pithecanthropus Erectus,* and further denoted that the remains on the island of Java must have been from the first inhabitants of Indonesia.[20] This was *Homo Sapiens* that lived in the Middle-Pleistocene Period (c. 300,000 years B.C.), in Java, when what is now an island was still part of continental Asia. After the last Glacial Period, the water level of the sea slowly rose. This caused the separation and formation of the island of Java from the continent of Asia.[21]

Following this, a human fossil found at Ngandong, Central Java, in 1930 revealed a more developed form of human being dating to the Neo-Pleistocene Period (40.000 years B.C.). They called it *Homo Soloensis.* This name derives from the Valley of the *Solo River* the site of the fossil remains, and where Ngandong lies.

These fossils are important evidence of Indonesian and especially Javanese origins. They also have significance in the pre-history of Southeast Asia, because ethnologists found human remains from the

---

[19] "Schädelfragment aus Java älter als angenommen", *Neue Zürcher Zeitung,* 26th February 1994, p. 8; see also Viviano Domenici, "Un Piccolo Homo Erectus di 5 anni, trovato a Giava, risulta più vecchio dei suoi antenati del Continente Nero, ma chi fu il primo emigrante che lasciò l'Africa? C'è un bimbo di 1 milione e 800 mila anni che sta confondendo la nostra storia", *Corriere della sera,* 6th March 1994, p. 37.

[20] H. Johardin, et al., (eds.), *Indonesia 1988. An Offical Handbook,* Jakarta, 1988, p. 15.

[21] A. Zecca, *Indonesia. Java Bali Sumatra Nias Siberut Sulawesi Lombok Sumbawa Komodo,* Milano, p. 11.

various Pleistocene periods only in this area.[22] Although it is not an adequate explanation of the entire pre-history of Indonesia, it constitutes the primary contribution to the ancient history of Indonesia. This sheds a light on the existence of many different groups that settled and spread throughout the Indonesian archipelago. From an ethno-historical point of view, these paleontological discoveries could provide an acceptable description of the origin of the people of Indonesia, and especially of the development of the Javanese.

The identity of Indonesia cannot be separated from its relationship with a wider geographical area. For centuries Indonesia had been a place of intercontinental immigration and emigration. Immigrants married with indigenous people and this influenced the subsequent identity of the Javanese as well as all Indonesians.

The indigenous Javanese lived as hunters, food-gatherers and fishermen. They moved from place to place and adapted themselves according to the available sources of food.[23] They used stone and wooden tools as knives for hunting and for collecting food. From archaeological remains of tools, we can further trace the progress from bone to horn. These indigenous people lived in small groups, and their lifestyle depended on the nature of their environment. This was the style of life that already existed at the time of *Homo Sapiens* of Wajak during the Late Pleistocene Period.

The first great immigration to the Indonesian archipelago as H.

---

[22] According to Thomassen, the chronology of the early Pre-historic period is as follows: *Homo Modjokertensis 600.000 years BC, Phitecanthropus erectus 300.000 years BC, Homo Soloensis (skull of Ngandong) 40.000 years BC.* The recent research stated that the fossils of *Homo Modjokertensis* dated 1.800.000 years BC. Cf. B.H.M. Vlekke, *Nusantara. A History of Indonesia*, Leiden, 1959, p. 4; Viviamo Domenici, "Un Piccolo Homo Erectus di 5 anni, trovato a Giava, risulta più vecchio dei suoi antenati del Continente Nero, ma chi fu il primo emigrante che lasciò l'Africa? C'è un bimbo di 1 milione e 800 mila anni che sta confondendo la nostra storia", *Corriere della Sera*, 6th March 1994, p. 37; "Schädelfragment aus Java älter als angenommen" *Neue Zürcher Zeitung*, 26th February 1994, p. 8.

[23] Cf. R.P. Soejono, (ed.), *Sejarah Nasional Indonesia I. Jaman Prasejarah di Indonesia* (National History of Indonesia I. Prehistoric Age in Indonesia), Jakarta, 1975, pp. 16-17.

Johardin has written: "During the Neolithic Period (3,000 - 2,000 B.C.), ... a grand scale migration from the mainland of Asia and originating from Yunnan in South China and Tonkin took place southwards,"[24] belonged to a Sub-Mongol people. They had a higher culture and civilization than that of the indigenous inhabitants, as was seen in the civilization at Wajak in East Java.[25]

It might be that the cultivation of rice, which in successive centuries has become the important element of the Javanese culture, was influenced by the migration from Yunnan, as the invention of the quadrangular adze has been attributed to the people of Yunnan in South China.[26] In fact the phenomena of cultivation and raising livestock had already emerged in 6,000 B.C.[27] If this assumption is right, it could be that the indigenous people also lived in dwellings. Perhaps this does not exclude the possibility of the Mongol influence in cultivating rice. They knew already a very elementary technique of agriculture which consisted of a primitive way of cultivating sweet potatoes (*Dioscorea Esculanta*) and the *keladi* root (*Colocasia Antiquorum*). In any case, after inter-marriage with the Sub-Mongols, the indigenous people advanced their methods of cultivation and there was trade through the exchange of things such as bronze and precious stones, during period from 3,000-500 B.C. Adriano Zecca gives similar information. He states that the Mongolians introduced a new form of culture, typical of the late Neolithic Period. The use of the quadrangular and the rostra axes and a different architectural

---

[24] Cf. H. Johardin, et al., (eds.), *Indonesia 1988. An Official Handbook*, Jakarta, 1988, p. 29; R.M. Sutjipto Wirjosuparto, *A Short Cultural History of Indonesia*, Djakarta, 1954, p. 2. Bambang Sumadio, (ed), *Sejarah National II. Jaman Kuno* (National History II. Ancient Age), Jakarta, 1976, p. 12; O.W. Wolters, *Early Indonesian Commerce*, New York, 1967, p. 37; Satyawati Suleiman, *Concise History of Indonesia*, Jakarta, 1975, p. 5.

[25] The fossil of Wajak man was found at Kediri's area in the East Java. Cf. R.P. Soejono, (ed.), *Sejarah Nasional Indonesia I. Jaman Prasejarah di Indonesia* (National History of Indonesia I. Prehistoric Age in Indonesia), Jakarta, 1975, p. 50.

[26] Satyawati Suleiman, *Concise Ancient History of Indonesia*, Jakarta, 1977, p. 5.

[27] Cf. R.P. Soejono, (ed.), *Sejarah Nasional I. Jaman Prasejarah di Indonesia* (National History of Indonesia I. Prehistoric Age in Indonesia), Jakarta, 1975, p. 23.

style characterized this period, which produced many megalithic monuments representative of proto-Malay culture.[28] This culture belonged to what was called "Melanesian".

The second wave of migration originated in the south of the sub-continent of India in 1,000 B.C..[29] M.P.M.Muskens and Johardin mention that these migrants were Indo-Aryan, and F.Krom points out that they were Indian traders. Prince Aji Çaka in A.D. 78, confirmed this evidence of Indo-Aryan migration.[30] The first Indian immigrants were mostly from Gujarat in West India. Most Indian emigrants came to Indonesia for trading purposes. For this reason they came as merchants and tried to establish relationships with local rulers. They also married indigenous women. Their marriages played an important role in the introduction of Hinduism into the culture and its development. This new combination of people brought about the Çaka period in Indonesia. The introduction of Sanskrit language and Pallawa Script demarcate this period.

Later the Indonesian Buddhist Kingdom of Sriwijaya had relations with Nalanda in South India.[31] The growth of a well-developed trade was based on such relations. In this period Indian immigrants also introduced a monarchic system of government.

There was a continuous influx of Indian settlers until the seventh century A.D. The Hindu religion peacefully and gradually spread among the upper classes of the Javanese people as well as throughout the

---

[28] Cf. A. Zecca, *Indonesia. Java Bali Sumatra Nias Siberut Sulawesi Lombok Sumbawa Komodo*, Milano, p. 12.

[29] H. Johardin, et al., (eds.), *Indonesia 1988. An Official Handbook*, Jakarta, 1988, p. 31.

[30] Both Sanskrit language and Pallawa Script were in a later period Javanesized and called *Kawi* language which has in its lexicon a number of additional Javanese words and phrases.

[31] Nalanda lay at Bihar, India. Here there were an ancient monastery and a great Buddhist university where thousands of students, numerous teachers of all schools, both Mahāyāna and Hīnayāna, thought, disputed and wrote. Cf. N. Farquhar and H.D. Grisword, *The Religious Quest of India*, Oxford, 1920, pp. 206-208.

12

archipelago. There was even an indigenous king[32] who embraced Hinduism.

Indian Buddhists also arrived in Indonesia between A.D. 100 and 200.[33] They introduced the Buddhist tradition and religion, especially the *Mahāyāna* and *Hīnayāna* sects. As the Chinese made their pilgrimages to India they went to Malacca and visited Indonesia to train and to develop their knowledge of the Buddhist religion. It was in this way that eventually both Hinduism and Buddhism joined in the syncretic form of *Śaiva-Buddha*.

B.   The Period of Kingdoms

A description of the period of the kingdoms indicates cultural and religious pluralism. Let us look briefly at the story of the kingdoms.

1.   The First Kingdoms in Indonesia

a.   The Kingdom of Kutai (c. A.D. 400)[34]

Based on Chinese sources, we have information that there was a kingdom at Kutai on the island of Kalimantan. Information from the T'ang dynasty (A.D. 618-906) and objects ascribed to the Han dynasty which were found in Kalimantan confirm the existence of this kingdom. The two successive kings of Kutai were Aswawarman and Mulawarman.[35] They were descendants of the indigenous king, Kundunga. Inscriptions in

---

[32] ".... , yang dapat dipastikan bahwa ia adalah seorang Indonesia asli, karena kakeknya masih menggunakan nama Indonesia asli, *Kundunga*". ("... , it can be certainly proved that he is a native Indonesian, because his grandfather used the original Indonesian name, *Kundunga*".) Cf. Bambang Sumadio, (ed.), *Sejarah Nasional II. Jaman Kuno* (National History II. Ancient Age), Jakarta, 1976, p. 30.

[33] H. Johardin, et al., (eds.), *Indonesia 1988. An Official Handbook 1988*, Jakarta, 1988, p. 21.

[34] B.H.M. Vlekke, *Nusantara. A History of Indonesia*, Leiden, 1959, p. 16.

[35] Satyawati Suleiman, *Concise Ancient History of Indonesia*, Jakarta, 1977, p. 14.

13

stone found in east Kalimantan at a place now called Muara Kaman attest to this history,[36] as Brahmans erected stone memorials to express their gratitude and respect for the king's kindness. Chizeled in the rock was their grateful testimony to Mulawarman's gift to the Brahmans of 20,000 cows for a Hindu ceremony.[37] The oldest proven date for this first kingdom is A.D. 400.[38]

b.   The Kingdom of Tarumanegara (A.D. 358 - ca. 669)[39]

The history of Tarumanegara's kingdom comes from Chinese sources[40] and in particular, from seven stone inscriptions. Chinese sources relate that Fa-shien, a Chinese Buddhist was driven by a storm and landed in *Ya-va-di*. Most experts agree that *Ya-va-di* is most likely an abbreviation of *Java-Dwipa* which alludes to the present Java island. This information is confirmed by inscriptions which show that the Kingdom of Tarumanegara lay near Cisedane. Its king was Purnawarman. Chinese source note: "There were few Buddhists, but many Brahmans and those who had indigenous religions."[41]

---

[36] B.H.M. Vlekke, *Nusantara. A History of Indonesia*, Leiden, 1959, p. 15.

[37] "Para ahli purbakala memperkirakan bahwa paling tidak prasasti itu berasal dari tahun 400 Masehi" ("The archaeologists estimated that the inscription was dated at least from 400 A.D."). Achadiati, Y.S., *Zaman Kutai Purba* (Ancient Age of Kutai), Jakarta, 1987, p. 12. Cf. Bambang Sumadio, (ed.), *Sejarah Nasional Indonesia II. Jaman Kuno* (National History of Indonesia II. Ancient Age), Jakarta, 1976, p. 35.

[38] Cf. M.P.M. Muskens, *Partner in Nation Building. The Catholic Church in Indonesia*, Aachen, 1979, p. 20.

[39] "Kerajaan Tarumanegara berkembang selama 311 tahun (358 - 669). Rajanya yang terbesar bernama Jaya Singhawarman (358 - 382 M) sedangkan raja terakhir Linggawarman (666 - 669 M)". ("The kingdom of Tarumanegara developed for 311 years [358 - 669]. The biggest king was named Jaya Singhawarman [358 - 382 M] and the last king was Linggawarman [666 - 669 M]"). Achadiati, Y.S., *Zaman Tarumanegara dan Sunda* (The Periods of Tarumanegara and Sunda), Jakarta, 1988, p. 10.

[40] W.P. Groenevelt, *Historical Note on Indonesia and Malaya. Compiled from Chinese Sources*, Djakarta, 1960, p. 6.

[41] W.P. Groenevelt, *Historical Note on Indonesia and Malaya. Compiled from Chinese Sources*, Djakarta, 1960, p. 7; Cf. Bambang Sumadio, (ed.), *Sejarah Nasional II. Jaman Kuno*

The people of the Kingdom of Tarumanegara accepted the presence of Hinduism and Buddhism among their indigenous religions on the island of Java, just as we have seen that they welcome the foreigners and other religions which they had already encountered.

2. The Period of Hindu and Buddhist Kingdoms

a. The Kingdom of Sriwijaya (500 - 1375)[42]

The Kingdom of Sriwijaya lay near Palembang on the island of Sumatra. Chinese sources dated from A.D. 502, refer to the island of Sumatra as *Kanto-Li* due to phonetic language barriers. Experts generally agree that *Kanto-Li* alludes to the Sriwijaya Kingdom,[43] and it was Sriwijaya is one of the Buddhist kingdoms in Indonesia. The king was Gautama Subadra. Later his son Pryawarman or Vinyawarman inherited his kingdom, and established relations with China.

The Sriwijaya Kingdom has been of no small significance either in a religious or cultural sense. This kingdom exerted its hegemony over the east coast of Sumatra, Malacca and West Java.[44] Sriwijaya was the centre of Buddhist learning and had many well-known scholars of Buddhist philosophy like Sākyakirti, Dharmapāla and Vrajabuddhi. I-Tshing, a Chinese Buddhist pilgrim, visited Sriwijaya in A.D. 671 for six

---

(National History II. Ancient Age), Jakarta, 1976, p. 43.

[42] Cf. Nia Kurnia Sholihat Irfan, *Kerajaan Sriwijaya* (Kingdom of Sriwijaya), Jakarta, 1983, p. 35; Bambang Sumadio, (ed.), *Sejarah Nasional II. Jaman Kuno* (National History II. Ancient Age), Jakarta, 1976, pp. 54-62.

[43] Uraian tentang negeri ini terdapat dalam Sejarah dinasty Liang (502 - 556) yang antara lain berbunyi: "Negeri *Kanto-li* terletak di sebuah pulau di laut selatan, adat istiadatnya sama dengan Kamboja dan Siam. Negeri ini menghasilkan pakaian berbunga dan pinang" (The information of this country was found in the history of Liang's dynasty [502 - 556] which said: "The country *Kanto-li* lay on an island in the south sea, its tradition is the same with Cambodia and Siam. This country produced the flowering textile and coconut"). Nia Kurnia Sholihat Irfan, *Kerajaan Sriwijaya* (Kingdom of Sriwijaya), Jakarta, 1983, p. 105.

[44] M.P.M. Muskens, *Partner in Nation Building. The Catholic Church in Indonesia*, Aachen, 1979, p. 21.

15

months.[45] He reported that Sriwijaya already had established relations with South India.

According to Muskens, there was Buddhist center of scientific study at Palembang with a thousand monks, which entertained a direct contact with the famous Buddhist university at Nālanda in India.[46] That is why the Kingdom of Sriwijaya has become something of the prototype for Indonesia; the unity of the archipelago derives from perhaps the very idea of a Buddhist principle of unity translated into ecumenism. It is not, afterall, infrequent in the history of humanity that religions exert a powerful influence on culture as well as on other parameters of society.

b.   The Kingdom of Shailendra (750 - 850)[47]

In Java there was a Buddhist Kingdom with the king of the Shailendra dynasty. The erection of many buildings bear testimony to the golden age of this kingdom. Buddhist monument of *Borobudur,* constructed in the eighth century, is filled with sculptures and reliefs which depict the religious doctrine of Mahāyāna Buddhism. This monument was originally a terrace sanctuary, according to ancient-Javanese tradition, in which an ancestor cult plays an important part. It was their belief that the spirits of the ancestors have their abode on the top of the mountains of the cosmos, and from there they contact their posterity.

In addition to a wealth of building, this kingdom of Shailendra had a naval power and advanced commercial relations and culture. Then the dynasty of Mataram took dominion of Central Java. Shailendra's successor, Panchapana, built the temples of Mendut, Kalasan and Pawon. As the art and architecture of Buddhism and the ancient Javanese religion

---

[45] Cf. Nia Kurnia Sholihat Irfan, *Kerajaan Sriwijaya* (Kingdom of Sriwijaya), Jakarta, 1983, p. 21.

[46] M.P.M. Muskens, *Partner in Nation Building. The Catholic Church in Indonesia,* Aachen, 1979, p. 21.

[47] Cf. A.J. Bernet Kempers, *Ancient Indonesian Art,* Amsterdam, 1959, p. 13.

had become amalgamated in the Borobudur, so elements of Hinduism and the ancient Javanese religion joined hands in the temple of Prambanan.[48]

Shailendra's downfall can be traced back to the end of the ninth century. At that time, there was a revival of Hindu cults. At the beginning of the ninth century the Kingdom of East Java had great power. Airlangga became its most famous king in the history of Indonesia. He was the son of King Udayana II of Bali and of the Javanese Princess Mahendradatta. He proclaimed himself king in 1019, and his power spread throughout the Kingdom of Mataram. Airlangga is described in an ancient Indonesian literary masterpiece as "Arjuna Wiwaha." He died in A.D. 1049.

After his death, the kingdom was divided into two parts, namely the Kingdom of Jenggala and the Kingdom of Kediri. The latter became stronger and extended its power to Bali, to Borneo and to the southern part of Sulawesi. Of the history of the Kingdom of Kediri, we know that they had an active commercial exchange with the Muslim Centre of Gujarati, as well as a flourishing trade relationships with Arabian and Chinese merchants who landed at the ports of Java.[49]

In 1222, Ken Angrok built his Kingdom of Singasari.[50] As king, he controlled the most important trade routes in the east and Malacca, the trade centre in the western archipelago. There was a succession of kings after Ken Angrok. The successor were Anusapati and Tohjaya, Wisnuwardhana and Kertanagara.[51] Kertanagara, who was the last king of

---

[48] M.P.M. Muskens, *Partner in Nation Building. The Catholic Church in Indonesia*, Aachen, 1979, p. 22.

[49] A. Zecca, *Indonesia. Java Bali Sumatra Nias Siberut Sulawesi Lombok Sumbawa Komodo*, Milano, p. 13.

[50] Cf. Bambang Sumadio, (ed.), *Sejarah Nasional II. Jaman Kuno* (National History II. Ancient Age), Jakarta, 1976, p. 250; v. also A.Zecca, *Indonesia. Java Bali Sumatra Nias Siberut Sulawesi Lombok Sumbawa Komodo*, Milano, p. 13.

[51] Bambang Sumadio, (ed.), *Sejarah Nasional II. Jaman Kuno* (National History II. Ancient Age), Jakarta, 1976, p. 251. Cf. Slamet Muljana, *Runtuhnja Keradjaan Hindu-Djawa dan Timbulnja Negara-negara Islam di Nusantara* (The Collapse of the Javanese-Hindu Kingdom and

Singasari, had self-proclaimed his rule in 1268. He was very influential in bringing a new trend of religious thinking.[52] His kingdom spread over a great part of Indonesia and laid the foundation of the Majapahit dynasty.[53]

c.   The Kingdom of Majapahit (A.D. 1293 - 1478 A.D.)[54]

After Kertanagara's death in a revolt in 1293, Wijaya, Kertanagara's son-in- law, became king. Wijaya established his kingdom in the town of Majapahit and rule there until A.D. 1309. He conquered the regions of Bali, Madura, Malaya and Tanjungpura.

This new Javanese empire reached its culmination under Hayam Wuruk (1350-1389) with Gajah Mada (1331-1364) as his Premier (*patih*). Together they succeeded in uniting the whole Indonesian archipelago under the name *Dwipantara*. During the forty years reign of Hayam Wuruk, Majapahit rose to a power and grandeur as had never taken place before in the archipelago.[55] His rule extended to include even Champa in North Vietnam and Kampuchea and the present Philippines.[56]

Yet Hayam Wuruk had no capable successor and according to tradition, Majapahit fell on account of an attack by a coalition of Moslem princes in A.D. 1478.[57] With the downfall of Majapahit, a new period

---

the Emergence of Islamic Countries in Nusantara), Djakarta, 1968, p. 175.; W. Fruen-Mees, *Sedjarah Tanah Djawa* (History of the Land of Java), Welkvreden, 1921, pp. 58-92.

[52] M.P.M. Muskens, *Partner in Nation Building. The Catholic Church in Indonesia*, Aachen, 1979, p. 24.

[53] A. Zecca, *Indonesia. Java Bali Sumatra Nias Siberut Sulawesi Lombok Sumbawa Komodo*, Milano, p. 13.

[54] Bambang Sumadio, (ed.), *Sejarah Nasional II. Jaman Kuno* (National History II. Ancient Age), Jakarta, 1976, p. 274.

[55] M.P.M. Muskens, *Partner in Nation Building. The Catholic Church in Indonesia*, Aachen, 1979, p. 25.

[56] H. Johardin, et al., (eds.), *Indonesia 1988. An Official Handbook*, Jakarta, 1988, p. 34.

[57] Satyawati Suleiman, *Concise Ancient History of Indonesia*, Jakarta, 1977, p. 36.

began of Islamic Kingdoms such as Demak, Tuban, Jepara, Surabaya, Madura and the Kingdom of Gresik (A.D. 1293-1520).[58]

3.   The period of the Islamic Kingdoms

There are three hypotheses for the advance of Islam. The first postulates that Islam came from China with the Islamic Chinese emigrants in the 6th century, when the emperor, T'sang drove them out of China. The second holds that Islam came with the Arabian merchants.[59] The third hypothesis is that Islam came from Gujarat with the Indian merchants who had embraced the Islamic religion and visited Indonesia in the 13th century.[60] Marco Polo, who came to Northern Sumatra in 1292, noted that the town of Perlak was Islamic.[61] In the 14th century, Malacca became the centre of the expansion of Islam.

The rulers of the northern shore of Java, i.e. in Cirebon, Demak, Tuban, Jepara, Gresik and Madiun, embraced the Islamic religion. The most prominent of them was Demak. Inroads were made from Demak to Malacca, West Java and East Sumatra.[62] Then Islam spread to the Moluccas, to Banjarmasin on Borneo and farther to Pasai and Perlak on Sumatra. In a later period, the island of Lombok was converted to Islam as well.[63]

---

[58] H. Johardin, et al., (eds.), *Indonesia 1988. An Official Handbook*, Jakarta, 1988, p. 35. Cf. M.P.M. Muskens, *Partner in Nation Building. The Catholic Church in Indonesia*, Aachen, 1979, p. 30.

[59] Cf. Uka Tjandrasasmita, (ed.), *Sejarah Nasional III. Jaman Pertumbuhan dan Perkembangan Kerajaan-Kerajaan Islam di Indonesia* (National History III. The Periods of Growth and Development of Islamic Kingdoms in Indonesia), Jakarta, 1976, p. 109.

[60] A. Zecca, *Indonesia.Java Bali Sumatra Nias Siberut Sulawesi Lombok Sumbawa Komodo*, Milano, p. 13. Cf. H. Johardin, et al., (eds.), *Indonesia 1988. An Official Handbook*, Jakarta, 1988, p. 35.

[61] B.H.M. Vlekke, *Nusantara. A History of Indonesia*, Leiden, 1959, pp. 55, 56.

[62] M.P.M. Muskens, *Partner in Nation Building. The Catholic Church in Indonesia*, Aachen, 1979, p. 30.

[63] H. Johardin, et al., (eds.), *Indonesia 1988. An Official Handbook*, Jakarta, 1988, p. 35.

The Javanese coastal princes viewed Islam as in keeping with tradition.[64] There were two reasons for this. First, Islam became a symbol of opposition to the Kingdom of Majapahit. It was an alternative to the Hindu view of the world. Second, they used Islam for strengthening their magical and spiritual power. As Vlekke tells us, "Javanese princes used to understand religious activities as instruments for advancing the inner power or their magic power."[65]

4.   The Period of Colonization and Independence

The arrival of the Portuguese marked a new period in which indigenous and Islamic inhabitants struggled to maintain their autonomy and identity through trade. The Portuguese were the first Europeans who came to Indonesia. Under the leadership of Diego Lopez da Sequeira, they came to Indonesia in 1511 in search of spices.[66] The Portuguese engaged war with the Islam Kingdom of Malacca on the Malay Peninsula.[67] From Jepara, Pati Unus sent 100 ships with an army of 10,000 to help Malacca against the Portuguese. The Portuguese, however, defeated these Javanese troops on the 1st of January 1513, and their position then became stronger on the Moluccas.[68]

Dutch navigators who had earlier helped the Portuguese during the contact in Ternate and Tidore, gained influence with the expansion of the

---

[64] M.P.M. Muskens, *Partner in Nation Building. The Catholic Church in Indonesia*, Aachen, 1979,   p. 30.

[65] B.H.M. Vlekke, *Nusantara. A History of Indonesia*, Leiden, 1959, p. 86.

[66] Uka Tjandrasasmita, (ed.), *Sejarah Nasional III. Jaman Pertumbuhan dan Perkembangan Kerajaan-kerajaan Islam di Indonesia* (National History III. The Periods of Growth and Development of Islamic Kingdoms in Indonesia), Jakarta, 1976, p. 333. Cf. Slamet Muljana, *Runtuhnja Keradjaan Hindu-Djawa dan Timbulnja Negara-Negara Islam di Nusantara* (The Collapse of the Javanese-Hindu Kingdom and the Emergence of Islamic Countries in Nusantara), Djakarta, 1968, pp. 200-201.

[67] Cf. H. Johardin, et al., (eds.), *Indonesia 1988. An Official Handbook*, Jakarta, 1988, p. 35.

[68] Uka Tjandrasasmita, (ed.), *Sejarah Nasional III. Jaman Pertumbuhan dan Perkembangan Kerajaan-kerajaan Islam di Indonesia* (National History III. The Periods of Growth and Development of Islamic Kingdoms in Indonesia), Jakarta, 1976, p. 335.

Dutch navy in 1529, and thereafter hindered any attempt by the Portuguese to extend rule over other Asian countries. The Dutch then established the Dutch East India Company (V.O.C.) in 1602, to get control of the Spice Islands in the Indonesian archipelago for the European market,[69] and on the 23rd of February 1605, the Dutch navy, under Steven van Haghen, defeated the Portuguese in Amboina.[70] In that same year, Dutch colonialism took a foothold in Indonesia. In 1619, the Dutch captured the port of Jakarta and renamed it *Batavia*. After the Dutch seizure of the Banda islands in 1623, the V.O.C. gained the Spice Islands trade monopoly.

The town of Malacca, supported by the Kingdom of Mataram, was also conquered by the Dutch in 1641.[71] However, there was unceasing resistance against the V.O.C. from the Indonesian kingdoms. For example, Trunojoyo of the Kingdom of Madura waged a war against the Dutch in 1680; Untung Surapati resisted the Dutch in 1706, yet after the bankruptcy of the V.O.C. in 1799,[72] the Dutch Goverment took over all territories in Indonesia on the 31st of December 1799.[73]

After a decade, Indonesia fell under the rule of the British East India Company (1811-1816), as a result of the loss of Dutch power following the French victory over the Netherlands in the Napoleonic wars in Europe. Later in 1814, the British in Indonesia built a fortress on the west coast of Sumatra or Bengkulu. The British stayed in Bengkulu until 1825.[74] Thomas Stamford Raffles became Governor General of Java and

---

[69] H. Johardin, et al., (eds.), *Indonesia 1988. An Official Handbook*, Jakarta, 1988, p. 36.

[70] Uka Tjandrasasmita, (ed.), *Sejarah Nasional III. Jaman Pertumbuhan dan Perkembangan Kerajaan-Kerajaan Islam di Indonesia* (National History III. The Periods of Growth and Development of Islamic Kingdoms in Indonesia), Jakarta, 1976, p. 350.

[71] M.P.M. Muskens, *Partner in Nation Building. The Catholic Church in Indonesia*, Aachen, 1979, p. 32.

[72] The Dutch company expired in 1799, leaving a debt of 134 million guillders. L. Fischer, *The Story of Indonesia*, London, 1959, p. 23.

[73] H. Johardin, et al., (eds.), *Indonesia 1988. An Official Handbook*, Jakarta, 1988, p. 37.

[74] H. Johardin, et al., (eds.), *Indonesia 1988. An Official Handbook*, Jakarta, 1988, p. 37.

introduced the "Land Rent System." At a convention in London on the 13th of August 1814, the British agreed to return to the Dutch the possessions which the Dutch had held from 1803 until the overthrow of the British. The Dutch finally reclaimed the Indonesian archipelago, but the Indonesians fiercely struggled to gain their independence, and revolts followed. Thomas Matulessy or Pattimura in Ambon (1816 - 1818),[75] Prince Diponegoro of Mataram (1825 - 1830), Imam Bonjol in the war of "Padri" in West Sumatra and Teuku Umar in Aceh (1873 - 1903), Sisingamangaraja, king of Batak in 1908, and Udayana from Bali, also in 1908, all fought for the cause of freedom.

These unsuccessful regional struggles inspired a more widely organized efforts. On the 20th of May, 1908, Dr. Wahidin Sudirohusada, Dr. Sutomo, Gunawan and Suraji founded the first national movement association called *Boedi Oetomo*. In the beginning, the aim of this association was merely to advance the Javanese Culture.[76]

There followed the founding of many economic, social and political organizations were founded after the *Boedi Oetomo* organization. In 1911 Haji Samanhudi began the organization called *Sarikat Dagang Islam* which was renamed *Serikat Islam* in 1913. In 1912 there emerged the progressive Moslem organization *Muhammadiyah*. In 1922 Ki Hajar Dewantoro founded an organization for Indonesian national education called *Taman Siswa*. Mohammad Hatta and Sukiman founded the Association of Indonesian Students (*Perhimpunan Mahasiswa Indonesia*) in 1924. Soekarno, Sartono and others formed the Indonesian Nationalist Party called *PNI* (*Partai Nasional Indonesia*) in 1927. Indonesian Youth made a pledge to strive for "one native country, one nation and one language," on the 28th of October 1928.

In 1942, the Japanese occupied several southeast Asian countries.

---

[75] Cf. Eka Darmaputera, *Pancasila and Search for Identity and Modernity in Indonesian Society*, Leiden, 1988, p. 147.

[76] R. Niel, van, *The Course of History*, in: Mc Vey, Ruth T, (ed.), *Indonesia*, New Heaven, 1963, p. 292.

Japanese forces invaded the Dutch East Indies whereupon the Dutch army surrendered to the Japanese in March 1942. Indonesian citizens continued to build the foundation for proclamation of its independence. After the Allies bombed Hiroshima and Nagasaki on the 6th and the 9th of August 1945, respectively, the Japanese surrendered unconditionally. Soekarno and Mohammad Hatta used this opportunity to proclaim Indonesia's independence on the 17th of August 1945. The first President was Soekarno and the Vice President was Mohammad Hatta. On the 18th of August, the *Pancasila* Principles were accepted as the ideological basis of the state. Meanwhile British troops and Dutch troops had returned to Indonesia. On the 10th of November 1945, fierce fighting between British troops and the Indonesian people ensued in Surabaya. The Indonesians continued their fighting and put pressure also on the Dutch troops. On the 2nd of November 1949, Holland recognized the sovereignity of the Republic of Indonesia. Indonesia succeeded in overcoming extremist rebellions such as *Darul Islam, PKI* (*Partai Komunis Indonesia*), and so on. On the 11th of March 1966, for due to ill health, president Soekarno requested that General Soeharto continued to govern for an interim, in his stead.

The New Order Government continued to make advances in Indonesia based on Pancasila and the 1945 Constitution. The government the framework of the "Five Year Development Plan" to realize its aims. Soeharto was elected president in 1968. Later he was reelected in 1973, 1978, 1983, 1988 and 1993. His main achievements towards the country's development were an extension of the road system and the improvement of existing roads. In 1976 Indonesia obtained its own space satellite which offered expanded possibilities for communications via telephone, radio, and television. Communication was and remains today the most elementary condition for further development.

Newly attained economic and social development and stability have enabled different tribes and religions to live together in harmony and to respect existing differences. Living in unity while recognising and accepting these differences creates a harmonious situation. This is the fruit of a culture and society based on Pancasila.[77] Such a history of Indonesia is closely akin to the struggle which has taken place in Java, Sumatra and the Moluccas and elsewhere.

This geographical and historical description of Indonesia as a whole reveals Java's role. Eka Dharmaputra points out that it is an objective reality that the Javanese culture had the most significant role in the history of Indonesia. Let us see a historical compendium of the position of Java and its culture as an inseparable part of Indonesian development.

III.   THE POSITION OF JAVA AND ITS CULTURE IN INDONESIA

As we have seen earlier, geographically and historically the island of Java played an important role in Indonesian progress. It is not purely accidental that the island of Java became great in the   Indonesian civilization. Her multi-faceted rise to importance happened over a long period of history. As we have mentioned, the traces of human origination and its development, from *Homo Modjokertensis* and *Pithecanthropus Erectus* to *Homo Sapiens,* were found in the land of Java. Evidence of her ancient relationship with the Chinese and with India can also be confirmed. There emerged also the mighty Javanese Sultans who had contact with Islamic thinkers. Dutch rulers chose to establish a centre of government on this island. Under the British, Thomas Stanford Raffles became Governor General of Java. Historian Bernard Vlekke even said:

> The history of the East Indies is, therefore, mainly the history of Java.
> Sumatra also has had great importance throughout history, especially
> its eastern and northern districts. The interior of Borneo and Celebes,

---

[77] M.P.M. Muskens, *Partner in Nation Building. The Catholic Church in Indonesia,* Aachen, 1979, p. 295.

24

however, have no history at all, since only coastal districts were drawn in the sphere of Javanese and Sumatra influences.[78]

This expression seems a bit exaggerated but it implies the truth that the Javanese culture and history have a significant place in Indonesia, while it does not exclude the roles of others such as Sumatra and Moluccas.

From the perspective of the Indonesian language, the Javanese were also influential. It may suffice to say that many Indonesian words and expressions have their roots in Javanese or Malayan. This influence of the Javanese language expanded, as Muskens wrote: "This influence grows stronger and stronger; it is not only a question of all kinds of words, but also of Javanese cultural elements, so clearly interwoven with Javanese language."[79] Indonesian as the national language is not yet definitive. Today, it still finds enrichment offered by local languages, among which Javanese is of major importance.

From the perspective of economic development, Java has developed faster than the other islands. There are two contributory factors. First, population figures show that two-thirds of the Indonesian population lives on Java. Second, government programmes and facilities have aided the development of Jakarta, Surabaya, Bandung and Semarang which in turn has enabled advancement in economic and industrial sectors. This progress, we might add, also has been made possible by continued adherence to the Indonesian cultural values of togetherness (*kekeluargaan*) and consultation aimed at producing mutual consensus (*musyawarah untuk mencapai mufakat*) in all matters of concern to society.[80]

However, we should view these facts from the perspective of the

---

[78] B.H.M. Vlekke, *Nusantara. A History of Indonesia*, Leiden, 1959, p. XIV.

[79] M.P.M. Muskens, *Partner in Nation Building. The Catholic Church in Indonesia*, Aachen, 1979, p. 58.

[80] Institute of Asian Affairs, (ed.), *Indonesia Seminar, Hamburg 22-23, 1976*, Hamburg, 1977, p. 66.

whole of Indonesia, in which regional roles are recognized. Such an approach to reality enables coexistence of ethnic groups and religions, a "unity in diversity" based on the concept of *Keselarasan*. In the following section, we shall investigate this dynamic culture further in the formation of the concept of *Keselarasan*.

CHAPTER II

THE FORMATION OF THE CONCEPT OF *KESELARASAN*

I. JAVANESE THOUGHT IN *WÉDHATAMA* AND *WAYANG*

The formation of the concept of *Keselarasan* takes place in a very long process, in which tradition and indigenous thought meet with external thought and influences. Accordingly, I would like to deal with Javanese thought and with Hindu, Buddhist, Islamic and Christian thought as they regard the concepts of *Keselarasan* and harmony.

As the basis for our observation of Javanese thought, we shall use written Javanese sources such as *Wédhatama* and *Wayang*, which cannot be separated from the treasure of the whole Javanese tradition. According to R. Harjono and C. Lekkerkerker, Javanese thought must be traced back to the period before the arrival of Hinduism and Islam in Java.[81] From the Pre-Islamic period, we can still find fragments in written sources. However it is not feasible to research periods prior to the appearance of Hinduism in Java, for which we have no adequate written sources.[82] The oldest written sources, *kakawin* and some Javanese literature that we called *piwulang*,[83] date from the 9th century and later.[84]

---

[81] Cf. J. Darminta, *"Mawas diri" (Self-Examination). A Dialogal Encounter of the Self-Examination of Ki Ageng Suryomentaram in the Perspective of the Javanese Religious life with the Ignatian Examination*, (Dissertation), Rome, 1980, p. 11; C. Geertz, *Islam Observed*, New Haven and London, 1968, p. 11.

[82] The description of Indonesia is discussed in the first chapter.

[83] *Piwulang* are Javanese teachings for daily life concerning good manners and morality as we found in *Niti Sastra, Wulang Reh, Wédhatama* and so on. Accordingly, such *Piwulang* are understood Javanese writings contain instructions on right behaviour and proper moral order which are akin to mysticism, social ethic and philosophical teaching. These ethical and moral teachings are communicated from generation to generation for daily life in society. Cf. G. Moedjanto, *The concept of Power in Javanese Culture*, Yogyakarta, 1990, p. 2; Eka Darmaputera, *Pancasila and*

P.J. Zoetmulder points out that our knowledge of Old Javanese history derives principally from early charters and inscriptions. The earliest inscription in Javanese is found in the Sukabumi inscription, dated 25 March 804.[85] Earlier documents were in Sanskrit. Zoetmulder says:

> The importance of 25 March 804 in Old Javanese studies is that it is the earliest date so far found at which Old Javanese was used. It thus marks the beginning of the history of the Old Javanese language. Although earlier inscriptions have been found in the area where Javanese is still spoken at the present day, the earliest dating from 732 A.D., they are all written in Sanskrit. The charter of Sukabumi is the first inscription known to us which uses Old Javanese, and from then on this is the language used in most official documents.[86]

For this reason, we discuss Javanese thought as expressed in *Wédhatama* which embodies the high point of *piwulang* and the tradition of *wayang*. Later we shall speak of the main teachings of Hinduism, Buddhism, Islam and Christianism in the light of unity in diversity and the idea of harmony. The concept of *Keselarasan* and the influences it received will be treated in the last part of this chapter. Now let us see Javanese thought, which is the basic seed of *Keselarasan*.

A. Javanese Thought in *Wédhatama*

First of all, I would like to determine the sense of "Javanese thought." Then the use of the expression "Javanese thought" has a significance in both thought and literature. The group of *piwulang*, such as *Kakawin, Niti Sastra, Wédhatama*, and so on, contains socio-ethical, mystical and philosophical teaching. It reaches its culmination in the *Wulang Reh* and *Wédhatama*. *Wédhatama* contains the most important ethical, philosophical and mystical works. S. Robson states that Javanese scholars of literature may well begin with *Wédhatama*, since it expresses profound Javanese thought.[87] *Wédhatama* with its context of Javanese

---

the *Search for Identity and Modernity in Indonesian Society*, Leiden, 1988, p. 108.

[84] Cf. Th. Pigeaud, *Literature of Java*, Vol.I, The Hague, 1967, p. 1.

[85] P.J. Zoetmulder, *Kalangwan*, The Hague, 1974, p. 3.

[86] P.J. Zoetmulder, *Kalangwan*, The Hague, 1974, p.3.

[87] Cf. S. Robson, *The Wédhatama. An English Translation*(with original text), Leiden, 1990, p. 3.

literature is a primary source in this study, due to the following reasons:
1) Both *Wulang Reh* and *Wédhatama* contains Javanese teaching, called *Piwulang*. From the perspective of Javanese content, *Wédhatama* has more comprehensive thought than *Wulang Reh* and other Javanese writings.

2) The book of *Wédhatama* is the most famous and highly valued product of Javanese literature. Pigeaud mentions that *Wédhatama* is a speculative poem ascribed to KGPAA[88] Mangkunagara IV.[89]

3) The *Wédhatama* also contains Javanese authoritative literature, because it is the product of the court activities. The author, Mangkunagara IV from Surakarta, was a princely author.[90] It is remarkable evidence that the courts of Surakarta and that of Yogyakarta are the highest centres of civilization found in the Javanese tradition.[91] Accordingly, *Wédhatama* is heavy with the authoritative teaching on sublime subjects such as philosophy and mysticism.[92]

The consequences of this approach are of note: the pluralism of

---

[88] KGPAA is the abbreviation of Kanjeng Gusti Pangeran Adipati Arya. It is the noble title in the Royal Court tradition.

[89] Cf. Th. Pigeaud, *Literature of Java*,Vol. I, The Hague, 1967, p. 110.

[90] Mangkunegara IV was born in 1809 and was the son of prince Hadiwidjoyo I of Kartosuro. As a young prince his name was R.M. Sudiro. From childhood he was educated directly by his grandfather who entrusted his further education to Kanjeng Pangeran Rio who later on became Mangkunegara III. When Mangkunegara III died on the 24th of March 1853, he was nominated to succeed him. Accordingly, he took the name Mangkunegara IV on the 16th of August 1857 and reigned over Mangkunegaran for 28 years. Mangkunegara IV was not only a great military expert and king, but he was also one of the great scholars of 19th century in Java. Beside *Wédhatama,* his other writings are *Tripana, Manuhara, Nayakawara, Yogatama, Parimita, Pralambang Lara Kenya, Pariwara, Rerepen Prayasmara, Sendhon Langenswara.* Cf. J. Darminta, *"Mawas Diri" (Self-Examination). A Dialogical Encounter of the Self-Examination of Ki Ageng Suryomentaram in the Perspective of Javanese Religious Life with the Ignatian Examination of Conscience,* Dissertation, Rome, 1980, p. 155; Th. Pigeaud, *Serat Anggitan Dalem Kandjeng Gusti Pangeran Adipati Aria Mangkunegara IV* (Letter of KGPAA Mangkunegara IV), Vol. III, Djakarta, 1953; Ki Padmasusastra, *Serat Piwulang Warni-warni Anggitan Dalem Swargi KGPAA Mangkunegara IV* (Letter of Various *Piwulang* of KGPAA Mangkunegara IV), Surakarta, 1965.

[91] Cf. S. Robson, *The Wédhatama. An English Translation* (with original text), Leiden, 1990, p. 3.

[92] S. Robson, *The Wédhatama. An English Translation* (with original text), Leiden, 1990, p. 3.

Javanese culture is recognized as fact; there is no uniformity of thought, habit and tradition. The eastern Javanese tradition, for example, is different from the central Javanese or western Javanese. The palace's civilization is not the same as urban civilization. This study is concerned with only one of the Javanese currents or traditions; it does not deal with that of the Javanese in urban society. In this section we rather concern ourselves with Javanese literature of the 19th century, especially *Wédhatama* from the palace of Surakarta, in which the author produced his golden work.

The second primary source is *wayang*. It is inevitable that in such an approach we limit the perspective of Javanese thought. The urban spector we shall leave aside, perhaps for another work at another time.

1. *Wédhatama* and Its Background

In dealing with *Wédhatama*, the concern of this study is not one of technical detail, such as the debate on the author,[93] the other printed versions of *Wédhatama*,[94] and so on. We concur with the traditionally accepted position of the majority of experts who maintain KGPAA Mangkunagara IV is the author of *Wédhatama*. We use the English translation of *Wédhatama* with its original texts as found in Robson's work. Robson is one of the most important experts on Javanese literature, and he uses all the previous works on *Wédhatama*.[95]

To interpret *Wédhatama*, we need to use both the previous and later works of *Wédhatama*. *Wulang Reh* and the Book of *Cabolek*, *Kalangwan* and *Manunggaling Kawula Gusti* of Zoetmulder shed some light for a clearer understanding of *Wédhatama*. Pigeaud"s *Literature of Java* has significantly contributed to this approach. The transmission of

---

[93] There is a polemic on KGPAA Mangkunagara IV or R. Ng. Wirya Kusuma as the author of *Wédhatama*. The traditional assumption and the majority of experts agree with KGPAA Mangkunagara IV as the author.

[94] The other version of *Wédhatama* adds 10 other stanzas of canto *Kinanti* after the canto *Gambuh*. We follow the original without addition as we find in the work of S. Robson.

[95] Cf. S. Robson, *The Wédhatama. An English Translation* (with original text), Leiden, 1990, pp. 55-57.

piwulang through the performance of *wayang* is also a remarkable source for comprehension of the philosophical ideas in Javanese thought. These are the foremost, yet few of the many Javanese works of literature that can help deepen the understanding of *Wédhatama.*

Wédhatama itself etymologically derives from the Sanskrit words *"Veda"* and *"uttama." "Veda"* means "knowledge or sacred knowledge or lore"; *"Uttama"* means "uppermost, highest and chief." Hence, the *Wédhatama* can be translated as "highest wisdom."[96] This book is filled with extra nuances of valuable esoteric knowledge, knowledge useful for the spirit. And so it is also philosophy or better, a philosophy of life.[97] It also contains an holistic perception of human being.

The date of *Wédhatama* is not known with any certainty. We do know that *Wédhatama* was written toward the end of Mangkunagara IV's reign, to whom authorship is generally credited. Critics agree that it was dated at the end of 1870s. The scholar-king also produced works of history, poems and a number of didactic works.[98]

Wédhatama used the form of Javanese poetry called *Macapat.* Pigeaud says:

> Originally the name *tembang Macapat* conveyed a similar idea, namely homely or home-made metres. *Macapat* and *Mancapat,* meaning "four fellows," are expressions referring to a group of closely-related units, located on the corners of a square, in accordance with cosmic order. To the Javanese mind the word *mancapat* suggests safety and the well-known order of the home district.[99]

We find four kinds of metre in these works. They are *pangkur, sinom, pucung and gambuh.*[100] *Pangkur* has 14 stanzas, *sinom* has 18

---

[96] S. Robson, *The Wédhatama. An English Translation* (with original text), Leiden, 1990, p. 48.

[97] S. Robson, *The Wédhatama. An English Translation* (with original text), Leiden, 1990, p. 14.

[98] Cf. Th. Pigeaud, *Literature of Java,* Vol. I, The Hague, 1967, p. 110.

[99] Th. Pigeaud, *The Literature of Java,* Vol. I, The Hague, 1967, p. 20.

[100] *Pangkur* is a name of a well known *macapat* metre. It is also the name of religious officials mentioned in some Old Javanese charters. *Sinom* metre and tune might contain remiscences of the appearance and activities of the traditional juvenile sesrvice groups in communal festivities. *Pucung* is one metre of the Javanese poem. It also means the bottle, carfe,

stanzas, *pucung* has 15 stanzas, and *gambuh* has 25 stanzas. Thus the total number is 72 stanzas.[101] Further, Javanese poetry's form of *Wédhatama* can be described as follows:

No.	Name of Metre	Number of stanzas	Scheme
I	Pangkur	14	8a, 11i, 8u, 7a, 12u, 8a, 8i
II	Sinom	18	8a, 8i, 8a, 8i, 7i, 8u, 7a, 8i, 12a
III	Pucung	15	4u, 8u, 6a, 8i, 12a
IV	Gambuh	25	7u, 10u, 12i, 8u, 8o

Every metre consists of stanzas (*pada*). Every stanza consists of lines (*gatra*). Each line is organized from a fixed number of syllables and vowels, as indicated in the scheme above.[102]

In the metre of the *pangkur*, we can find the motive of the author of *Wédhatama*. KGPAA Mangkunagara IV wrote *Wédhatama* in order to give instructions to all his sons to gain the prosperity of the noble science.[103] According to *Wédhatama*, everyone who attains *ngèlmu* becomes a wise man who likes to give in. Such a person observes the appearances of reality and hides his feelings behind good expressions. Accordingly, his conversations are always in good taste. He is not afraid to be called "blockhead." Such a condition gives happiness to those who

---

glas container, or the name of the small animal. *Gambuh* means experienced or expert. This name is also connected with certain dances which occupied an important place in ancient Javanese communal festivals. (Ibid. pp. 20-21)

[101] Cf. S. Robson, *The Wédhatama. An English Translation* (with original text), Leiden, 1990, p. 8.

[102] S. Robson, *The Wédhatama. An English Translation* (with original text), Leiden, 1990, p. 8.

[103] The idea of noble science is expressed in canto *Pangkur* 1. Cf. S. Robson, *The Wédhatama. An English Translation* (with original text), Leiden, 1990, pp. 20, 21.

already possess *ngèlmu*; and they can use it as *kasekten*.[104]

There is an assumption in society that without *ngèlmu* a human person does not grasp the essence of reality. And so he is empty. KGPAA Mangkunagara IV, therefore, instructed his sons and all youths to strive for *ngèlmu*. The acquirement of it is characterized by a quality of austere life, auspicious example and of the capacity of restraining one's desires.[105] For example, one receives an inspiration from God with the capacity to gather up the scattered pieces of himself through the ways of austerity. Accordingly, he is free from his desires and has a clear insight into the *two in one* or "unity in diversity" in the precise example of the unity between a human being and God.[106] This is the end of *ngèlmu*, expressed in the term *sepuh* in Javanese thought. *Pangkur* 12 points out that "Liring sepuh sepi hawa. Awas roroning atunggal." (*Old* is in a sense free from passions or desires and has a clear insight into the *two-in-one*.) Thus the term "old" is taken not only in the sense of "have many years in age," but moreover, it has a philosophical and mystical meaning. It is that moment in which a human being is in the state of experiencing no difference between sleeping and waking. He is in the realm of the void, in which a human being is reduced to his first origin.[107]

The canto *sinom* contains a description of a perfect human being.

---

[104] *Kasekten* is an extraordinary capacity of a human person, gained through self-discipline, fasting and esoteric practices. It is described in the canto *Pangkur 9*. The ancient Javanese authors (*Pujanggas*) believe that *kasekten* is a mediumistic phenomenon coming out from macrocosmos and concentrating as a mysterious power. Cf. S. Robson, *The Wèdhatama. An English Translation* (with original text), Leiden, 1990, pp. 22-23; Sang Harumjati, *Pustaka Radja Mantrajoga. Saka Kitab "Ilmu Kasekten Gaib"* (Pustaka Radja Mantrajoga. From the book of "Knowledge of Mysterious *Kasekten*"), in: AAvv, *Baboning Kitab Primbon. Bundelan 10 Kitab Primbon Pusaka Sumber Ilmu Kejawen Taksih Asli dening Para Pujonggo Jawi* (Motherbook of *Primbon*. Collection of 10 Primbon's Heirloom Books. Sources of the *Kejawen* Knowledge derived from Javanese Authors), Solo, 1946, pp. 1-8.

[105] The acquirements of *ngèlmu* are described in the canto *Pangkur 11*. Cf. S. Robson, *The Wèdhatama. An English Translation* (with original text), Leiden, 1990, pp. 24-25.

[106] The idea of "unity in diversity" might be expressed by the term *sepuh* in canto *Pangkur 12.*. Cf. S. Robson, *The Wèdhatama. An English Translation* (with original text), Leiden, 1990, p. 24.

[107] We find this description in the canto *Pangkur 13-14*. Cf. S. Robson, *The Wèdhatama. An English Translation* (with original text), Leiden, 1990, p. 24.

34

The example of the perfect human being is Panembahan Senapati, the figure who one characerizes as having good manners and devoting oneself to lessening desires and passions.[108] One reaches a clear insight into the right course of action so that one sees the core of one's own self. The mind's eye ranges limitlessly.[109] With a remarkable personality, such a person strives to be gentle and comforting to others. One retires to solitude and is captivated by peace of mind. Firmly and steadfastly, one controls the desire for food and sleep.[110] Capacity is rooted in solitude with the attitude of strengthening the will and discipline. The *ngèlmu* of Panembahan Senapati is very deep, so that even the *Queen of the South*[111] came to beseech him.[112] This perfect being is a human paragon and zealous in philosophy.

We find differences between the Javanese tradition and Islamic teaching. *Wédhatama* is an invitation to the Javanese to follow the teachings of the ancestors. They teach three basic principles of life. They are *wirya, arta,* and *winasis,*[113] meaning status, property or money and skill, respectively. The absence of these three principles in human beings results in a loss of all traces of humanity.

The canto of *pucung* contains a description of *ngèlmu* as a knowledge which exists in company with practice. This knowledge is exercised with firmness, with the strong will to master evil urges. It helps some to love tranquillity, to forgive one's errors, and to devote oneself to

---

[108] Cf. S. Robson, *The Wédhatama. An English Translation* (with original text), Leiden, 1990, pp. 26-27.

[109] Cf. S. Robson, *The Wédhatama. An English Translation* (with original text), Leiden, 1990, pp. 32-33.

[110] S. Robson, *The Wédhatama. An English Translation* (with original text), Leiden, 1990, pp. 26-27.

[111] *Queen of South*, who is also called *Ratu Kidul*, is a goddess of the South Sea in Javanese legend. Cf. G. Moedjanto, *The Concept of Power in Javanese Culture*, Yogyakarta, 1990, pp. 109-110; Sartono Kartodirdjo, *Modern Indonesia. Tradition and Transformation*, Yogyakarta, 1988, p. 219.

[112] Cf. S. Robson, *The Wédhatama. An English Translation* (with original text), Leiden, 1990, pp. 30-31.

[113] Cf. S. Robson, *The Wédhatama. An English Translation* (with original text), Leiden, 1990, pp. 32.

highest gentleness. The aspiration of knowledge is accepted by judgment; it becomes effective through asceticism. Through asceticism one cultivates (a) acquiescence (*lila ora gegetun*), (b) acceptance of self and of the bitter experience of others through internal reflection, and (c) a humble surrender and trust in God.[114] Such practice of *ngèlmu* is like a pure retreat in which God is seated at the pinnacle of one's heart.

Gambuh is the canto of worship. The four objects of human worship are the body, thought, the soul, and essence.[115] The worship of body concentrates on physical rites and orders. According to the *Wédhatama,* practice of the Islamic religion belongs to this form of worship.[116] The worship of body is useful to achieve peace of mind and to banish inner confusion.[117] The author underlines that the worship of body is not the only worship. There are possibilities of different paths; Human beings are not all alike and the warp and weft of life are varied.

The worship of heart or thought is a way of practising asceticism. This worship engenders the certainty of knowledge that brings about the acknowledgement of providence. The practice of the worship of heart leads one to see that particularity fades away with the revelation of a higher world. Human feelings die away; hence a human being finds the righteousness of the All-Seeing.[118]

Beside the types mentioned above, there is the worship of soul, called the culmination of the way. The practitioner turns to his inward being as this worship consists of insight and mindfulness.[119] A human

---

[114] Cf. S. Robson, *The Wédhatama. An English Translation* (with original text), Leiden, 1990, pp. 38-39.

[115] S. Robson, *The Wédhatama. An English Translation* (with original text), Leiden, 1990, pp. 38-39.

[116] This idea is expressed in canto *Gambuh* 2, 7. S. Robson, *The Wédhatama. An English Translation* (with original text), Leiden, 1990, pp. 40-41.

[117] The state of peaceful mind is precisely described in canto *Gambuh* 8. Cf. S. Robson, *The Wédhatama. An English Translation* (with original text), Leiden, 1990, p. 40.

[118] Cf. S. Robson, *The Wédhatama. An English Translation* (with original text), Leiden, 1990, pp. 42-43.

[119] Cf. S. Robson, *The Wédhatama. An English Translation* (with original text), Leiden, 1990, pp. 44-45.

being is said to be bound to three worlds. The microcosm mastered the macrocosm and the underworld; at the same time consciousness is swept into the universe, and it becomes like a glittering star, in which a human person contains and is contained. At this moment the human heart opens.

The last worship is the worship of essence, which is the core of creation. A human being performs the worship of essence by inner firmness. This worship takes place when a human being simply trusts in providence and anxieties have vanished from his heart.[120]

2. The Ideas of *Keselarasan* in *Wédhatama*

The ideas of *Keselarasan* are expressed in the canto of *gambuh*. It sings of the possibility of differences and a spirit of tolerance. The description of a perfect human being, for instance, points to the importance of the capacity to gather up the scattered pieces of self. The perfect human being is further able to have a clear insight of the *two-in-one*. There is a noble manner which acquiesces, accepts bitter reality in peace, and fully surrenders the person to the Lord. According to the Javanese, the human person can reach an ultimate state of mastery of his world.

We can also accompany the ideas of *Keselarasan* with the idea of human beings in unity with the universe. A human being should see the self in relation to the surrounding reality. Person and environment are the two realities; nevertheless they constitute a union. Existence unites a human being to the world, and according to Javanese thought, it is a fact that as long as one exists, there is a union to the other things in the world.

In gaining the highest end of human life, a human being should roll up the *triloka*,[121] so says canto *gambuh* 18, that microcosm and macrocosm become one, and universe and human beings unite. Thus, a

---

[120] Cf. S. Robson, *The Wédhatama. An English Translation* (with original text), Leiden, 1990, pp. 46-47.

[121] *Triloka* literally means "the three worlds". It is a Javanese expression for the totality of the universe, consisting of heaven, earth and the underworld.

human being constitutes the unity of the universe, and by this constituency has an harmonious reciprocal relationship with the universe. It is this very relationship that forms the seed from which grows *Keselarasan*.[122]

The essence of a human being is not different than the essence of the universe, which is *alam suwung* or *kosong*.[123] In canto *Gambuh* 17, *alam suwung* means an eternal and permanent realm. This realm, in which human beings live, is the realm of changing and becoming. The essence of points out that human beings live in the process and development of a changing world. A human being is distinguished from other things because humans are conscious of their existence. This consciousness leads to virtue and perfection in human life.[124] A human being does not sink into or depend on the universe; his identity is always relational. That is why the essence of a human being is called *bhinneka tunggal, majemuk tunggal* or *monopluralis*.[125] The essence of human nature as *monopluralis* signifies many elements as one unity.

Let us consider *monopluralis* in the relationship between the body and the soul. *Wédhatama* states that a human being consists of body and soul.[126] The word *"Jiwangga"* in canto *Sinom* 16 and *Gambuh* 12 alludes to this duality.[127] *Jiwangga* consists of the word *"jiwa,"* meaning "soul" and *"angga,"* meaning "body." The expression *Jiwangga* maintains that body and soul are one reality. We cannot think of the existence of a soul

---

[122] Cf. Endang Daruni, et al., *Gambaran Manusia menurut Wédhatama. Laporan Penelitian,* (The Concept of Man in *Wédhatama*. A Report of Research), Yogyakarta, 1984, pp. 37-38.

[123] The expression *"alam suwung* or *kosong"* means the realm of nothing, without content or nothingness. Cf. S. Robson, *The Wédhatama. An English Translation* (with original text), Leiden, 1990, p. 38.

[124] S. Robson, *The Wédhatama. An English Translation* (with original text), Leiden, 1990, pp. 41-42.

[125] The Indonesian expressions of *"bhinneka tunggal, majemuk tunggal* or *monopluralis"* mean "two or many various things in one". Cf. S. Robson, *The Wédhatama. An English Translation* (with original text), Leiden, 1990, p. 42.

[126] *Pangkur* 8, 13; *Gambuh* 8; *Sinom* 16, *Pucung* 11. Cf. S. Robson, *The Wédhatama. An English Translation* (with original text), Leiden, 1990, pp. 22-23, 24-25, 40-41, 32-33, 38-39.

[127] Cf. S. Robson, *The Wédhatama. An English Translation* (with original text), Leiden, 1990, p. 32.

38

without thinking of the existence of a body. Both the body and the soul are important elements of the human essence[128] which constitutes the reality of human life.

The control of human reason, feelings and will, which in Indonesian expression we call *akal, rasa* and *kehendak,* brings out the equilibrium between soul and body. The teaching of *Wédhatama,* therefore, guides human beings to the attainment of good manners and a noble quality of human life.[129] In this way human beings fulfill their nature by striving for beauty and goodness.[130] Human beings also have to be in equilibrium with the universe. Only then can they have an attitude of acquiescence and trust in the Lord, who shrouds everything.[131]

Wédhatama contains a remarkable, percise conception of a human being as God's creature, as a unity of the soul and body, as an individual and social being.[132] Accordingly a human being has a social nature, nevertheless one is at the same time also an individual.[133] Thus, human beings should think of others or of society, by mere consequence of human nature. In juxtaposition to this, it is necessary for a Javanese person to find one's own personality by retreating in solitude or *tapa brata.* And so one gains the self confidence to be one, to choose one's preferences and make personal decisions[134] within society. The basic principles which guide human life in society are power, property and

---

[128] Cf. Endang Daruni, et.al., *Konsep Manusia dalam Wédhatama. Laporan Penelitian* (The Concept of Man in *Wédhatama.* A Report of Research), Yogyakarta, 1984, p. 54.

[129] Cf. Endang Daruni, et al., *Konsep Manusia dalam Wédhatama. Laporan Penelitian* (The Concept of Man in *Wédhatama.* A Report of Research), Yogyakarta, 1984, p. 55.

[130] Cf. S. Robson, *The Wédhatama. An English Translation* (with original text), Leiden, 1990, p. 42.

[131] Endang Daruni, et al., *Konsep Manusia dalam Wédhatama. Laporan Penelitian* (The Concept of Man in *Wédhatama.* A Report of Research), Yogyakarta, 1984, p. 44.

[132] Endang Daruni, et al., *Konsep Manusia dalam Wédhatama. Laporan Penelitian* (The Concept of Man in *Wédhatama.* A Report of Reasearch), Yogyakarta, 1984, pp. 6, 34.

[133] Endang Daruni, et al., *Konsep Manusia dalam Wédhatama. Laporan Penelitian* (The Concept of Man in *Wédhatama.* A Report of Research), Yogyakarta, 1984, p. 63.

[134] Endang Daruni, et al., *Konsep Manusia dalam Wédhatama. Laporan Penelitian* (The Concept of Man in *Wédhatama.* A Report of Research), Yogyakarta, 1984, p. 64.

skill.[135] Consciousness of these basic principles is manifest in one's association with others.

B.   Javanese Thought in *Wayang*

We deal with the *wayang* because the wayang is full of old Javanese teachings and philosophical thought. As Lee Khoon Choy states: "The shadow play is an important part in Javanese philosophy."[136] We, therefore, complement the philosophical thought of *Wédhatama* by the philosophical thought in *wayang*.

Besides, the *wayang* demonstrates the concept that human development still is on going.[137] Choy teaches: "To understand *wayang* is the first step to understand the Javanese. There is at least one *wayang* group which performs regularly for viewers of all ages in every village throughout Java. It has become a way of life."[138] For this same reason we use the *wayang* as an important source for our study.

1.   The *Wayang* and Its Background

Wayang is a dramatic performance in which a story is presented by means of puppets or dancers. The term *wayang* has the same etymological background as the Javanese word for shadow. It alludes to the form of *wayang's* performance on a shadow screen. There are several kinds of *wayang* such as *wayang orang, wayang golek, wayang purwa, wayang klitik* and so forth.[139] Of special concern is *wayang purwa*; it is

---

[135] Cf. S. Robson, *The Wédhatama. An English Translation* (with original text), Leiden, 1990, p. 33.

[136] Lee Khoon Choy, *Indonesia between Myth and Reality*, London, 1976, p. 3.

[137] Cf. H. Ulbricht, *Wayang Purwa. Shadows of the Past*, Kualalumpur, 1970, p. 20.

[138] Lee Khoon Choy, *Indonesia between Myth and Reality*, London, 1976, p. 3.

[139] *Wayang orang* is a dramatic performance in which a story is presented by dancers. This name is given to the theatre with male and female, playing *wayang* plays, which developed in central Java at the Royal and princely Court in the last decade of the nineteenth century. *Wayang golek* is the *wayang* in which a story is presented by the use of dolls made from wood. It follows the *wayang purwa* in popularity. *Wayang golek* uses polychroned round, wooden puppets with movable hands and arms. Heads made by gifted woodcarvers can be very expressive. The story

considered as first and most popular in Javanese society.

The *wayang purwa* is an art form of which it can be said that it has become the innermost heart of Javanese society. Its stories appeal to the entire population, and to the rural population above all. As mentioned above, there are many kinds of *wayang*; however, it is *wayang purwa* which is the classic *wayang*, the most attractive, and which resonates deeply in society. It is very attractive because it encompasses the philosophy of life which best accords with the Indonesian way of looking at reality. It also presents spiritual teachings, morals, instructions in etiquette that belong to their unique civilization, and patriotism and heroism.

Wayang purwa as the traditional or classical Javanese shadow play has its origin in ancient times. H. Ulbricht and Victoria M. Clara van Groenendael affirm that it originated in Neolithic times from the practices of ancestor worship.[140] Sri Mulyono accepts the assumption that *wayang* included the figure of Semar dated from c. 1500 B.C.[141] This former assumption that it dates from Neolithic times lacks sound reasons. First we do not have remnants of *wayang* from the Neolithic times, and second, the Javanesese *gamelan,* the most important music in *wayang,* dates only from A.D. 347.[142] Therefore, it might rather be that *wayang purwa* is a product of a later civilization. According to Choy, *wayang* has its origin from the ancient Hindu King Joyoboyo in 861.[143] At the time, King Joyoboyo ordered his artists to make drawings on palm leaves, called *lontar,* of the stone figures of his ancestors. This fact is confirmed by information from Pigeaud to which he adds:

---

of *wayang purwa* is presented by puppets on a screen. *Wayang klitik* uses flat wooden boards with flexible arms as puppets. V. Pigeaud, *Literature of Java,* Vol. I, p. 246.

[140] H. Ulbricht, *Wayang Purwa. Shadows of the Past,* Kualalumpur, 1970, p. XV; Cf. Victoria M. Clara van Groenendael, *The Dalang behind the Wayang,* Dordrecht, 1985, p. 1.

[141] Cf. Haryanto, S, *Bayang Bayang Adhiluhung. Filsafat, Simbolis dan Mistik dalam Wayang* (Beautiful and Noble shadows. Philosophy, Symbols and Mystic in *Wayang),* Semarang, 1992, p. 104.

[142] Cf. Inge Skog, *North Borneo Gongs and the Javanese Gamelan,* Stockholm, 1993, p. 112.

[143] Cf. Lee Khoon Choy, *Indonesia between Myth and Reality,* London, 1976, p. 140.

The strange proportion of wayang figures belong to an antique style of drawing, which represented the divine character of mythical heroes by a sacral rigidity and exaggerated proportions of important limbs and parts of the body: arms, eyes and noses.[144]

I think it is quite right that at the beginning *wayang purwa* was closely connected with ancestor worship. Both Ulbricht and Choy have the same perception. Choy further states that the present word of *wayang* was borrowed from a word which originally referred to the image of the ancestors.[145]

Later *wayang* was connected with religious exorcist rites, which might be dated from the eighteenth century or later.[146] A considerable number of *wayang* plays deal with the exorcism of evil beings and victory over demons. Some are relate to ancient myths. This development has not changed the essence of *wayang*. Suffice it to say that although the tendencies of exorcist rites are not fundamental in *wayang*, however, as Pigeaud finds: "All have the idea of struggle against evil powers and victory by means of religious exorcist rites or practices in common."[147]

The whole performance of *wayang* is also connected with moral, religious teaching known as *piwulang*. That is why the key figure in the shadow theatre game is called *dalang*, which is a shortened form of *ngudal piwulang* or in English, "to teach." Rassers points to the conviction frequently expressed by the Javanese that *wayang* has something to do with the education of the young.[148] According to Hazeu, the word *dalang* refers to "the man wandering about to give *wayang* performances from place to place."[149]

The existence of *wayang purwa*, preserved well during the many

---

[144] Th. Pigeaud, *Literature of Java*, Vol. III, The Hague, 1970, p. 46.

[145] Cf. Lee Khoon Choy, *Indonesia between Myth and Reality*, London, 1976,, p. 140.

[146] Cf. Th. Pigeaud, *Literature of Java*, Vol. I, The Hague, 1967, p. 205.

[147] Th. Pigeaud, *The Literature of Java*, Vol. I, The Hague, 1967, p. 205.

[148] Rassers W.H., *Panji, the Culture of Hero. A Structural Study on Religion in Java*, The Hague, 1959, p. 152; Cf. Victoria M.Clara van Groenendael, *The Dalang behind the Wayang*, Dordrecht, 1985, p. 5.

[149] Cf. Victoria M. Clara van Groenendael, *The Dalang behind the Wayang*, Dordrecht, 1985, p 4.

years up to now, shows us that it has deep roots in the core of Javanese culture and civilization. It is based on local myths from ancient native literature, as Pigeaud tells us:

> Indeed several plays belonging to all cycles of the Javanese theatrical repertoire apparently are based on folk-tales or myths, survivals of ancient native literature. Only the names of heroes and heroines were borrowed from the great epics and classical romances of Indian literature.[150]

Besides, the *wayang* is full of ancient Javanese treasures. Sri Mulyono maintains:

> For all these centuries wayang has played an important role in the lives of those who follow it. It is a rich source of folk sayings, a medium of education, a store house of knowledge, a mine of musical fantasy, a library of poetic imagery, and a living treasury of religion and spiritual teachings that can thrill the soul into its awakening when the time is right and the hearer is ready.[151]

The various teachings of *wayang* are expressed in a great number of themes. Some of the very old themes are inspired by the Indian epics *Rāmāyana* and *Mahābhārata*.[152] Th. Pigeaud confirms this assumption when he says: "In the Pre-Islamic period, belletristic Court literature consisted mainly in Old Javanese poetic adaptations of epic tales borrowed from Indian literature."[153] The Javanese author, on one side, borrows the subjects of Indian epic literature; on the other side, the fundamental concept of social and cosmic order pervades all original literature.

Through the mythical characters of *Mahābhārata* and *Rāmāyana*,

---

[150] Th. Pigeaud, *The Literature of Java*, Vol. I, The Hague, 196, p. 247.

[151] Sri Mulyono, *Human Character in the Wayang. Javanese Shadow Play*, Singapore, 1981, pp. 270-271.

[152] *Rāmāyana* is is a classical Indian epic poem written by Wālmiki. The tale of Rma's struggle with Dasamuka for the possesion of Sita (often called Sinta) has been known in Java from ancient times and in various versions. Perhaps Indian civilization was introduced into Java by men belonging to a cultured class of society. *Mahābhārata* might be a counterpart of the *Rāmāyana*. Its subject matter is the struggle of *pandawas* and *kurawas*. In Javanese society it is known as *Bharata Yudha*, in which the content is an account of the final battle. The Javanese *Bharata Yudha* was composed by Mpu Sedah (1157) and finished by Mpu Panuluh. Their Royal patron was King Jaya Bhaya of Kediri. Cf. Th. Pigeaud, *Literature of Java*, Vol. I, The Hague, p. 178.

[153] Th. Pigeaud, *Literature of Java*, Vol. I, The Hague, 1967, p. 176.

the *dalang* conveys to the viewers and listeners the Javanese concept of the universe. He also expounds poetically the existential position of the Javanese personality and the importance of maintaining harmony and stability in a world of conflict.[154]

The Arjuna Sasrabahu theme forms a kind of prelude to the Rama cycle. It deals with the events leading up to the great battle between Rama, as a manifestation of the god Wisnu, and the demon King Rawana, which in a previous incarnation of god Wisnu, had fought over the possession of Dewi Sinta (Sita) who is abducted by Dasamuka (Rawana) but is liberated by Rama with the support of Hanuman and his monkey army.[155]

There are a great number of *wayang* themes which have well known, deep philosophical and spiritual contents. Some examples follow: 1) *Dewa Ruci*: this theme speaks about Bima who looks for the water of life, the path of understanding, the origin and meaning of life. The theme of *Dewa Ruci* is based on a legend written at the end of the Majapahit Kingdom. S. Haryanto states that the theme of *Dewa Ruci* was creation of Mpu Siwamurti. It was known in the 1450s.[156]
2) *Arjuna Wiwaha*: this theme speaks about Arjuna who fasts and meditates in order to get divine aid. He wants to achieve great virtue and strength so that he cannot be defeated by anything in the whole world and can control the whole world and save it. This theme is the work of Mpu Kanwa during the reign of King Airlanga (1020 - 1035).

There are other numerous themes which also express the symbol of human life. Using those themes, *wayang* has reached a highly aesthetic level both in music and in form. The *wayang* performance requires the use of a number of instruments, such as a *gamelan* orchestra, puppets, *gedebok* or the trunk of a banana tree, screen, lamp, and so on. The

---

[154] Cf. Lee Khoon Choy, *Indonesia between Myth and Reality*, London, 1976, p. 137.

[155] Cf. Sunardjo Haditjaroko, *Ramayana. Indonesian Wayang Show*, (8th Edition), Jakarta, 1993, p. 101-112.

[156] Haryanto, S., *Bayang Bayang Adhiluhung. Filsafat, Simbolis dan Mistik dalam Wayang* (Beautiful and Noble Shadows. Mystic, Symbol and Philosophy in *Wayang*), Semarang, 1992, p. 122.

44

essential instruments of *wayang* also reveal Javanese thought and philosophical reflection on reality.

The *gamelan* orchestra, for instance, used to express the mood of the particular moment becomes the symbol of harmony of all worldly activities.[157] *Serat Centini* agrees that the *gamelan* is a symbol of the harmony of events.[158] The puppets with their art forms are capable of portraying the deep realities behind human character. The screen alludes to human life as the place and the witness of all events in the world. The shadow on the screen is used to illustrate the invisible world. It has two dimensions: it is real and at the same time unreal. Through the use of shadow they can project the spirit of their ancestors which, they believe, exist but are not visible to our eyes. In philosophical terms, the illuminated screen is the visible world and the puppets represent the variety of God's creation. The *dalang* also uses the shadow to convey the meaning of life and the destiny of man.[159] The trunk of a banana tree, on which the puppets are placed, is a symbol of the surface of the world. Meanwhile the lamp above the head of the dalang is an image of the light of life.

2. The Idea of *Keselarasan* in *Wayang*

In the *gamelan's* ambience, we find the term *laras*,[160] which

---

[157] Cf. Lee Khoon Choy, *Indonesia between Myth and Reality*, London, 1976, p. 139.

[158] *"Kelir jagad gumelar wayang pinanggung / asnapun makluk ing Widi / gedebog bantala wegung / belèncong pandama ing urip / gamelan gending ing lakon"* ("The Screen is the visible world, the puppets on the left and right sides are the categories of God's creatures. Trunk of banana's tree is the earth. The *blèncong* is the lamp of life. The *gamelan* is the harmony or Keselarasan of the events"), *Serat Centini* V, 359-367; Cf. P.J. Zoetmulder, *Pantheïsme en Monisme in de Javaansche Soeloek-Literatuur*, (translated by Dick Hartoko), Jakarta, 1991, pp. 287, 291; P.J. Zoetmulder, *Pantheism and Monism in Javanese Suluk Literature. Islamic and Indian Mysticism in an Indonesian Setting*, (edited and translated by M.C. Ricklefs), Leiden, 1995, pp 242, 245.

[159] The *dalang* entertains the essential purpose of life which is to serve the community. Besides, the *dalang* also assists the country-men in their quest of the true significance of human existence. Cf. Sunardjo Haditjaroko, *Ramayana. Indonesian Wayang Show*, Jakarta, 1993, p. 112.

[160] In the Old Javanese or Kawi, *laras* means beautiful, nice, fascinating, appropriate and concordant voice.

indicates the concord of one instrument with the others. *Laras* is generally translated as "tuning system". as the term *laras* is akin to the word *nglaras*, meaning "to tone."[161] Sometimes it is used in contrast with *blero* which refers to a discordant voice with accompanying music. In this sense the word *laras* has some rich nuances, such as "enjoyable", "relaxing" and "aesthetic sense of contemplation." According to R. Anderson Sutton, in Java the musical term *laras* also has non-musical associations with ideas of harmonious appropriateness and agreement.[162] From this word comes the word *selaras*, which means "in the same rhythm or melody of music," "compatible," and "harmony." Thus there is remarkable evidence in the gamelan that *Keselarasan* has a profound meaning, and captures within it the harmony as of an array of instruments used in one composition of music.

According to Choy, the *gamelan* orchestra symbolizes the harmony of all worldly activities.[163] The *gamelan* consists of a number of instruments, such as the *kendang, demung, gong, kenong, rebab* and so on. They are played together for the performance of one whole melody according to the circumstances or scene in the story. There can be a slow and express sadness when the scenario is sad. The music can express heroic dynamism when there is war or fighting in order to defeat the evil one. At such a moment the melody is fast. It can change abruptly and become slower, so that it helps the audience to fllow the story with feeling and imagination. The music of the *gamelan* has a different quality for every different situation. Sri Mulyono says: "The compositions played by the gamelan each have a distinctive quality of their own: noble, elegant, sacred, arrogant, or splendid, and not only are they delicious to hear and teach the soul to explore aesthetic pleasure,..."[164] *Gamelan* as

---

[161] Cf. Walter Kaufmann, *Selected Musical of Non-Western Cultures: A Notebook-Glossary,* Michigan, 1990, p. 420.

[162] R. Anderson Sutton, *Variation in Central Javanese Music Dynamic of a Steady State,* Illinois, 1993, p. 20.

[163] P.J. Zoetmulder, *Pantheïsme en Monisme in de Javaansche Soeloek-Literatuur,* (Translated by Dick Hartoko), Jakarta, 1991, p. 139.

[164] Sri Mulyono, *Human Character in the Wayang. Javanese Shadow Play,* Singapore, 1981, p. 20.

46

the symbol of harmony implicitly teaches the stages of the mystical experience, painting the bliss of divine grace through its melodies together with the story.[165]

In short the nature of the *gamelan* orchestra itself presents the image of *Keselarasan*, as all the instruments are combined harmoniously in a beautiful whole. No one element may predominate, but every instrument has its role in creating this atmosphere of a beautiful whole. It is not the individual formal element that determines the success of the *wayang* performance, but rather the union of the *gamelan* instruments which constitutes that quality of performance which has endured for centuries.

Besides the *gamelan* orchestra, there is one principal stage property of the Javanese *wayang,* called the *gunungan*. It is made of stiff buffalo leather, perforated and coloured. The *gunungan,* fastened to a stick made of buffalo horn, is planted upright in the middle of the stage at the beginning and at the end of the performance. It is manipulated in various ways at turning points of the play. The upper half of the *gunungan* shows the branches of the tree-of-life, which stands for the source of life (God), who is concealed behind a door. The two giants are guarding the door. They are supposed to represent the powers of hunger and sex. As a whole the picture is meant to represent man as having to master his longing for food and his carnal desire before he is able to see God. Only vanities are visible, symbolized by the monkeys and birds which bustle about in the branches of the tree-of-life. Two snakes and two other big animals are shown in combat with each other, in a demonstration of power and strength which, if uncontrolled, are a menace to peace.[166]

According to A. J. Bennet Kemper, the mountain is the seat of gods and ancestors, a world full of mysteries. The mountain is the source of life giving, fertilizing water and the border between the human world

---

[165] V. P.J. Zoetmulder, *Pantheism and Monism in Javanese Suluk Literature. Islamic and Indian Mysticism in an Indonesian Setting*, (edited and translated by M.C. Ricklefs), Leiden, 1995, p. 242.

[166] Cf. H. Ulbricht, *Wayang Purwa. Shadows of the Past*, Kualalumpur, 1970, pp. 5-7.

and that of the dead.[167] J.J. Ras sees the *gunungan* as the symbolic representation of the process of creation which plays an important role in all religious ceremony.[168] Brandes and Sutterheim point out the importance of the celestial tree. Furthermore, Choy interprets the *gunungan,* whose form looks like a mountain, as an instrument representing Javanese thought on life in all its aspects. This idea is also agree upon by Pigeaud who writes: "It is a symbol of Cosmic Order, the basic concept of Javanese philosophic and religious thinking".[169]

An interesting figure which always appears in every *wayang* performance is Semar. He is a servant of the five *Pāndavas*, especially of Arjuna. Semar's instruction from God, *Sang Hyang Tunggal*, is to see that his masters keep a good balance among their senses and that they are not swayed by their emotions. Semar's role also exposes deceptive appearances in human character. He looks ugly but he is kind-hearted. He is powerful but humble, brave but faithful. He appears stupid, but is often brilliant and wise.

Semar has many side characters and means different things to different people. As a clown he is known as Semar. As Guru, he is called *Batara Manikmaya.* And as a saint, he is known as *Sang Hyang Ismaya.* It is commonly believed that Semar is the brother of Śaiva, a god of many attributes and functions.[170] These diversified characters also provide mental guidelines for interpreting personalities who they happen to encounter.[171] The character of Semar, which is rife with honesty and dedication, can be a Javanese inspiration for perservation of prosperity and peace. Endowed with supernatural powers, Semar never once misuses them, and always comes to the rescue of the helpless. Whenever a good kingdom is about to fall, he is there to save the day.[172]

---

[167] A. J. Bennet Kemper, *Ancient Indonesian Art*, Amsterdam, 1959, p. 21.

[168] Cf. J.J. Ras, "The Panji Romance and W.H. Rassers' Analysis of its Theme", *BKI* 129/4 (1973), pp. 444-445.

[169] Th. Pigeaud, *Literature of Java*, Vol. III, The Hague, 1970, p. 48.

[170] Lee Khoon Choy, *Indonesia between Myth and Reality*, London, 1976, p. 146.

[171] Lee Khoon Choy, *Indonesia between Myth and Reality*, London, 1976, p. 138.

[172] Lee Khoon Choy, *Indonesia between Myth and Reality*, London, 1976, p. 146.

Such mythology and mysticism makes a great impact on the minds of the Javanese people through *wayang*. Mythological stories of war between the *Pāndavas* and *Kuravas*, between right and wrong, and stories of the supernatural powers of the warriors, derived from their *ala*, as well as stories of reincarnation, cannot but influence the Javanese mind, particularly, that of the younger ones. Most Indonesians, therefore, believe in the existence of the soul. They believe that death is not the end of everything and that there is such a thing as a soul, or we may call it super-consciousness, which can be contacted by a well-trained mystic.[173] The objective of the mystic is to break through the world of history and time into that of eternity and timelessness. Mysticism takes its form from the raw material of all religions and adds its inspiration from much of philosophy, poetry, art and music, and becomes a consciousness of something beyond. Mystical experience or speculation is not limited to one religion.[174]

That mystical experience coupled with and mythological expression goes beyond one religion can be illustrated in several examples. One obvious illustration is the invention or development of such key elements of Pre-Islamic culture as *wayang* or the *gamelan* orchestra by the *wali,* the proselytizing saints of Old Javanese Islam. Another well-known example is the common interpretation of the name of King Judistira's *pusaka,*[175] the *serat kalimasada,* as the *kalimah Sahadat,* namely, the Qur'ānic confession of faith.[176] Islam becomes more Javanized and fuseswith some elements of Javanese. Actually not only Muslims, but some adherents of other religions also, believe that Semar, the ugly but supernaturally powerful clown in the *Mahābhārata,* is the guardian of Java.[177] They also respect ancestors' tombs and even try to

---

[173] Lee Khoon Choy, *Indonesia between Myth and Reality*, London, 1976, p. 8.

[174] Lee Khoon Choy, *Indonesia between Myth and Reality*, London, 1976, p. 9.

[175] *Pusaka* is heirloom such as some instruments of *gamelan* orchestra, *Criss*, or any thing considered has particular forces for the human capacity.

[176] Cf. B.R. O'G., Anderson, *The Idea of Power in Javanese Culture*, in: C. Holt, *Culture and Politic in Indonesia*, New York, 1972, p. 58.

[177] Cf. Lee Khoon Choy, *Indonesia between Myth and Reality*, London, 1976, p. 4.

49

invoke the spirits of their ancestors.[178]

Apart from conveying mythical tales and mysticism, the *wayang* has also more serious philosophical connotations. The *wayang* in fact represents the whole of Javanese philosophy of vagueness and their ideas of man and God. The use of the shadow to show one's philosophy is typical of Javanese genius. The shadow itself is a vague thing so that it is perhaps the only thing in the world that one can see but cannot touch or feel. Through the shadow the *dalang* tries to convey the meaning of life and the destiny of human beings. The *dalang* tries to teach people about universal order and the cosmos, as well as their relationship to the Divine. The *wayang* implants in the Javanese mind the philosophy that everyone has a different role in society, and all must know their his own role. In other words, a king must behave like a king and a clown like a clown. A king should never act like a clown, nor a clown like a king.[179]

There is another philosophical aspect of *wayang*. It is related to the two audiences present at each *wayang* performance - one group sitting in front of the screen, and the other group is behind the screen. Those in front see only shadows; they are the majority, the masses who only see things superficially. Those viewing from behind, the privileged few, see how the *dalang* operates and are aware of what is going on behind the screen. Perhaps the privileged few can be considered as having a deeper understanding of the feeling, behaviour and aspirations of the decision maker.[180] This opinion is enriched by the figure of *dalang*.

The dalang is the key figure in all the above mentioned shadow theatre performances. He is the narrator of the stories, the singer of the song (*suluk*), the interpreter of the mood of the particular moment, and the conductor of the accompanying *gamelan* orchestra. Above all, he is the commentator of the puppets or human actors.[181] In preparation, the *dalang* must perform some particular practices. The young *dalang*, in wandering from teacher to teacher searches especially for that secret,

---

[178] Lee Khoon Choy, *Indonesia between Myth and Reality*, London, 1976, p. 4.

[179] Lee Khoon Choy, *Indonesia between Myth and Reality*, London, 1976, pp. 138-139.

[180] Lee Khoon Choy, *Indonesia between Myth and Reality*, London, 1976, p. 139.

[181] Victoria M. Clara van Goenendael, *The Dalang behind the Wayang*, Leiden, 1985, p. 2.

50

jealously guarded knowledge (*ngèlmu*) that is the key to success as a *dalang,* and, aside from professional skill, to an honoured position in society. *Dalangs* only acquire this knowledge after preparing themselves for initiation into this sacred science by practising asceticism (*tapa*).[182] The practice of asceticism by the *dalang* derives from the necessity for spiritual strength which is considered as capable of exerting power over visible force. It is this power that ensures for the *dalang* that elusive property called success.[183] The *dalang* with the instruments and the story, together form one complete, beautiful composition. Such a composition implies to the totalistic, dualistic and hierarchical world-view in the *wayang* mythologies, and reveals the solidarity celebrated in the *slametan* ritual which is based on the ethical values of the Javanese society.[184]

The practices of the *dalang* allude to *Keselarasan* in a human being, as a conflux of various elements. Each human person becomes a centre and can regulate the forces to attain a good manner and personality. According to Choy, the fundamental philosophy of the Indonesian, especially of the Javanese, is to strike a balance between material and spiritual happiness.[185] Such an assumption is also found in the *Kebatinan* as a metaphysical search for harmony with one's inner self, harmony between one's inner self and one's fellow men and nature, and harmony with the universe and with the almighty God. It is a combination of occultism, metaphysics, mysticism and other esoteric doctrines. Choy says it is a typical product of the Javanese genius of synthesis.[186]

I am in the opinion that Choy exaggerates when he says, "No one can give an official definition of *Kebatinan*. The essence, however, is

---

[182] Victoria M. Clara van Goenendael, *The Dalang behind the Wayang*, Leiden, 1985, p. 24.

[183] Victoria M. Clara van Goenendael, *The Dalang behind the Wayang*, Leiden, 1985, p. 2.

[184] *Slametan* is a communal socio-religious meal, in which neighbours along with relatives and friends participate. The *slametan* is held at the important moments of personal or social life. Cf. Eka Darmaputera, *Pancasila and the Search for Identity and Modernity in Indonesian Society*, Leiden, 1988, p. 177.

[185] Cf. Lee Khoon Choy, *Indonesia between Myth and Reality*, London, 1976, p. 11.

[186] Cf. Lee Khoon Choy, *Indonesia between Myth and Reality*, London, 1976, p. 180.

peace of mind."[187] There are two things to say heres. First, it is possible to define the *Kebatinan* because there are efforts to give the *Kebatinan* a formal place in society. This makes possible the recognition of the 209 organisations of *Kebatinan*.[188] Second, it should be said that in addition to "peace of mind" there are other essential elements, such as religious and social relationships and a method of self-integration that inhere in the defintion of *Kebatinan*.

The Javanese mind, therefore, is essentially flexible and pragmatic, as far as a person's spiritual life is concerned. The complexity which is present in their thought is perhaps the result of the complicated cultural background and its influence. Javanese thought characteristically takes an individualistic approach, one in which a person communicates with the supernatural and realizes the philosophical value of self-discipline in relation to society and the universe.[189] This reality is what is so well expressed in civilization and in the culture of the *wayang* performance.

C.   Some Important Thoughts In Connecting with *Wédhatama* and *Wayang*

In this section, we deal with some Javanese thoughts and even traditions which are closely connected to ideas in *Wédhatama* or *Wayang*. These thoughts or traditions can be divided into three main ideas, as follows: the Javanese mysticism which is characterized by magical thoughts and *kasekten*,[190] the unity of existence, and *slametan*.

Some of the elements of these ideas have been mentioned briefly in the previous section. For the purposes of our study, we still need further clarification of them, so that we can have a comprehensive sense of Javanese thought. In the following we discuss the Javanese concept of mysticism.

---

[187] Lee Khoon Choy, *Indonesia between Myth and Reality*, London, 1976, p. 181.
[188] Cf. Abd. Mutholib Ilyas - Abd. Ghofur Imam, *Aliran Kepercayaan dan Kebatinan* (Currents of Belief and *Kebatinan*), Surabaya, 1988, pp. 187-195.
[189] Cf. Lee Khoon Choy, *Indonesia between Myth and Reality*, London, 1976, p. 181.
[190] Supra, p. 34.

1.　　Javanese Mysticism

Mysticism generally means a form of religious experience which puts emphasis on awareness of relationship with the ultimate reality or mysterious transcendence, an intimate consciousness of the Divine presence. According to W.R. Inge, mysticism is an interior feeling of the unity of self with God. R. Otto sees mysticism as the dynamic of *tremendum* and *fascinans*, an awe of fascinating mystery. Oriental mysticism emphasizes the aspect of existential experience and the feeling of the unity of self with the mysterious absolute.

We, herein, shall consider mysticism as an existential experience of what the Javanese understand as the divine reality or divine elements through a deep interior reflection. Thus Javanese mysticism consists of a process of an interior journey and reflection. We shall concentrate our discourse on how the Javanese practise and understand mysticism. There is remarkable evidence that Javanese mysticism includes the practice of magic and the *kasekten*.[191] This practice of magic consists of "white magic" and "black magic." White magic denies the desire of gaining the worldly aims, of passion, greed and material property. That is why white magic is characterized by good aims and instruments. The practice of magic gives an extraordinary capacity to a human being. In white magic this capacity is based on the power of God; they therefore practise it with the consciousness and conviction of surrendering to God, because in reality, a human being is like a grain of sand before God, the Almighty.

On the contrary, black magic is characterized by its extraordinary capacity based on spirits which practitioners use consciously. It animates the passions and material aims. That is why they become instruments for the lower forces and for evil.[192] We might say that an evil basis, bad aims and instruments constitute this black magic.

In our discourse on mysticism we find a mixture of magic and

---

[191] Through self-discipline, fast, and esoteric practice, someone is able to develop the realization of his human capacity in a more complete way.

[192] Cf. N. Mulder, *Kepribadian Jawa dan Pembangunan Nasional* (Javanese Personality and National Development), Yogyakarta, 1984, p. 16.

kasekten which produces an extraordinary human capacity. It consists of the fruits of words (*mantra*), actions (*laku*), and attitude of avoiding something (*patrap/sirikan*).[193] The magical practices are very complicated because of their esoteric dimension, and therefore in our study we shall concentrate only on the main ideas of Javanese mysticism.

There is remarkable evidence that Javanese mysticism permeates Javanese lifestyle and culture, or as S. de Jong said, the world of Javanese life is animated by the mystic.[194] Thus we might say that mysticism is the basic vision of Javanese culture. Culture should be understood as defined by Lévy Bruhl. According to him, culture is every product of human minds in group or society. Consequently, we can induce that Javanese mysticism has a remarkable anthropocentric dimension.

This anthropocentric dimension is understood as a tendency of the Javanese mystic to look for the true reality of his being (*kasunyatan jati*). Most Javanese believe that a human being consists of spiritual and material elements. The material element, the body, is finite and not eternal. Meanwhile, the spiritual element is the soul (*sukma*) or the personality, and originates from the divine; as such the soul is the true reality of a human person. The latter expression should be understood as the basic orientation of Javanese thought, which has a tendency to follow spiritualism. Javanese spirituality is manifested in the practice of mysticism, and this creats a distance from material reality. The Javanese unceasingly endeavour to understand their true essence, which transcends matter. They devote themselves to mental exercises, *tapa* and ascetical discipline. For example, the ancestors of the Javanese used to concentrate on the essence of reality in grottos, rivers, forest and seashores.

A human being has an origin, purpose and direction, which the

---

[193] Sang Indrajati, *"Kitab Wedha Mantra"* (The Book of Wedha Mantra), in: AAvv, *Baboning Kitab Primbon. Bundelan 10 Kitab Primbon Pusaka Sumber Ilmu Kejawen Taksih Asli dening Para Pujongo Jawi* (Motherbook of Primbon. Collection of 10 Primbon's Heirloom Books. Sources of the *Kejawen* Knowledge Derived from Javanese Authors), Solo, 1979, p. 3.

[194] Cf. S. de Jong, *Salah Satu Sikap Hidup Orang Jawa* (One of the Javanese Attitudes of Life) Yogyakarta, 1976, pp. 11-12.

Javanese call *sangkan paran*. This expression points out the idea that God is the force of life surrounding us. He is the necessary principle on which our existence is based. That is why God is the origin of human beings. Along with this, the life of a human being is a process or an accumulation of events, moving towards its destination, namely, God. For this reason, the Javanese perceive human life as a sojourn here, a mere a mere transitory. The Javanese use the following expression: *"Urip iku mung mampir ngombé,"* human life is a stop on the road where we pause to have a drink. The task of life is to seek the continuance of the flow of life from origin to destination. The Javanese assume that God exists in the heart, it is the "god" they feel; God is "Life" (with a capital letter), in the sense that Life itself animates the order of the earth and the cosmos, the changes of the seasons, and so forth. Life is its essence and secret and human beings are part of it.

The process of mysticism cannot be separated from reflection on *rasa* (feeling), self-discipline and exercises for managing "intuitive inner feeling" which is a property of every person. Some people have a refined *rasa* that makes them sensitive to things that escape the attention of others. It is also fundamental to the nature of substance or true being. *Rasa* also becomes a personal instrument which leads to true insight into reality. In this mysticism, it seems there is a relationship between intuitive inner feeling and mystery. *Wayang,* which is full of symbolical idioms, has a special place in the Javanese tradition. As a myth it can express a vision which transcends historical truth. In this case the cultivation of one's inner being and deep self is central to the essence of *Kebatinan.* It constitutes the microcosm of all-encompassing life. The movement of this cultivation is from exterior to interior. It is like a journey from origin to destination, from birth to reabsorption with all, from becoming sensitive to one's social surroundings to becoming sensitive to the presence of Life and the realization of it in one's inner being. Self-mastery, therefore, becomes the capacity to shape one's life and to coordinate self with the higher truth. N. Mulder explains:

> The basis of Javanese culture lies in self mastery and because of it, in the capacity to shape life beautifully. In this deeper dimension it centres on the cultivation of the self in order to realize the perfection of life, irrespective of one's social need not be religiously expressed,

although it always entails the cultivation of the *batin* and exercise to refine one's intuitive inner feeling, or *rasa*, to sense the true dimension of existence.[195]

In the inner being, one can carry a spark of the essence of life that animates the earth and the cosmos. That is why the inner being (microcosm) in relation with the macrocosm constitutes Life. The passions and rationality tie human beings to the material world. The task of a human being is to free his energies, to develop his inner core and to train his intuitive inner feeling to become attuned to higher truth. The ultimate ground of one's experience is the self-centered conviction that one lives in step with Life, and that one has access to truth in a direct and immediate way, drawing power from "God" at the same time that one is independent from sources of truth outside the deep self. Here a human being builds up strong inner resources and divine revelation, the ultimate truth (*kasunyatan*), inspires one's life and actions. We might say that the inner feeling is the important realm of existence. The cultivation of the intuitive inner being is expressed in the general tendency to reserve oneself, to be at home with oneself, in such a way that whatever happens outside cannot disturb one's life. Here a human being with his personal character becomes autonomous, as Mulders says:

> Most Javanese authors describe society as a vague accident of history in which their individual characters become autonomous centres of their own world, inwardly directed while often having recourse to religion or mystical feelings which relate their lives to superior truth.[196]

A human being becomes complete in himself and he potentially encompasses Life with its centre in his deep secretive self (*batin*). A human being does not only master phenomenal existence but rather he can achieve the essence of Life, in which exists the realization of self and the realization of truth in the depths of self. Such mastery and self possession are seen as sources of power to produce intended results. In Javanese mysticism, a person generates wisdom, inspiration and power because of his fusion with its sources; and consequently, a person is guided by Life itself.

---

[195] Cf. N. Mulder, *Individual and Society in Java. A Cultural Analysis*, Yogyakarta, 1992, p. 18.

[196] N. Mulder, *Individual and Soceity in Java. A Cultural Analysis*, Yogyakarta, 1992, p. 76.

The concept of a leader is one who has a relationship with strong inner resources, or individual potency, and divine inspiration (*wahyu*). A leader has to manifest effective action in which he appears motionless and quiet while in full command of events. For this reason, the Javanese have found a way to an individual-centred expression of the self, irrespective of the demands of their social lives, in which subjective feeling is the legitimate and true measure of all things. This thinking has important ethical and behavioural consequences, and sustains involvement in the social process. The Javanese movement of *Kebatinan* tries to realize the full capacity of the inner human being so that the Javanese mystic tries to pass through the sensory realm to enter the ultimate depth of his personality. According to Koentjaraningrat, a leader has to have the human qualities which are idealized by the majority of the members of society and which therefore have deep moral implications.[197] That is why self-discipline and various exercises prepare a human being to listen to his inner voice and to stimulate the way of the mystery of *rasa*. Here one perceives the reality behind phenomena.

The movement of *Kebatinan* directs a human being to advance self-integration and participation in the human extraordinary capacity, in which it transcends the common quality of a human being. This is what we call the human transformation which is the end of *Kebatinan,* and in which one has a deep consciousness and experiences a new identity. In Javanese expression, this new quality is known as *budi luhur* (noble thought) , *waskita* (keeping the eyes open) and *susila* (good morality). In this state, one transcends egocentrism. One can dedicate individual talents so that inner harmony and work are universally shared with for all beings.

By the ethical, cosmical and pantheist way of mysticism, a human being remains open to the divine and to social values. In the philosophy of *Dewa Ruci*[198] we see that in the ultimate reality there is no place for

---

[197] Koetjaraningrat, *Javanese Terms for God and Supernatural Beings and the Idea of Power*, in: R. Schefold, J.W. Schoorl and J. Tennekes, (ed.), *Man, Meaning and History*, Leiden, 1980, p. 133.

[198] *Dewa Ruci* is the story of Bima looking for the water of life as the path to understand the origin and the meaning of life. This story was written at the end of the Majapahit Kingdom (c.1473). Cf. Sri Mulyono, *The Human Character in the Wayang. The Javanese Shadow Play*,

duality, and the personality is absorbed in the universal realm in which a human being is but a small part of reality. A human being is a part of the wholeness. In a very close relationship with God or even a non-dual union between man and God, a human being gets his autonomy from union with the most autonomous. They use the expression *jumbuhing kawula-Gusti, pamoring kawula-Gusti.* Supomo calls it total mystical oneness.[199]

Union with the Lord or *jumbuhing kawula-Gusti* is an expression of mystical experience, which is always inadequate in explaining its essence. That is why we mentioned the expression *mysterium tremendum* and *fascinans* in the terminology of Otto. However it must be understood that what is united are two wills and not two substances, as by the idiom "a teacup cannot hold the ocean." Human beings are finite, while God is infinite. It is impossible that the finite encompass the substance of the infinite. It must be understood that both substances have a very close relationship. That is why *Wédhatama* exhorts that only through inner strength of purpose and with courageous endurance can a human being ultimately encounter the genuine reality of things. Thus even though human beings and the Lord unite, they do not become identical. Here we find unity in diversity because in this mystical experience, they remain *two-in-one*. As Sri Mulyono says: "All that unites is the two wills, the two forces, for the creature cannot become the Creator, and the ruled cannot be both subject and monarch."[200]

The state of such a union is described as if "dead to the world" and self-will is gone, dissolved in the will of the Almighty. Such a state is pure and filled with awareness of the eternal aspect of all things. *Wédhatama* describes that while a worship is in this state one will one day suddenly find oneself dazzled by great light, between consciousness and unconsciousness, and here is where one will experience directly the

---

Singapore, 1981, p. 23.

[199] Cf. Rahmat Subagya, *Kepercayaan - Kebatinan, Kerohanian, Kejiwaan - dan Agama* (Belief - Kebatinan, Spirituality, Kejiwaan - and Religion), Yogyakarta, 1976, pp. 55-56.

[200] Sri Mulyono, *The Human Character in the Wayang. Javanese Shadow Play*, Singapore, 1981, p. 87.

58

true nature of things.[201]

Here is expressed the ideal of a human being as "dead while still living" (*mati jroning ngaurip*). It means dead to the attractions of this world, dead to the human appetites and passions, but alive, very much alive. *Wédhatama* understands this in the sense that the ideal human being is a human being who is free from attachment to the things of this world and yet at the same time includes them in his life, for the sake of life. In this sense, a human being still needs property, position and knowledge (*arta, wirya and winasis*).

2.   The Unity of Existence

The thought of the ancient Javanese is used to look for unity amidst many varied phenomena. They thought that sensory things could be separated; they are not the ultimate reality. The Javanese seek the essential unity which includes everything. Every human person constitutes a spark of the essential unity, in which human beings take part. The unity of existence presupposes the idea of total existence. Total existence is called Life. A human being is a part of this whole existence and must be related to the whole existence. Here relationship with others is a necessity. Persons find themselves somewhere in the middle. Existence is interwoven with others. Social existence is inevitable for human existence. Such a state of being demands *rukun* (peace, cooperation without quarrel or conflict) which refers to harmony on a number of different levels, between God and humans, person and person, between the contrary forces of *lair* and *batin* within the individual.[202]

To explain further, human being consists of an outward appearance that we called *lair* and of the inner being that we call *batin*. Both *lair* and *batin* belong to the unity of existence and all people have

---

[201] Cf. Sri Mulyono, *Human Character in the Wayang*, (translated by M.M. Medeiros), Jakarta, 1977, p. 97; Sri Mulyono, *Human Character in the Wayang. Javanese Shadow Play*, Singapore, 1981, p. 94.

[202] Cf. Patrick Guinness, *Harmony and Hierarchy in a Javanese Kampung*, Singapore, 1986, p. 175.

an inner core, through which they potentially share in the essence of life. The unity of existence is essentially mysterious. That is why life on earth is seen as a shadow (*wayangan*) of the higher truth. This reality is also expressed in the *wayang,* in which we can see the lofty truth of the character of human life.

In this idea of unity, all existence has to run its fixed course and life is an inescapable project in which all have to participate while setting limits to lot, purpose and volition. Life is an ordered and coordinated whole which people must accept and to which they should adapt themselves. That is why Mulder says: "After all, it can only be wise to live in tune with that which is greater than oneself."[203]

That is why in the Javanese traditional society, a human being cannot be separated from his environment. A human person finds identity in the environment or in society. Social relationship is closely akin to the surrounding universe. The changes of the seasons and the realm of the universe constitute the thought of society; the Javanese cannot be separated from that reality.[204] The idea of a perfect human being is one who can embrace the whole of reality. Here the figure of Panembahan Senopati becomes an example. Panembahan Senopati enters this reality, and he succeeds in reaching harmonious unity with the universe and his neighbours. For this reason, then, a king such as Panembahan Senopati becomes the figure of a perfect human being. In this case, distance is used to overcome worldly disharmony. Self-discipline, concentration and exercises prepare a human being to reach true harmony with the ultimate reality.

Here we find a system of ideas regarding the nature of a human being and of society which gives a universal meaning to an integrated body of knowledge. The Javanese use this to interpret life as it is, and as it appears to be. Consequently, it refers to an ethics and a lifestyle which is basically characteristic of a culturally induced attitude toward life that

---

[203] Cf. N. Mulder, *Individual and Society in Java. A Cultural Analysis*, Yogyakarta, 1992, p. 11.

[204] Cf. S. de Jong, *Salah Satu Sikap Hidup Orang Jawa* (One of the Javanese Attitudes of Life), Yogyakarta, 1976, p. 80.

transcends religious diversity. In turn, there is a strong tendency to be conscious of the existence of others and of the reality that one is not alone. A human being is continually moving into and out of, another's space. Acknowledging the existence of others means accepting and respecting others; this is essential in maintaining good order while achieving a personal measure of undisturbed continuity (*tentrem*). According to Patrick Guiness, the achievement of genuine *tentrem* within each individual is considered the best way of ensuring harmonious social relation, for a *tentrem* person is unaffected by rude or impolite behaviour.[205]

The two perspectives of looking at reality (*batin* and *lair*) bring about two attitudes toward life. First, the outside world means suffering and struggle where one often experiences the need to give in and a feeling of powerlessness and of losing. Second, the interior world means self-sufficiency and autonomy, a world in which one develops his *batin* as a stable inner core and a source of integrity.

A parental view of the world has an important role in the idea of "unity of existence," hierarchy, order, phenomena and essential existence. The inner life is protected by the maintenance of order and the willingness to cultivate mutually harmonious relationships. Social life becomes the stage of autonomy in which one presents himself in a status position. This induced self-respect appears to be an ingredient of individual consciousness as well as consciousness of others.

The cosmological ideas of *Kebatinan* bring about the idea of "unity of existence" regarding the reality of society, of *lair* and *batin*. A human being needs to practice the exercises in order to prevent those incidents which alienate a human person from identity of self. For this, we used Javanese terminology such as *olah rasa, mawas diri, samadi eneng eling, meleng mantheng, eling, nyawiji, manunggal, manekung ing tyas,* and the like.[206] The priority of unity with the universe is prominent

---

[205] Cf. Patrick Guinness, *Harmony and Hierarchy in a Javanese Kampung*, Singapore, 1986, p. 129.

[206] *Olah rasa* means "exercise of feelings". *Mawas diri* means "self-reflection". *Samadi eneng eling* means "a deep meditation". *Meleng mantheng* means "a serious concentration". *Eling*

in ancient Javanese thought. Sometimes they interpret this realm of nature as the divine nature. By self-discipline one reaches identification with the soul of the universe, the cosmic mind, which is followed by the extraordinary power that we call *kasekten*.

Accordingly, a human being experiences a union of the subject with his Lord or a union of man with God. Such a reality is also expressed in Sunan Bonang's dialogue with Sunan Kalijaga and Wujil as follows:

> You two must look like one, and completely.
> You two must feel as one, be of one heart,
> and in all things be united.
> Once you are one, and not two,
> once you're one in faith and life, truly,
> nothing's forbidden at all
> regarding clothes and food.
> Since His Will is joined to your heart, as one who's loved,
> you may no longer choose or pick, proving you're one with His law.[207]

A human being ultimately encounters the genuine reality of things[208] and experiences the unity of existence.

3.   The *Slametan*

Slametan in Javanese society is understood as a communal socio-religious meal in which neighbours, along with some relatives and friends, participate. It is undertaken in a set of ritual ceremonies at important moments in life. The central element of the *slametan* is having a meal together. It is a realization of Javanese social relationship in which we find the differences of the hierarchical principle. We also find paradoxical thought similar to that expressed in the mythological figures

---

means "remember". *Nyawiji* or *manunggal* means "being one or join together in a unification". *Manekung ing tyas* means prayer or worship in one's own heart. Cf. Rachmat Subagya, *Kepercayaan - Kebatinan, Kerohanian, Kejiwaan - dan Agama* (Belief - *Kebatinan*, Spirituality, *Kejiwaan*, - and Religion), Yogyakarta, p. 48.

[207] Sri Mulyono, *The Human Character in the Wayang*, (translated by M.M. Medieros), Jakarta, 1981, p. 52.

[208] Cf. Sri Mulyono, *The Human Character in the Wayang. The Javanese Shadow Play*, Singapore, 1981, p. 76.

of the Javanese. Those that we call the paradoxical figures are the *Punakawan* which always appear at the entertainment of *wayang*. The *Punakawan* is the Semar's family which has an important role in the solution of conflicts. These figures are very important so that the *wayang* is not complete without their presence. Most of the Javanese people eagerly wait for the scene when the figures of the *Punakawan* appear. In like manner, the Javanese discuss their life from the perspectives of the mythology of *wayang purwa*.

The purpose of the *slametan* is to achieve the state of *slamet*,[209] the maintenance of order and the constraining of danger. The state of *slamet* can be described as a state without any disturbance from gods, spirits and ancestors, in which events will run their fixed course smoothly and nothing untoward will happen to anyone.[210] That is why the *slametan* brings about an harmonious community that promotes a good social relationship, the state of *slamet*'s condition. In this sense, there is the idea of the absence of disaster and accident.

The heart of the *slametan* is the reconciliation of the essential unity with individualization, and self-correction which promotes harmonious development. Many Javanese appreciate the *slametan* as an important socially integrative mechanism in which everyone has the social obligation to visit their parents' grave.

Behind this religious and social rite of *slametan* is the Javanese sense of order, where the great order of Life is felt as mysterious and beyond human understanding. The best that human beings can do is attempt to shape the experience of life in a disciplined manner as a means to establishing a maximum of order and security. Consequently a human being should shape life actively (*rame ing gawe*) in order to create good

---

[209] The word *slamet* might derive from Arabic word "*Salāma*", meaning safety, security, blamelessness, smooth progress; success. The adjective word *Salima* means safe, secure, faultless. Accordingly, the Javanese word "*slamet*" points out a state of being free from danger, security, and safety. Cf. H. Wehr, *A Dictionary of Modern Written Arabic*, (edited by J. Milton Cowan), Wiesbaden, 1979, pp. 495-496.

[210] Cf. N. Mulder, *Individual and Society in Java. A Cultural Analysis*, Yogyakarta, 1992, p. 15; A. Maryadi Sutrisnaatmaka, *The Slametan and the Eucharist. Towards the Inculturation of the Eucharistic Celebration in the Javanese Cultural Context*, (Dissertation), Rome, 1987, p. 5.

order and to shape one's own existence.

A human being has in oneself an individual will, emotions and self-interest. To reach the state of *slamet,* a human being must suppress self-interest and cultivate the feeling of shame in doing evil to society and must also cultivate politeness and agreeable manners. According to the Javanese, it is wise to go with the flow (*ngeli*) of social life, to show respect and tolerance, to restrain what causes disturbance.[211] Consciousness of others and interpersonal relations tend to become distant and impersonal. However, the ritualization of interaction, an elaboration of politeness, and the wisdom to go with the flow are a rich repertory of life. From the perspective of a deep indigenous psychology and anthropology, the Javanese appear to have found a positive way to live with consciousness of others and interaction. The true centre of existence is located in the inner self.[212]

Social morality plays an important role in Javanese thought. That is why we see the tendency of returning to the indigenous system of morality, to the ancestors' simplicity with mottos such as *budi luhur* and *sepi ing pamrih.*[213] It is the *slametan* which motivates the Javanese to protect themselves from the forces that cause obstacles and troubles. The *budi luhur* and *sepi ing pamrih*, which are also advanced in the *slametan*, can harmonize and neutralize disturbing events. It provides the system of harmonizing the supernatural powers which bring about the harmonious relations among themselves, the gods and the spirits. Herein lies the concept of the world in Javanese thought. The salvation of a human being depends on his behaviour in regard to that concept of the world, and as Franz Magnis Suseno relates, that proper behaviour, on which human salvation depends, brings about unity.[214]

---

[211] Cf. N. Mulder, *Individual and Society in Java. A Cultural Analysis*, Yogyakarta, 1992, p. 145.

[212] N. Mulder, *Individual and Society in Java. A Cultural Analysis*, Yogyakarta, 1992, p. 161.

[213] *Budi luhur* means "noble thought"; *sepi ing pamrih* means "without the motives of one's own personal interests"

[214] Cf. F. Magnis Suseno, *Etika Jawa. Sebuah Analisa Falsafi tentang Kebijaksanaan Hidup Jawa* (Javanese Ethic. A Philosophical Analysis on Javanese Wisdom of Life), Jakarta, 1984, p. 84.

II.   HINDU THOUGHT OF "UNITY IN DIVERSITY" AND "HARMONY"

A.   The Teaching of Hinduism in Veda.

First of all, we shall deal with the significance of Veda and its history; and will follow the principle teaching of "unity and diversity." Such an approach is quite helpful and reveals the principles of Veda which regards "unity in diversity" and harmony.

The word *Veda* means "knowledge". R.C. Zaehner states that the "canon" of Hindu Scripture is collectively known as the Veda, a Sanskrit word which means "knowledge" or "wisdom."[215] Further, *Veda* is that name given to the Hindu Scriptures which consist of four kinds of collections or samhitās. They are Rgveda, Sāmaveda, Yajurveda, and Atharvaveda. These Vedas originally consisted of a single collection of sacred hymns of praise, entitled "Rgveda."[216] Then they appended the Sāmaveda which is the collection of melodies used by the priest who acts as cantor at the sacrifice. The Yajurveda consists of sacrificial formulas, and the Atharvaveda is the collection of magic formulas or *mantras*.[217]

From the historical perspective, the Veda should be seen in the light of the Āryan invasion of India in the second half of the second

---

[215] Cf. R.C. Zaehner, *Hindu Scriptures,* London, 1992, p. ix.

[216] R.C. Zaehner, *Hindu Scriptures*, London, 1992, pp. x-xi; R.N. Dandekar, *Insights into Hinduism,* Delhi, 1979, pp. 14-21.

[217] According to R.C. Zaehner, the Atharvaveda is later in date than the other three, since even in later times three Vedas are usually spoken of, not four. Cf. R.C. Zaehner, *Hindu Scriptures,* London, 1992, p. x.

millennium B.C.,[218] which brought with it the Sanskrit language and the Vedic religion. The Aryans went from Caucasia to the Indus valley where they met the Dravidian people. This meeting created the Hindu culture, civilization and religion. For a long time, the main source of our knowledge for Pre-Aryan civilization was the Veda itself. With the excavation of the sites of Mohenjo-Daro and Harappa in the Indus valley, our knowledge of the pre-Aryan people has increased.[219] As to the date of the Vedic Scriptures in their present form, we have a consensus that the Veda dates from about 1500 B.C.

In Hindu literature, two kinds of revelation can be distinguished: 1) *Śruti* which means "to hear," and 2) *Smrti* which means "the human tradition." The Veda belongs to the *Śruti*. This *Śruti* has the following characteristics: first, the characteristic of *Nityā* which means "eternal"; Hindus believe that the Veda is eternal, and second, the Veda is said to be *Apuruseya* which means "without human authorship." This latter characteristic maintains the legitimacy and absolute authority of the Veda.

The understanding and thought in the Vedic literature has gradually changed from that of an absorbing self-concern to a new centering in the supposed unity of reality and value that is deemed to be God, Brahman or Dharma. Thus the concept of liberation is the transformation of human existence from self-centeredness to union with the ultimately transpersonal Absolute, who is the eternal reality of Brahman.

Brahman, according to the *nirguna* aspects,[220] however, is beyond conception. He is unconditionally one as a transcendent-immanent reality. Only through the negative way which we call *neti-neti* (not this, nor that), we can say that Brahman is not anything that we experience objectively in our world. The Brahman is an absolute reality which transcends space and time. As Michael Brück says, Brahman is supra-temporal, which is everlasting existence, a manifestation and attraction of love in

---

[218] Cf. R.C. Zaehner, *Hinduism*, Oxford, 1992, p. 14.
[219] Cf. R.N. Dandekar, *Insight into Hinduism*, Delhi, 1979, p. 9.
[220] *Nirguna* means "beyond qualities or attributes," an epithet applied to the *brahman*.

66

temporal appearance.[221]

In the Rgveda we find the exaltation of nature and cosmic powers in a mythological framework. The world of natural powers, such as the strength of horses, fascinates people. In contact with natural powers they experience a manifestation of the divine. That is why in the Veda we can trace the developing social structure of a tribal society and the functional deities in its mythology. In addition, the combination and integration of all powers or forces into an orderly whole, into what the Veda calls *rta*, "right order" and "truth," refer to the idea of *dharma*.[222] Thus *rta* is a term designating the cosmic order on which human order, ethics and social behaviour depend.[223]

This thought of wholeness provides a coherent model for the unity of truth. It is also clear in the Sankara's *advaita*, as J.B. Chethimattam writes:

> The vision of the secondless Self, however, cannot go hand in hand with the path of action since it implies distinctions of action, instrument and effect, which are subversive of notions derived from such declarations as "The real is without a second." All this is Self alone.[224]

The world has a practical meaning and reality of its own. Only reaching a certain internal balance and harmony within the world can bring about the full manifestation of the Self in its place. *Advaita* means non-dual, a way to experience reality as oneness. For this reason some experts interpret Hinduism as a monism, which underlines "non-duality." Some experts have objected to the designation of "monism" for this thought, they would rather call Hinduism *panentheism*. They used *panentheism* in the sense that God is found in everything. Nevertheless,

---

[221] Cf. Michael von Brück, *Unity of Reality. God, God-Experience, and Meditation in the Hindu-Christian Dialogue*, New York/Mahawah, 1990, p. 8.

[222] About this *dharma*, R.C. Zaehner said that everything is bondage to the fetters of time and the fetters of desires, the desire above all to live and the desire to do (*karma*=doing).Cf. R. C. Zaehner, *Hindu Scriptures*, London, 1992, pp. 4-5, 18.

[223] R. C. Zaehner, *Hinduism*, Oxford, 1992, p. 18.

[224] J.B. Chethimattam, *The Pre-Aryan Roots of Sankara's Advaita*, in: Thomas Mampra (ed.), *Religious Experience. Its Unity and Diversity*, Bangalore, 1981, p. 66.

the problems still remain. The main question here is how the world of many should be understood if we accept the "non-duality".

Veda uses a mythological pattern of thought. The literature expresses the reality of many by the names of gods such as *Indra, Agni, Varuna, Soma* and so forth. For the reality of One they use Brahman as the ultimate reality. In this mythological thought the Hindus understand reality in a global way. I am of the opinion that perhaps this is characteristic of all myth. This thinking, contained in the Veda, has a more advanced form in the upanisads. The next section deals expressly with this.

B.   The Teaching of Hinduism in the Upanisads

Etymologically, Upanisad derives from the Sanskrit word *upa* which means "supplementary," "additional," and *ni-sad* which means "to sit down (near a teacher)." Thus the Upanisads are supposed to indicate a disciple sitting at the feet of the master and the discourse of the master to his disciple.[225] According to Sri Swami Shivananda, the Upanisads are metaphysical treatises which are replete with sublime conceptions of Vedānta and with intuitions of universal truths.[226] They are the source of Vedānta philosophy. For this reason, the Upanisads are known as Vedānta, which means the end of Vedas, the final stage of Vedas.[227]

Theoretically there are many texts which contain the esoteric teachings that are considered as Upanisad.[228] The richest and the most original of the Upanisad are the *Brhad-Aranyaka* and the *Chandogya*, dated from the sixth century B.C.. Besides, there are other texts such as *Aitareya, Taittirīya, Kathaka, Śvetāsvatara, Mahā-Nārāyana, Isā, Mundaka, Mandūkya* and so on. These texts were composed between the

---

[225] Cf. Eknath Easwaran, *The Upanishads,* London, 1988, pp. 11-12.

[226] Sri Swami Shivananda, *The Principal Upanishads. Isa, Kena, Katha, Prasna, Mundaka, Taittiriya, Aitereya and Svetasvatara Upanishads with Text, Meaning Notes and Commentary,* Shivanandanagar, 1983, p. x.

[227] Cf. R.C. Zaehner, *Hindu Scriptures,* London, 1992, p. ix; Bede Griffiths, *The Cosmic Revelation,* Illinois, 1983, p. 10-11.

[228] Cf. Bede Griffiths, *The Cosmic Revelation,* Illinois, 1983, p. 47.

68

seventh and third century B.C..[229] However, we shall not be too much involved in such technical problems, since in this study we would like to concentrate on the discourses on "unity in diversity" and "harmony" which exist in the Upanisads. All these are investigated in the light of Brahman, Atman and *Purusa*.[230]

The Upanisads teach a philosophy of absolute unity. We find two principal teachings in the Upanisads: 1) *Brahma Jñāna*, which means that final emancipation can be attained only by knowledge of the ultimate reality, or Brahman. 2) There are four means of salvation: viz., discrimination (*Viveka*), dispassion (*Vairgya*), the six-fold treasure and self-control, and yearning for liberation (*Mumuk shuttva*), which help someone in attaining Brahman. The knowledge of Brahman destroys ignorance, the seed of samsāra. The knowledge of Brahman can remove all sorrows, delusion and pain. That is why the Upanisads lead to Brahman and help the disciple to attain Brahman. This means immortality, eternal bliss, and everlasting peace.

The peace and tranquillity of oneness subjugates the phenomenal experience of the many and differentiated things in space. According to Śankara, the purpose of the Upanisads can only be to point to one Self without beginning and end, in contrast to the relative universe. By looking around the world Atman was discovered, Self as the foundation of all consciousness; and then the discoverer rose to the conception of the *Purusa* and saw how Brahman, Atman and *Purusa*, the Personal God are all one. According to *Māndukya* Upanisad, nothing at all exists except the One. The "One" is not the "All" as it usually is in the earlier Upanisads, because the "All" signifies plurality and this must be totally denied to the one.[231]

According to *Chandogya* Upanisad, the Brahman indicates inexpressible mystery. This is beyond the phenomena that are called *neti-neti* (not this, nor that). In later reflection they call Brahman *Tat tvam*

---

[229] M. Winternitz, *A History of Indian Literature*, Calcuta, 1927, p. 209.

[230] *Mundaka* Upanisad speaks of Brahman, Atman and Purusa. Cf. R.C. Zaehner, *Hindu Scriptures*, London, 1992, p. xviii.

[231] Cf. R.C. Zaehner, *Hindu Scriptures*, London, 1992, p. xvii.

asi, meaning "That thou art." The self as the foundation of being is one with the Brahman. It is the object of the Upanisads to have human beings discover themselves and search for something immortal within them. In the other words, they are seeking the immortal self. The basic orientation of the Upanisads is found in the search of this inner self, which is beyond the body and mind. That is why *Chandogya* Upanisad searches for a true liberation or "release" from space and time.[232]

Meanwhile according to *Katha* Upanisad, beyond the unmanifest, there is the *Purusa*; beyond the *Purusa*, there is nothing which is called the highest end, the goal. This is the course of the ascent of the mind of man, to the *budhi*, to the cosmic order, the cosmic consciousness, to the unmanifest beyond, and finally to *Purusa* himself. This is the self of peace. The state of beyond the phenomena is the final stage that is beyond all dualities, to the One Self, who is in all.[233]

The teaching of *Katha* Upanisad is different from the teaching of Sāmkhya philosophy. The latter has two main principles, namely *Purusa* and *Prakrti*. *Purusa* is masculine, and refers to person, the spirit and the consciousness. *Prakrti* is feminine and refers to matter and nature. The union of the *Purusa* and *Prakrti*, of the male and female, becomes the basis of the whole of creation. It also indicates the union of the active and passive principles. In this perspective, yoga is viewed as the art of uniting in oneself the male and female principles, the conscious and the unconscious, spirit and matter, so as to bring the duality within our nature into unity.[234]

These teachings of Upanisads are developed further in the Bhagavad-Gītā. In this epic the vision of unity has a very deep meaning. We shall discuss this in the following section.

---

[232] Such true liberation is a form of existence than can only be compared to the wind in its freedom to roam at will, unhampered by material things. Cf. R.C. Zaehner, *Hindu Scriptures*, London, 1992, p. xvii.

[233] In the state beyond the phenomena is intuitively realized that Brahman is identical with the inmost self of man. Cf. R. C. Zaehner, *Hindu Scriptures*, London, 1992, p. xx; Bede Griffiths, *The Cosmic Revelation*, Illinois, 1983, p. 79.

[234] Cf. Bede Griffiths, *The Cosmic Revelation*, Illinois, 1983, p. 89.

C.   The Teaching of Bhagavad-Gītā

Bhagavad-Gītā derives from the Sanskrit words *Bhagavan* which means "Lord" and *Gītā* which means "song." The Bhagavad-Gītā, therefore, means "the song of the Lord."[235] For this reason the Bhagavad-Gītā develops the devotion to a personal God.

In the Bhagavad-Gītā the experience of God has its roots in the Vedas, which comes to light in the Upanisads. The experience of God has its fullest and most perfect expression in the Bhagavad-Gītā.[236] This epic poem is of very deep meaning. Bhagavad-Gītā does not belong to the Vedic period, nor to the Upanisad period; but rather it belongs to the later age that we call the "epic period." The Bhagavad-Gītā was inserted in the great epic *Mahābhārata*, which is dated 300-200 B.C..[237] The Baghavad-Gītā actually is separated from the *Mahābhārata*, which is the longest poem in the world, and of which the Bhagavad-Gītā is an episode.[238]

The *Mahābhārata* contains the story of the Pāndavas and the Kuravas. The Pāndavas are five brothers who have the right to the throne. However the Dhrtarasta of the Kuravas and his son Duryodhana usurped their throne. The Pāndavas were condemned to go into exile as a result of losing a game of dice. At the same time the Kuravas and Duryodhana claimed the right to the throne. Later when the Pāndavas returned from exile, they reclaimed their kingdom. The tension between the Pāndavas and the Kuravas leads to a point where the two are seated in chariots facing each other. Arjuna cannot fight a battle against the Kuravas who are his own relations and friends. He lays down his arms in desperation. At that time Krsna comes to Arjuna to advice him. It is the discourse of Krsna to Arjuna that we call the *Bhagavad-Gītā*.

Krsna's discourse or advice to Arjuna is given by means of

---

[235] Cf. Eknath Easwaran, *The Bhagavad Gita*, London, 1986, p. 47.

[236] Cf. Michael Brück, *Unity of Reality. God, God-Experience, and Mediation in the Hindu-Christian Dialogue*, New York/Mahawah, 1990, p. 61.

[237] Bede Griffiths, *The Cosmic Revelation*, Illinois, 1983, p. 87.

[238] Cf. Sarvepalli Radhakrishnan, *Bhagavad Gītā*, (translated by Icilio Vecchiotti), Rome, 1964, p. 32; R.C. Zaehner, *The Bhagavad Gītā*, Oxford, 1973, p. 5.

instructive symbolism, in which Krsna counsels and teaches Arjuna how to fight in battle. Arjuna must fight because Dhrtarasta is has usurped the throne. He symbolizes the ego, the false self. Dhrtarasta is the symbol of the blind self, of useless desires and appetites. The Pandavas, as rightful owners of the throne, are the symbol of the true self. The chariot is the symbol of the body, and Arjuna is the symbol of the soul. Krsna, the charioteer, is the lord who comes to guide and instruct the soul. That is why this battle is the symbol of life's battle in restoring the spirit to its proper place. Every human being must face this battle of life.

The end of the Bhagavad-Gītā is a concise account of progress toward human perfection, which insists on inquiry into the truth of being, devotion to God, cleansing of the heart and dedicated action.[239] We can divide the Bhagavad-Gītā into three parts. According to Bede Griffiths, "The first six books are concerned with *Karma Yoga*, the yoga of action; the next six books with *Bhakti Yoga*, the yoga of love; and the last six books with *Jñāna Yoga*, the yoga of wisdom."[240] R.C. Zaehner explains that the teaching of Bhagavad-Gītā consists of teachings on the human being, Brahman and God.[241]

The teaching on the unity of the ways of action, devotion, and intellectual contemplation is the philosophical basis of the Bhagavad-Gītā. Moreover this teaching is also a guide to spiritual fulfilment which incorporates important elements along the path to unity.

Furthermore, the Bhagavad-Gītā has to be understood as a very forceful, concrete and existential presentation of the general religious quest of man. It presents identity and diversity, as K.T. Kadankavil says: "Identity or at least unity in this general quest and programme of religious man involved, and diversity in its concrete expressions, is what I believe, the *Gītā* presents."[242] The Bhagavad-Gītā also draws on the

---

[239] Cf. K.T. Kadankavil, *Gita and the Synthesis of Hindu Religious Experience*, in: Thomas Mampra, (ed.), *Religious Experience. Its Unity and Diversity*, Bangalore, 1981, p. 84.

[240] Bede Griffiths, *The Cosmic Revelation*, Illinois, 1983, p. 92.

[241] Cf. R. C. Zaehner, *The Bhagavad Gītā*, Oxford, 1973, pp. 10-42.

[242] K.T. Kadankavil, *Gita and the Synthesis of Hindu Religious Experience*, in Thomas Mampra, (ed.), *Religious Experience. Its Unity and Diversity*, Bangalore, 1981, p. 96.

72

darśanas, the early Indian system of Philosophy, especially the Sāṃkhya and Yoga. The supreme *Purusa*, in the great symphonic vision, is our model and compass as well as our chariot driver of life.

In the *Karma Yoga*, Bhagavad-Gītā maintains that freedom from selfish desires, the inner balance as a harmony of mind, is the first condition for not seeking the fruit of work. However one has to work with the whole heart and soul. That is why the *Karma Yoga* guides one to serenity of mind. Man finally can reach the capacity to be the same in good or evil, in pleasure or pain, in success or in failure, in honour or dishonour. In this sense, *Karma Yoga* is not a method of suppression, but is rather a kind of an inner control. Griffiths says:

> The Gītā says that all work which has a selfish end is binding, and its consequences are inescapable, but all the work which is done with an unselfish purpose and in the service of others not only does not bind, but in trying to do our work without seeking a reward, we leave the results to God; we offer our work in sacrifice, uniting ourselves with the action of God.[243]

The *Bhakti Yoga* is interpreted as a firm, intense devotion to God. It is full of overwhelming affection for God with a full sense of His greatness. There are several phases of devotion as follows: love of the Lord's grandeur, love of His beauty, worship of Him, meditation on Him, service to Him, the love of Him as a friend, as a child, as a wife, loving Him in full self-surrender, awareness of unity with Him, and the feeling that one cannot live without Him.[244] Zaehner interprets the Bhagavad-Gītā as the union of love and liberation.[245]

The *Jñāna Yoga* must be connected to the epilogue, especially the last chapter of the Gītā, verses 64-66. This knowledge is a participation in a timeless mode of existence. "Centre thy mind on Me, be devoted to Me, sacrifice to Me, revere Me, and thou shall come to Me. I promise thee truly, for thou art dear to Me"(18,65). For this reason, a human

---

[243] Cf. Bede Griffiths, *The Cosmic Revelation*, Illinois, 1983, p. 93.

[244] Cf. K.T. Kadankavil, *Gita and the Synthesis of Hindu Religious Experience*, in Thomas Mampra, (ed.), *Religious Experience. Its Unity and Diversity*, Bangalore, 1981, p. 87.

[245] K.T. Kadankavil, *Gita and the Synthesis of Hindu Religious Experience*, in: Thomas Mampra, (ed.), *Religious Experience. Its Unity and Diversity*, Bangalore, 1981, p. 93.

being recognises who he is and in that knowing is everything. The mind observes the external world and sees its structure. It perceives that the world consists of a multiplicity of separate objects in a framework of time, space and causality, because these are the conditions of perception. Through our mind, we see diversity in unity. The mind is transcendent; therefore, it enters a mode of knowing where duality disappears. In this sense, the phenomena of the world are not an illusion or unreal, but they appear in a sense of separateness.

Finally we must understand that the Bhaghavad-Gītā does not introduce a system of philosophy, but a path of self-realization and a guide to action. In other words, we can conclude that the Bhagavad-Gītā begins with a way of selfless action, passes into a way of self-knowledge, and ends with a way of love.

D. Some Important Hindu Ideas with Regard to Harmony

The idea of *rta* maintains "right order" of cosmos on which human order, ethic and social behaviour depend.[246] Accordingly, *rta* represents the immanent dynamic order or inner balance of the cosmic manifestations of the selves. It also points out the combination and integration of things into an orderly whole. This idea is very close to the idea of *dharma* as eternal law, truth, morality, righteousness and religious duty.[247] Both *rta* and *dharma* are important ideas which might bring the perception of the wholeness and harmony within the world.

The final participation in the ultimate reality or Brahman, as taught by Brahma Jñāna in Upanisad, might be an important element for the unity of things. Besides, *Katha* Upanisad teaches a basis of the whole creation in the unison of male-female, *Purusa-Prakrti*. Accordingly, this teaching is open to the possiblity of the unity between the very contrasting things such as the passive and active.

The Bhagavad-Gītā teaches the important path which brings about

---

[246] Cf. R.C. Zaehner, *Hinduism*, Oxford, 1992, p. 18.
[247] M.Dhavamony, *Classical Hinduism*, Rome, 1982, p. 333.

inner control and action according to the dignity of one's identity. Action without self-interest, the intuitive knowledge of the One, and fervent devotion to God are deep teachings in the discourse of Krsna to Arjuna. These teachings constitute the realization of harmonious life with one's self, society and God.

III. BUDDHIST THOUGHT

The main Buddhist thought can be summarized in the teaching of *Triratna*, namely Buddha, Dharma and Sangha.[248] In this part, we will deal only with the idea of Buddha and *dharma*. Accordingly we will not discuss Sangha. Instead, we will deal with some important ideas regarding the idea of harmony in Buddhism. It might be that these ideas have also influenced the process of the Javanese thought of *Keselarasan*.

A. Buddha

The word *Buddha* means "enlightened," "awakened."[249] Hence the word *Buddha* is used as the title of a person who knows the highest object of knowledge, Supreme Truth. The Buddhists believe that there have been many Buddhas. Every period of time has its own Buddha, who receives the illumination or enlightenment.

One of the most important Buddhas is Sidharta Gotama, the historical founder of Buddhism. He was born in 563 B.C.. Nevertheless the Buddhists assume that it was not the first time that he came into the world. Behind this assumption there is a belief that every human being has been born many times. A person can be reincarnated as an animal, a

---

[248] Cf. Harun Hadiwijono, *Agama Hindu dan Buddha (The Religion of Hindu and Buddha)*, Jakarta, 1987, p. 54.

[249] The word *buddha* is near to the Sanskrit word *buddhi* which has two meanings: firstly, it means "relating to intellect or understanding". Secondly, *buddhi* is a faculty of supreme understanding as distinct from the understanding itself.

human being, or as a *deva*.[250]

According to Buddhism, the illumination of Sidharta Gotama was reached after several reincarnations. At every level of reincarnation he attained higher knowledge, so that he eventually became *Bodhisattva*. *Bodhisattva* means that his essence or being is the wisdom resulting from direct perception of truth, with compassion awakened thereby. A *Bodhisattva* remains in the world, not because of the momentum of undischarged karmic debt, but due to the momentum of the initial compassionate resolve to help free all beings from the coils of suffering. Later, with the rise of Mahāyāna, the *Bodhisattva* ideal became generalized.[251] *Bodhisattvahood* is a way of self-transcendence in which human beings experience a transformation from self-centeredness to reality-centeredness.[252] It is like the turning from ego to reality. They are illuminated and enabled by the *anattā* doctrine.

The *anattā* doctrine states that there is no existence of ego. It teaches the doctrine of the inseparableness of all forms of life, the opposite of that of an immortal and personal soul. With *anattā* there is no permanent ego which makes up the personality. Buddha denied the existence of an ego or soul, and taught that no permanent entity can be found in any human faculty. The reality behind the flux of *Samsāra*[253] is an indivisible unity, with no separate possession of any part of it.

Further, S. Collins interprets *anattā* as "not self,"[254] in which the body is not an independent entity and consciousness is not self. With regard to the idea of *nibbāna*, Collins says, "In any case, the term applies

---

[250] The Sankrit word *Deva* means "shinning one". It is a celestial being, good, bad or indifferent in nature. Devas inhabit any of the three worlds. They can be compared with the angelic powers of Western theology.

[251] J. Snelling, *The Buddhist Handbook*, London, 1989, p. 82.

[252] Cf. J. Hick, *Interpretation of Religion*, London, 1991, p. 41.

[253] *Samsāra* is the 'bondage of life, death and rebirth'. According to Buddhism, human beings live in the world of flux, change and ceaseless. The purpose of the *Noble Fold Path* is to enable one to step off the wheel of becoming, in which human beings turn life after life, into the state of *Nirvāna*.

[254] Cf. J.M. Koller and P.Koller, *A Sourcebook in Asian Philosophy*, New York, 1991, pp. 222-225; S. Collins, *Selfless Person*, Cambridge, 1982, p. 96.

to any and every item of the Buddhist conceptual universe (*dhamma*), whether parts of the karmic conditioning process or the unconditioned *nibbāna*: impermanent are all conditioned things, unsatisfactory, not self, and constructed; and certainly *nibbāna* also is a description meaning not-self".[255]

Nibbāna is a strategic denial of any definitive description of self, without affirming or denying the existence or non-existence of something transcendent, indefinable self. Like many others, Collins emphasizes occasional remarks in the texts to the effect that there is no point in discussing the problem of the existence of the self. In this sense perhaps *anatta* simply advises against uselessly trying to conceive of it.

The attainment of enlightenment or *nibbāna* can be accomplished through the exercise of knowledge. Liberation from the circle of reincarnation, the understanding of the Four Noble Truths and the practice of the Eightfold Noble Path, fundamentally depend on knowledge. Knowledge, therefore, is regarded as essential in Buddhist thought.[256]

That is why the figure of Buddha is also described as a person with a broad mind. He valued social virtues and toleration. According to S. Tachibana, Buddha was a person with a tolerant nature who did not use harsh language in rebuking his disciples.[257] Buddha was strict, but in his strictness there was something which attracted others to him. He saw his disciples with fatherly eyes. Between him and his disciples there were feelings similar to those existing between parents and children.[258]

2. Dharma or Dhamma

To understand the teaching of *dhamma* in Buddhism, we should have a background knowledge of Hinduism. The reason is because Buddhism is a reaction to Hinduism in which Brāhmaṇas over-

---

[255] S. Collins, *Selfless Person*, Cambridge, 1982, p. 96.
[256] Cf. S. Tachibana, *The Ethics of Buddhism*, London, 1975, p. 9.
[257] S. Tachibana, *The Ethics of Buddhism*, London, 1975, p. 237.
[258] S. Tachibana, *The Ethics of Buddhism*, London, 1975, p. 239.

accentuated the rites and ceremonies.[259]

In Indian philosophical and religious literature, the Sanskrit word *dharma* also has many rich meanings. For example, according to *Rāmāyana*, *dharma* guides a human being in moral situations. It is described as consisting of the highest moral principles such as learnedness, austerity, self-sacrifice, faith, sacrificial ceremony, forbearance, purity of emotion and pity, truth, and self-control. The *dharma* demands obedience to the commands of *gurus*,[260] parents, the king and other elders. Besides, the *dharma* is also a characteristic property of science, morality, legality, religion with all its proper implications, the psycho-physical relationship and spirituality. It is also a property of righteousness and of law generally, but above all, of duty. Therefore, *dharma* is the fulfilment of one's duty to others.

According to *Vedānta*,[261] *dharma* is the form of things as "they are" and the power that keeps them as "they are."[262] *Dharma* is the foundation of the entire universe at both macro-cosmic and micro-cosmic levels. All the concepts of *dharma* have their origin in Veda as the primary source and in *smṛti*, the human tradition which consists of many works produced by human authors, as the secondary source.

Instead of *dharma* in Sanskrit, Buddhism uses the Pali term *dhamma*, which means the right course of human conduct, the doctrine or teaching of Buddha, righteousness, law and justice, condition of antecedent and the ultimate reality. According to Nakamura Hajime, *dhamma* has a relationship to the doctrine of righteousness, cause, thing and cosmic order, which Buddhists consider as unchanged truth.[263] C.

---

[259] Cf. S. Collins, *Selfless Person*, Cambridge, 1982, pp. 29-40.

[260] *"Guru"* is identical with the teacher.

[261] *Vedānta* literally means "the End of Veda". The Upaniṣads are the *Vedānta*, because they come at the end of Vedic literature, and because they form the culmination of Vedic wisdom. *Vedānta* is also one of the six orthodox systems of Indian Philosophy. It teaches the doctrine of Brahman as Reality unifying all phenomena, and the identity of man's real Self with that ultimate Reality.

[262] M. Dhavamony," Vedantic Philosophy of Religion", *International Philosophy Quarterly* 21, 1981, p. 52.

[263] Cf. Nakamura Hajime, *Ways Thinking of Eastern Peoples: India, China, Tibet, Japan,*

Eliot adds that this doctrine has the function of creating a mood and a habit of life.[264]

The knowledge of human beings is limited and imperfect. That is why there are many different perceptions and understandings of *dhamma*. It should be noted here that the truth of *dhamma* as an eternal and universal concept is considered a higher spiritual realization which transcends space and time. Thus there are many and various definitions and explanations of the concept of *dhamma*.

Accordingly, *dhamma* has no single or general meaning in Buddhism. However, it can be grouped into four different senses of *dhamma*. They are as follows: 1) reference to good conduct; 2) moral instruction; 3) doctrine of Buddha as contained in the scripture; and 4) cosmic law.

Besides these, the doctrine of Buddhism on dhamma can be summed up in the Four Noble Truths. The Buddhist practise of these Four Noble Truths can be described as follows:

1) Life is *dukkha*, meaning suffering and dissatisfaction. The reality of *dukkha* permeates what is called life. There are many forms of *dukkha* or suffering which belong to physical or mental pain, such as the agonies of cancer, aches and pains, the anguish of total despair, dislikes and frustration. That is why *dukkha* touches everything that exists.

The beginning of the road to wisdom begins with a realistic recognition of the fact of *dukkha*. In other words, it is notable that Buddhism starts with the dark side of life in order to see and appreciate the grandeur and challenge of human existence. However, it is not pessimistic but it is rather a realistic assumption based on the problem of human suffering.

2) *Dukkha* has an identifiable cause. The origin of suffering lies in craving or grasping. Buddhism uses the term *Tanhā* for this. It means "thirst," which can be described as an obsessive lust for money and

---

Delhi, 1991, p. 114.

[264] Cf. C. Eliot, *Hinduism and Buddhism. A Historical Sketch*, London, 1962, p. 185.

sensual pleasure. *Tanhā* is implanted in everything that exists and so it is entirely natural. *Tanhā* is also described in the wheel of life as a power of rolling motion of life. It drives human beings from one moment to the next, from one life to the next in the cycle of incarnation. Every human being wants to get off the wheel of life and thereby liberate himself from *dukkha*.

3) Cessation of suffering is possible. It means that there is a method or a way to attain ultimate freedom.[265] This ultimate freedom is known as *Nibbāna* in Pali or *Nirvāna* in Sanskrit. This is the supreme goal of Buddhism, in which a human being is free from the limitations of existence. In other words, *Nirvāna* is a state attainable by right aspiration, purity of life, and elimination of egoism.

4) Practical way to liberation. There are some practical steps in order to root out the causes of *dukkha*. In order to attain liberation, Buddhism proposes eight steps as follows: right understanding, right thought, right speech, right action, right livelihood, right effort, right mindfulness, and right concentration. These steps are called the *Noble Eightfold Path*.

Further, these steps can be grouped in three sections , i.e., wisdom, morality and meditation. "Wisdom" contains the first two steps concerning the preliminary frame of mind of the aspirant. "Morality" includes the next three steps concerning the ethical requirement. "Meditation" contains the last three steps concerning meditative training.

The exercise of self-control, therefore, plays an important role in Buddhism. Tachibana says:

> To begin with, the six sense organs are usually regarded as the 'doors' (*dvāra*) through which evils may intrude into the human mind; and therefore guarding and protecting them, conquering them, tranquillizing and pacifying them is everywhere commanded as praiseworthy conduct. To control one's sense organs and to prevent them running their natural course forms an important part of Buddhist culture.[266]

---

[265] Cf. J. Snelling, *The Budhist Handbook*, London, 1989, p. 54.
[266] S. Tachibana, *The Ethics of Buddhism*, London, 1975, p. 102.

The restraint and the direction of human sense-organs constitute the way of rising higher on the steps of life. This will preserve morality, mental concentration, knowledge and insight in order to attain full enlightenment.

C. Some Important Buddhist Ideas with Regard to Harmony

Buddhism sees reality as a continuous, self-energizing process rather than a series of permanent states. It can be illustrated as a fire which consists of the burning of new elements. It begins and dies out. The continuously new elements which are added to the fire form the reality of the fire. The middle way is the right view that existence is the continuous process of two extremes: arising and perishing. Both arising and perishing depend on previous conditions and give rise to new conditions. This point deals with dependent origination in which the elements depend on each other and act in unison. The factors wich constitute dependence simultaneously originate the element of being. That element of being is karma.

Buddhism sees itself as taking a middle way between two extremes of the ordinary man's enjoyment of pleasure and the intense self-mortification practised by many ascetics. Buddha taught his renunciatory followers thus to avoid the extremes of self-mortification and simple immersion in self-indulgent sense-gratification.

Harmony in the sense of absolute interdependence is important in Buddhism. This interdependence maintains reality. In addition, there is the important idea of *suñyatā* which means emptiness or nothingness. This is the ultimate explanation of the not-self. The essence of all phenomena is nothing or zero. It is important on the ontological level. On the field of *suñyatā* the selfness of the self has its being in the home-ground of all other things.[267] All things are considered in interdependence. On the mental level, we might say that emotions are determined in a context which is caused by other thoughts. The term *Prajñā Pāramitā* is a dynamic idea of nothingness, the sacred revelation of a transcendent knowledge or inspiration. The idea of harmony as the state of

---

[267] Cf. J.M. Koller and P. Koller, *A Sourcebook in Asian Philosophy*, New York, 1991, p. 394.

interdependence emerges from the basis of the commonplace experience of nothingness, not-self, and the idea of impermanence or *anicca.*

Accordingly, the consequence is that human beings must be adaptable. Because reality is sustained by absolute interdependence and there is "not self", everybody must adapt to the same situation. From this idea derives the term *upāya,* meaning the creative efforts of wisdom. With this in view, Buddhism offers a particular dynamic for adaptation and penetration into various cultures.

Buddhism emphasizes participation in the current affairs of the world for the realization of absolute virtue. And so, the importance of unity among individuals is maintained in society of fellow beings.

IV.   ISLAMIC THOUGHT

This section concerns the teaching of the Qur'án and some Islamic philosophers' views on harmony, as observed from the perspective of Indonesian Islam. Here, I would like to deal only with the medieval philosophical opinions, as from the 13th century Islam shows its appearance in society.

A.   The Teaching in the Qur'án on Harmony

The Qur'án is the sacred book of Islam, the word of God revealed to Muhammed. The Muslims believe that the Qur'án has the final authority on how to lead life on this earth, and that the earthly Qur'án is a direct copy of an eternal Qur'án inscribed in heaven. This is why the Muslims treat the Qur'án with great respect. Accordingly, the rules and maxims of the Qur'án become the basis of the *shari*ᶜ*a.*[268]

The foundation of Islam, the Qur'án is believed to contain everything. All the problems in the world have been clarified in the Qur'án. We will concentrate on the teachings in the Qur'án in regard to harmony.

We are dealing with the harmony of nature, which is seen in the

---

[268] *Shariᶜa* is Islamic law based on divine revelation. The laws of the *shariᶜa* are drawn from the Qur'án, the *Sunna* (example and saying of Muhammad in his life), the *Ijmaᶜ* (the consensus of Islamic community) and *Qiyás* (a term for the deduction made about law on the basis of the Qur'án). Cf. H.A.R. Gibb, *Mohammedanism*, translated by Abusalamah in: *Islam dalam Lintasan Sejarah*, Jakarta-New York, 1983, pp. 66-79; H.R. Moedjono Sosrodirdjo, *Ungkapan dan Istilah Agama Islam* (Terms and Expressions of the Islamic religion), Jakarta, 1985, pp. 122-123.

seriousness of the divine project. The Qur'an says:

> Unto Him is the return of all of you; it is a promise of Allah in truth. Lo! He produceth creation, the reproduceth it, that He may reward those who believe and do good works with equity; while, as for those who disbelieve; theirs will be a boiling drink and painful doom because they disbelieved (Qur'an 10,4).[269]

The Qu'ran also says, "whoso doeth right, it for his soul, and whoso doeth wrong, it is against it. And afterwards unto your Lord ye will be brought" (Qur'an 45,15).

The quotations above state that human beings are created by God, and they will return to God. God exercised all this creative activity and continues to act in this world. The world possesses a seriousness which derives from the end for which God has destined it from the beginning and which will last until the Day of Judgment.[270] On the last day there will be a gathering of mankind before the Judge. The graves will be opened and human beings of all ages, restored to life, will join the throng. This description points out that the Qur'an does not assert a natural immortality of soul, because the existence of human beings are dependent on God's will.[271]

The duty of human beings and creation is to glorify the Almighty God. The Qur'an says: "All that is in the heavens and all that is in the earth glorifieth Allah, and He is the Mighty, the Wise" (Qur'an 59,1). Besides, human beings have the duty to give thanks to God for His bounty. The Qur'an says:

> And He it is Who hath constrained the sea to be of service that ye eat fresh meat from thence, and bring forth from thence ornaments which ye wear. And thou seest the ships ploughing it that ye (mankind) may seek of His bounty, and that haply ye give thanks (Qur'an 16,14).

---

[269] The translation of the Qur'an cited in this study is taken from *The Meaning of The Glorious Qur'an*, translation by Muhammad Marmaduke Pickthall, Cairo-Beirut, 1972. For further comprehension I use A. Yusuf Ali, *The Holy Qur'an. Text, Translation and Commentary*, Leicester (UK), 1975.

[270] Cf. T. Michel, "The Teaching of the Qur'an about Nature", Pontificium Concilium pro Dialogo Inter Religiones, *Bulletin* 79 (1992), p. 90.

[271] Cf. W. Montgomery Watt, *Islamic Surveys*, Edinburgh, 1970, p. 159.

Proceeding from God with a mission to fulfill, man's destiny is ultimately to return to Him. That is why man should worship Him. The Qur'ān says:

> Lo! Your Lord is Allah Who created the heavens and the earth in six Days, then He established Himself upon the Throne, directing all things. There is no intercessor (with Him) save after His permission. That is Allah, your Lord, so worship Him. Oh, will ye remind? (Qur'ān 10,3).

In the context of creation, a human being should refer to God as the source and witness to his purpose. He had not been "created for naught" (Qur'ān 23,115); he has a mission and he is God's "viceroy in earth" (Qur'ān 2,30). According to Achilles deSouza, the whole cosmos is laid out for human beings, and a human in its centre points to God.[272]

From the Qur'ānic point of view, a human being has exceptional power and a privileged position inside creation, because he receives the Spirit. And so, the teaching of the Qur'ān on the concept of a human being is as follows: a human being is a privileged being with "spiritual favours" (Qur'ān 17,70). In reference to this, M. Talbi says:

> Among the whole range of creatures only man has duties and obligations. He is an exceptional being. He cannot be reduced to his body, because man, before everything else, is a spirit, a spirit which has been given the power to conceive the Absolute and to ascend to God. If man has this exceptional power and this privileged position inside Creation, it is because God "breathed into him something of His spirit"(Qur'ān 32,9). Of course man, like all living animals, is matter. He has a body created "from sounding clay, from mud moulded into shape"(Qur'ān 15,28). But he received the spirit.[273]

The Qur'ān recognizes the existence of spiritual beings, such as Jinn and Satān. These are shadowy spirits who seldom assume a distinct personality or name. Satān is the same person as Iblīs who is an angel deposed for his pride (Qur'ān 2,34). They are associated with deserts, ruins and other various places, and might assume such forms as those of animals, serpents and other creeping things. They are vaguely feared, but are not always malevolent. Though created from fire, and not like man, from clay (Qur'ān 55,14; 15,26) their end is likewise to serve or worship God (Qur'ān 51,56).

---

[272] Cf. Achilles de Souza, "Creator of the Universe", *Focus* 1 (1989), p. 30.

[273] M. Talbi, "Religious Liberty: A Muslim Perspective", *Islamochristiana* 11 (1985), p. 102.

It is said in the Qur'an that on one occasion a company of Jinn listened to Muhammed proclaiming the Qur'an and that some of them became Muslims (Qur'an 72,1-19; 46,29). The Jinn, hence, warned the people to believe in God (Qur'an 46,31). In contrast to the recognition of spiritual beings, the Muslims have an obligation and duty to believe in the One God Almighty.

The foundation in association with others, is the favour of God who has saved the people and thus they must unite one another, as the Qur'an teaches:

> And hold fast, all of you together, to the cable of Allah, and do not separate. And remember Allah's favour unto you: how ye were enemies and He made friendship between your hearts so that ye became as brothers by His grace; and (how) ye were upon the brink of an abyss of fire, and He did save you from it. Thus Allah maketh clear His revelation unto you, that haply ye man be guided (Qur'an 3,103).

Regarding a harmonious coexistence with other religions, the Qur'an invites each of the adherents to live their own religion. The Qur'an says:

> Say: O disbelievers! I worship not that which ye worship; nor worship ye that which I worship. And I shall not worship that which ye worship. Nor will ye worship that which I worship. Unto you your religion, and unto me my religion (Qur'an 109,1-6).

Besides, the Qur'an advises its adherents not to argue, except with those who do wrong. The Qur'an says:

> And argue not with the People of the Scripture unless it be in (a way) that is better, save with such of them as do wrong; and say: We believe in that which hath been revealed unto us and revealed unto you; our God and your God is One, and unto Him we surrender (Qur'an 29,46).

Talbi says that the attitude of respectful courtesy, recommended by the Qur'an, must be extended to the whole of mankind, believers and unbelievers, except for those who do wrong in the sense of those who are unjust, violent and resort deliberately to the argument of the fist, either physically or in words.[274]

---

[274] Cf. M. Talbi, "Religious Liberty: A Muslim Perspective", *Islamochristiana* 11 (1985),

It is the best conduct that becomes the criteria of nobleness. This good conduct is addressed to all human beings, male and female, tribes and nations. The Qur'an says: "O mankind! Lo! We have created you male and female, and have made you nations and tribes that ye may know one another. Lo! the noblest of you, in the sight of Allah, is the best in conduct. Lo! Allah is Knower, Aware" (Qur'an 49,13). According to A. Yusuf Ali, these verses are addressed to all mankind, and not only to the Muslims. The tribes, races, and nations are convenient labels by which human beings may know certain differing characteristics.[275] The reason is that they are all one and the noblest is the best in conduct.

The Muslims are invited to join those who are inclined to peace, meanwhile they also trust in God. The reasons for this are that God is the Knower, the Almighty and the most Wise. The Qur'an says:

> And if they incline to peace, incline thou also to it, and trust in Allah. Lo! He, even He, is the Hearer, the Knower. And if they would deceive thee, then Lo! Allah is sufficient for thee. He it is Who supporteth thee with His help and with the believers. And (as for the believers) hath attuned their hearts. If thou hadst spent all that is in the earth thou couldst not have attuned their hearts, but Allah hath attuned them. Lo! He is Mighty, Wise (Qur'an 8,61-63).

In short, the Islamic description of harmony expresses that God is the Creator and the destination of every human being and all creation. He still has many names, such as the Knower, the Almighty, the Wise, and so forth.[276] Human beings should live in good relationships in the sense of "not to argue" and to "unite with those who are inclined toward peace."

B.   The View of Some Islamic Philosophers

We will deal only with the important Islamic philosophers' views as far as they help us to understand the influence of Islamic thought in

---

(1985), pp. 105-106.

[275] Cf. A. Yusuf Ali, *The Holy Qur'ān. Text, Translation and Commentary*, Leicester (UK), 1975, p. 1407.

[276] The most beautiful names which are called *al-asmā'al-ḥusnā* have tended to play a large part in later Islamic thought. Cf. W. Montgomery Watt, *Islamic Surveys*, Edinburgh, 1970, p. 152.

the formation of *Keselarasan*. Accordingly, we speak about the ideas of Al-Kindī, Al-Fārabī, Al-Ghazālī, and Avicenna (Ibn-Sīnā). Their thought might shed light on the development of Javanese thought during centuries.

Al-Kindī (870) adopted the doctrine that the world emanates from the One, which is identified with the God of the Qur'ān. In a lengthy argument he offered proof to demonstrate both God's existence and oneness. Unless there is a being who is utterly one, devoid of all multiplicity, there can be no variety and multiplicity in the world. But, Al-Kindī argued, multiplicity and variety in the world is a fact which we experience and cannot dismiss. Hence, the being who is utterly one, namely God, must exist.[277]

It was al-Fārabī (875-950) who more than anyone else shaped the general character of Islamic philosophy. According to him, the earth was the centre of the universe. In the order of existence it was the most remote from God and hence, in order of value, lowest. But within our earth, by virtue of being endowed with reason, man stood highest in the scale of value. Around the earth revolved the heavenly spheres. The closest was the sphere of the Moon, then the spheres of Mercury, Venus, the Sun, Mars, Jupiter and Saturn, respectively. Beyond Saturn was the sphere of the fixed stars; finally there was an outermost sphere assumed to be without stars.[278]

God is the one or the First from whom all existence proceeds; and in this sense al-Fārabī accepted the Islamic doctrine that God is the Creator of the world. In the relationship between creation and God there is a hierarchical order. The head is also described as commanding but not obeying; all the intermediate grades obey those above and command those below, and the lowest grade only obeys.

This entire emanative process is for al-Fārabī an eternal one. The

---

[277] M.E. Marmura, *God and His Creation: Two Medieval Islamic Views*, in: *Introduction to Islamic Civilization*, Cambridge, 1973, p. 50.

[278] Cf. M.E. Marmura, *God and His Creation: Two Medieval Islamic Views*, in: *Introduction to Islamic Civilization*, Cambridge, 1973, p. 50.

universe is an orderly, rational one, emanating in degrees from a supreme mind, God. Humankind, on this earth, being endowed with voluntary action, must order its own life and society to be in tune with the rational, harmonious order of the universe. Only thus can a human being attain happiness. Just as the universe is ordered by a supreme rational being, God, and each heavenly sphere is governed by an intelligence, so a human being is a small universe in his own right, out to govern himself by his reason. The same holds for human society. The state should be organised in such a way that each level of society performs its proper function, all acting as a harmonious whole.[279]

Al-Fārābī teaches that everything in the world emanated from the divine pre-knowledge: it previously existed in the form of an idea. This emanation takes place in five stages. A human being is the sixth stage, which is separated, because his soul might be reunited with the essence of divinity through transcending the form of unreal plurality. Consequently, the form of all creation is actually the essence of the Creator.[280] Everything which has form is considered as a manifestation of divine mystery. This doctrine is called *taṣawwuf wujūdīyah*.[281]

In so far as they are humans, the claim would be true of people that they all have a common sense by the free exercise of which they can arrive at the essence of all religious truth. Without this natural endowment, man would not be man at all. The universalism of this aspect of Islamic belief knows no exception whatever. On this basis of *religio naturalis*, Islam has founded its universal humanism. All men are ontologically the creatures of God, and all of them are equal in their creatureliness as well as in their natural ability to recognise God and His law. Nobody may even be excused from knowing God, his Creator, for each and every one has been equipped at birth with means required for

---

[279] M.E. Marmura, *God and His Creation: Two Medieval Islamic Views*, in: *Introduction to Islamic Civilization*, Cambridge, 1973, p. 51.

[280] Cf. Gustave E. von Grunebaum, (ed.), *Unity and Variety in Muslim Civilization*, (translated by E.N. Yahya), Jakarta, 1983, p. 330.

[281] Cf. P.J. Zoetmulder, *Pantheism and Monism in Javanese Suluk Literature. Islamic and Indian Mysticism in an Indonesian Setting*, Leiden, 1995, pp. 103, 209.

such knowledge.[282]

Concerning religion, Ismail al-Faruqi says:

> To have religion is to have access to a whole hierarchy of values. These values are ultimate, they concern the ultimate dimension of existence and life. Nothing is more valuable than what religion teaches about, namely God, and His disposal of the lives of humans, knowledge, adoration and love of Him, obedience to Him, fulfilment of His will, graces, vicegerency of God, the reward of eternal happiness in paradise are of ultimate value.[283]

He adds that religion does not only give us access to ultimate values, but it also introduces us to ultimate truths about our life and existence, about heaven and earth. It convinces us of these truths, for it presents them not as one opinion among others, but as the truth. Some religions hold a relativist theory of truth, maintaining that their truth is theirs and need not be necessarily the view of others.[284]

Al-Ghazāli (1050-1111) in his last treatise, deals with the influences of the heavenly bodies on terrestrial affairs. He states that the function of astrology is to show that when the planets are in harmonious relationship, affairs in the sublunar world of "Generation and Corruption" go well; when the planets are out of harmony affairs go ill. Furthermore, certain conjunctions of the planets point to the occurrence on earth of specified situations and conditions.[285]

According to him, the universe or the macrocosm, which consists of the seven heavens and the seven earths and what lies between, bears a resemblance to the individual human being or the microcosm, with all one's parts and members. The universe is, moreover, endowed with a single spirit which directs the powers of each part of it in the same way that the soul of the individual man directs all one's members.[286]

---

[282] Cf. Ismail al-Faruqi, "Rights of Non-Muslims under Islam: Social and Cultural Aspects", *Journal Institute of Muslim Minority Affairs* 1 (1979), p. 92.

[283] Ismail al-Faruqi, "Rights of Non-Muslims under Islam: Social and Cultural Aspects", *Journal Institute of Muslim Minority Affairs* 1 (1979), p. 94.

[284] Cf. Ismail al-Faruqi, "Rights of Non-Muslims under Islam: Social and Cultural Aspects", *Journal Institute of Muslim Minority Affairs* 1 (1979), p. 94.

[285] Reuben Levy, *The Social Structure of Islam*, Cambridge, 1969, p. 477.

[286] Reuben Levy, *The Social Sructure of Islam*, Cambridge, 1969, p. 477.

Avicenna (Ibn-Sīnā), one of the most important of Muslim philosophers, elaborated one of the most cohesive, subtle, and all embracing systems of Medieval history. In the Muslim world, his system is still taught in traditional centres of Islamic learning. Avicenna devised a theory of the distinction between essence and existence. Concerning this theory he refined the implications of the Islamic doctrine of creation, which al-Kindī had crudely asserted, into an integrated philosophical system.

Avicenna asserts a single, universal process of outward movement, and he posits three factors: matter, form and existence. Hence he postulates a Necessary Being as the basis for the world process. Because of Islam's demand for a fundamental distinction between God and the world, he implies that God is so distinct from the world by the fact that His being is necessary and simple; God cannot be composed of matter for material being is a composite of essence and existence. Material beings are composed of matter and form, which constitute their essence, and the fact of their existence. All existence flows from God.

Some important ideas concerning the formation of *Keselarasan* can be noted as follows:

We can begin with the idea that everything which has form is a manifestation of God. Some thinkers reduced this to the extreme conclusion of identification of the self with God. The same conclusion was drawn by both Al-Ḥallāj and Sheik Siti Jenar, one of the Walis. They proclaimed the deep experience of unity with God in public. Then they reduced this assumption to the conviction which identified themselves with God. For this reason, Al-Ḥallaj and Sheik Siti Jenar were condemned to death.[287] However, these ideas have constituted an expression of human longing for a close unification between human beings and the Creator.

The image of God as creator and purpose of human life is well

---

[287] Cf. P.J. Zoetmulder, *Pantheism and Monism in Javanese Suluk Literature. Islamic and Indian mysticism in an Indonesian Setting*, (edited and translated by M.C. Ricklefs), Leiden, 1995, pp. 301, 307.

known. This Islamic thought has maintained or influenced the Javanese understanding of human life. It inspired the Javanese image of human life as a journey. We recall that we have said that human life in the world is a moment for rest to drink or, in Javanese expression, *mampir ngombe*.

In this sense, the image of a human being is also described as a spark of divinity in the process of emanation. Happiness is the return to its sources, the unity between a human being and God. This idea has contributed to the importance of knowing human identity and its place in the universe and in society. It contributes a significant element in realizing the aspiration of harmony.

V.   CHRISTIAN THOUGHT

There is remarkable evidence of the influence of Christian thought in Indonesia since the sixteenth century. At the end of the fifteenth century, the Portuguese found a nautic route to Asia by means of South Africa.[288] This discovery of a nautic route facilitated the coming of missionaries, together with Portuguese and Dutch navigation for trade. In 1511, the Portuguese came to the town of Malacca and also reached the islands of Moluccas.[289] G. Schurhammer noted that Francis Xavier had come to the islands of Maluku (Mollucas) in 1546-1547.[290] We shall speak of the central ideas of harmony in the Bible and in some philosophical ideas of the Christian tradition.

A.   Teachings in the Bible on Harmony in the Judaeo-Christian Tradition

The Bible is the book of the story of God's revelation and salvation plan, which reachs its culmination in the historical event of Jesus Christ. Christians believe that the authors were inspired by the Holy Spirit, and so, the Bible is often described as the Word of God.[291] This Word of God is expressed through the words of men with the inevitable

---

[288] Cf. M.P.M. Muskens, *Sejarah Gereja Katolik Indonesia* (History of Indonesian Catholic Church), Vol. I, Jakarta, 1974, p. 44.

[289] Cf. M.P.M. Muskens, *Partner in Nation Building. The Catholic Church in Indonesia*, Aachen, 1979, p. 38.

[290] M.P.M. Muskens, *Sejarah Gereja Katolik Indonesia* (History of Indonesian Catholic Chruch), Vol. I, Jakarta, 1974, p. 46.

[291] Cf. Dei Verbum 5. *I Documenti del Concilio Vaticano II*, Torino, 1987, p. 180.

limitation of all human words. By means of faith as an intuitive understanding, readers of the Bible can go beyond the letter to the spirit of the Prophets' experiences and the truth to which they sought to bear witness. In this section we deals with some ideas in the Bible, such as Paradise, Šalōm, and the Kingdom of God, which are important for both Jews and Christians.

1. Paradise

The Greek word *paradeisos* means "garden." The Old Persian word *Pairidaēza* means "an encircling wall, circular enclosure, garden." According to the tradition of the religions in the Middle East, a god's life can be described in the following way. Gods have palaces, surrounded by gardens where the "water of life" flows.[292] Besides many beautiful trees, there is a flourishing "tree of life." The image of the temples of the gods with their sacred gardens might have been a prototype for the paradise in the Bible.

In short, the image of paradise can be described as follows: In the beginning God created heaven and earth (Genesis 1,1), and within six days he finished them with all the beings which they contain. Among them were human beings, whom God created male and female, in His own image (Genesis 1,27). After the Creator had completed his work, He saw all the things that He had made, and they were good (Genesis 1,31). On the seventh day God rested from all the work He had done and, for this very reason, He blessed that day and sanctified it (Genesis 2,3).

God created man and had a purpose for which He placed him in this world. God planted a garden for him in Eden (Genesis 2,8) that is identified as paradise.[293] Man was put into a paradise of pleasure, to dress it and to keep it. Man's life in this garden included labour (Genesis 2,15), but at the same time it had the character of ideal happiness. C. Westermann says that human existence includes work and community

---

[292] Cf. C. Westermann, *Genesis 1-11*, (translated by J.J. Scullion), London, 1984, pp. 212-214.
[293] Cf. A. Clarke, *Clarke's Commentary*, Vol. I, Nashville, 1828, p. 42.

with other human beings.[294] The circumstances are described as full familiarity with God, free use of the fruits of the Garden, mastery over all animals (Genesis 2,19), harmonious union of the primitive couple (Genesis 2,18,23), moral innocence that is signified by the absence of shame (Genesis 2,25) and the absence of death.

Death came into the world as a result of sin (Genesis 3,19). Sin happened when man did not want to recognise his different identity from that of God. Man wished to "be like gods" (Genesis 3,15).[295] Later, sin spread because there was no respect for the differences between Cain and Abel, pointing out variety in work and occupation.[296] But the way of the tree of life shall be opened once again to man (Revelation 2,7; 22,2). The promised paradise as the restored paradisiacal life shall show forth a characteristic equivalent to the first paradise. There shall be marvelous fertility in nature (Amos 9,13; Jeremiah 31,23-26; Joel 4,18). Christians believe that Jesus Christ has realized the promised paradise, which brings about universal peace, not only among themselves (Isaiah 2,4), but also with nature and animals (Hosea 2,20; Isaiah 11,6-9; 65,25).

The Bible has its own images and concepts, symbols derived from the unique experiences of the people of Israel. The myth of paradise leads to the myth of the new creation, culminating in St. John's Revelation of a "new heaven and new earth." From that time on, paradise is opened to all who die in the Lord.

Thus paradise is a symbol of the original harmony of man's environment. Man was originally a child of nature. He was formed "of the dust of the ground," the same ground from which "the Lord God made to grow every tree that is pleasant to the sight and good for food." And so, man is part of the universe and creation. He, therefore, has a close relationship with his environment in paradise.

---

[294] Cf. C. Westermann, *Genesis 1-11*, (translated by J.J Scullion), London, 1984, p. 220.

[295] Cf. C. Westermann, *Genesis 1-11*, (translated by J.J Scullion), London, 1984, pp. 242-248.

[296] Cf. C. Westermann, *Genesis 1-11*, (translated by J.J. Scullion), London, 1984, p. 293.

96

2.　　Šalōm

The Hebrew word *šalōm* is derived from a root which points out two things. First, the word *šalōm* is used to designate the fact of being intact or complete. For example 1 Kings 9,25 indicates *šalōm* as "to complete a house." In other words, it indicates the action of re-establishing things to their integrity. The basic idea is totality; so everything which is in connection with totality relates to *šalōm*.[297] Second, the word *šalōm* also indicates the well-being of daily existence, the state of one who lives in harmony with nature, with oneself, with God. This forms a community which participates in God's blessings. *Šalōm* contains a kind of harmony and opportunity for improvement for everybody. Accordingly, everybody as a member of a community can develop integrity, creating *šalōm* in the whole community. Besides, it contains the ideas of health and prosperity (1 Samuel 10,4; Psalms 38,3). Somebody who lives in *šalōm*, enjoys health, prosperity, strength and integrity.

Christians believe that Christ is a realization of the idea of *šalōm*. The reason is that Jesus reconciles all creatures through Himself, whether on the earth or in the heaven, making peace through the blood of His cross (Colossians 1,20). And the God of peace who has raised up Jesus (Hebrews 13,20), having destroyed Satan (Romans 16,20), will restore all things in their original integrity. St. John's Gospel shows that Jesus is the source and reality of peace (John 14,27; 20,19-23). Christians acknowledge the lordship of Jesus Christ, whose coming at the end of time will establish definitive and universal peace. Jesus was sent by God to be a prince of peace (Isaiah 9,6) who would "proclaim peace to the nations" (Zechariah 9,10).[298]

In Jesus Christ, the destiny of mankind has been fulfilled. In Him the conflict has been overcome, body and soul have been restored to a unity with the Spirit, a power of unification.[299] The fulfilment of human

---

[297] Cf. Herman Hendrickx, *Peace anyone?*, (translated by F. Rudiyanto), Jakarta, 1994, p. 10.
[298] R.E. Brown, *The Gospel according to John XIII-XXI*, Vol. 29A, Garden City, 1970, p. 653.
[299] Cf.R.E. Brown, *The Gospel according to John XIII-XXI*, Vol. 29A, Garden City, 1970,

life in Christ constitutes a good relationship of beings which reduces their multiplicity to unity. The unity of peaceful convivialty was expressed in the life of the first Christians (Acts 2,41-47). In addition, St. Paul also advised the early Christians to associate with one another in a peaceful way of life (Romans 12,15-18; 15,1-4; 2Corinthians 13,11). Jesus who has redeemed the world constituted a Christological foundation for *šalom*, so that humans might live in harmony with nature, with self and with neighbour, and with God.

c. Kingdom of God

The main purpose of Jesus' coming into the world is to proclaim the kingdom of God. The kingdom of God is a mysterious reality which is revealed by Jesus' words and works. Sometimes Jesus uses parables for describing the reality of the kingdom of God. This kingdom comes where the Word of God is addressed to humanity; such seed, once thrown on the ground, is meant to grow (Matthew 13,3-9; 18-23). It will grow by its own power, like a grain of wheat (Mark 4,26-29). The kingdom of God ought to become a great tree where all the birds of the air will come and shelter in its branches (Matthew 13,31). And so, it becomes "good news" for all nations.

The kingdom of God and the messianic kingship are closely connected because the Messiah King is the son of God Himself. In His kingdom, God becomes all in all. The universe was transformed and newly ordered by the same power which had appeared in Jesus Christ. They all radiated the transforming power of God's Spirit (Romans 8,17).

The coming of the kingdom of God is the fulfilment of creation. It will come to its fulfilment in the last day of the world. At that moment the crucified Jesus will bear the title of the universal Lord of creation (John 1,3; Colossians 1,16). The realization of the kingdom of God includes all creatures, such as animals, plants, and even so-called "inert matter" such as stones and water. Accordingly, salvation is seen within the horizon and scope of the history of the universe and of creation.

---

p. 1051.

B.   Some Philosophical Views in Christian Tradition

Some philosophers in the Christian tradition try to explain and maintain biblical truth and their faith in their historical context. Consequently, some of the Christian philosophers and thinkers speak about God, creation and the reality of human life. We concentrate on some ideas from St. Augustine (A.D. 354-430)[300] and St. Thomas Aquinas (A.D. 1225-1274) regarding the influence of Christian thought in Indonesia, and especially Javanese thought.

The background of St. Augustine should be seen in the influence of Neo-Platonic philosophy which maintains "duality," in the sense that there are ideas which are eternal, unchanged, and there is a tangible reality which is not eternal, and thus can be changed. Besides, Manicheism with its two principles of good and evil also influenced his thoughts.

St. Augustine spoke of the world as being created with its "causes" or seminal principles implanted in nature. From their beginning created beings look like seeds, which are destined to develop their specific forms according to the laws or tendencies inherent in them. According to St. Augustine, God is the Creator of all beings; He created humankind in likeness to Himself, as His image.[301]

It starts from the external reality such as universe, memory, and so on to the interior reflection. He said that God created everything from "nothing." Therefore, creation is "ex nihilo."[302] God created the world and creatures as traces of Himself. All things, therefore, speak of God. In God there are divine ideas and the world was created according to these

---

[300] The quotations of Augustine's Confessions cited in this study are taken mainly from *Le Confessioni* in Latin and Italian translation by Carlo Vitali, Milano, 1992. For further notes and comparison I also use the translation of Henry Chadwick, Oxford, 1992.

[301] Confessiones XIII, xxii. Cf. Sant'Agostino, *Le Confessioni*, translated by C. Vitali, Milano, 1992, pp. 698-701; Saint Augustine, *Confessions*, (translated by H. Chadwick), Oxford, 1992, pp. 291-292.

[302] Confessiones XI, v. Sant'Agostino, *Le Confessioni*, (translated by C. Vitali), Milano, 1992, pp. 545-457; Saint Augustine, *Confessions*, (translated by H. Chadwick), Oxford, 1992, pp. 224-225.

ideas. Creation is a manifestation of the participation in divine ideas. Being is a sign of something beyond, so that man can know God through reflection on things.[303] The world, thus, is a description of divine ideas which have beauty and harmony.

A human being can actively participate in divine ideas by knowledge of God. Knowledge has been included in the reality of love. Accordingly, someone who knows the truth, knows eternity and love.[304] In the heart and unity of consciousness, time is reconnected to unity: through the heart time is felt as a continuity uniting the past and the future. Mankind's method of thinking is interior reflection, commencing from tangible reality to inner reflection. This principle of participation constitutes the process of contemplation and knowledge.[305]

In Book XIII, xxxii, St. Augustine described the harmony of the universe. According to him, the universe consists of the entire mass of the world or the entire created order absolutely. He says : "We see the beauty of the waters gathered in the expanses of the sea, and the dry land whether bare of vegetation, or given form so as to be 'visible and ordered,' the mother of plants and trees."[306] In addition, he says : "we see that each particular point and the whole taken all together are very good."[307]

According to St. Thomas Aquinas, philosophy might be called "natural philosophy," because he recognizes that the mind can observe truth. Reason alone is enough for knowing the world or even God. He

---

[303] Cf. Confessiones X, vi. Sant'Agostino, *Le Confessioni*, (translated by C. Vitali), Milano, 1992, pp. 450-455.

[304] Nec ita erat supra mentem meam, sicut oleum super aquam nec sicut caelum super terram, sed superior, quia ipsa fecit me, et ego inferior, quia factus ab ea. Qui novit veritatem, novit eam, novit aeternitatem. Caritas novit eam. Confessiones VII, x. Cf. Sant'Agostino, *Le Confessioni*, (translated by C. Vitali), Milano, 1992, p. 318.

[305] Confessiones VII, vii. Cf. Sant'Agostino, *Le Confessioni*, translated by C. Vitali, Milano, 1992, pp. 308-311; Saint Augustine, *Confessions*, (translated by H. Chadwick), Oxford, 1992, pp. 119-120.

[306] Confessiones XIII, xxxii. Saint Augustine, *Confessions*, (translated by H. Chadwick), Oxford, 1992, p. 302.

[307] Confessiones XIII, xxxii.Saint Augustine, *Confessions*, (translated by H. Chadwick), Oxford, 1992, p. 302.

defends the right of the mind and the free mind in its own field. Faith is a method of gaining knowledge beyond the reason of the mind. Even though faith is beyond the mind, it is not in contrast with the mind. Consequently he states the existence of two kinds of knowledge: natural knowledge and knowledge of faith. Natural knowledge can be reached by the activity of reason; while the knowledge of faith can be reached by revelation and divine truth as found in the Holy Scripture.

St. Thomas Aquinas uses Aristotelian terminology such as act and potentiality. According to him, God is a Perfect Being. He is *Actus Purus*, in which everything has come to perfect realization so that there is no development in Him. He is pure act, in which his essence and existence are identical. In contrast with this, a human being consists of essence and existence, which constitutes a metaphysical principle of all finite things.

The teaching of St. Thomas Aquinas on creation based on Augustinian-Neo-Platonism, contains a tenet of participation. Accordingly, all beings participate in God, the Divine Being. The reason is not because of emanation as in Neo-Platonism, but because of creation. St. Thomas Aquinas underlines the thoughts of St. Augustine that the world is created from nothing. The relationship from God to creature is a mental relation of reason (*relatio rationis*) attributed to God by the human intellect. The important point is that the creature depends on God and God does not depend upon creatures. Consequently the rational relation between creatures and God is a relationship of dependence, which is found in the reflection on creatures alone.[308]

The existence of God as Creator is explained in five philosophical ways. These ways become the most well-known proofs for God's existence. The first way is an analysis of the tangible universe ascending to God. From this process of reflection, one finds an unmovable motor which causes change and movement. St. Thomas calls this unmovable motor "God." The second way is based on the nature of causation. In this analysis God is seen as sufficient cause which is not caused. The third

---

[308] Cf. F. Copleston, *History of Philosophy*, Vol. II, London, 1966, p. 364.

way is an analysis of what needs to be and what must be. God, therefore, is necessary Being. He is one who is something which must be, and owes this to no other thing than Himself.[309] The fourth way is an analysis based on the gradation observed in things. Things are found to be more good, or more beautiful and so on. Finally, the observation comes to the perfect being who we call "God." The fifth way is the analysis of the guidedness of nature, its orderedness of action to an end. Everything is directed to its goal by someone with understanding, and this someone we call God.[310]

The five ways to know God not only demonstrate the existence of God but also show that God is the Creator of the world. For St. Thomas, created nature has its concrete individuality. Things have a connection with God's will. St. Thomas Aquinas introduced the concept of nature into Christian philosophy, and brought it to an examination of nature and beyond nature to reason and faith, freedom and grace.

The arrival of Christian missionaries in Java brought Christian thought into the Javanese tradition. Nevertheless those ideas were filtered by the culture of the people, which is rooted in the heart of Javanese society. K.A. Steenbrink states that Christianity in Java originated not as the result of the work of foreign missionaries, but as a consequence of the spiritual quest of Javanese people themselves.[311] The contact with Christian tradition enriches habits and Javanese thought, as it was also enriched by Hindu, Buddhist and Islamic thought. This integration of thought took place over a very long period of history, in which however, the original Javanese characteristics remain evident.

The dynamic of integration has brought about the very rich concept of *Keselarasan*. We have seen the origin of *Keselarasan* in the previous chapter which speaks about *Wédhatama* and *wayang*. We shall speak further about the sense of *Keselarasan* in a more comprehensive way in the next section.

---

[309] Cf. P. Sherry, (ed.), *Philosophers on Religion*, London, 1987, p. 50.

[310] P. Sherry, (ed.), *Philosophers on Religion*, London, 1987, p. 50.

[311] Cf. K.A. Steenbrink, "Rehabilitation of the Indigenous. A Survey of Recent Research on the History of Christianity in Indonesia", *Exchange* 22/3 (1993), p. 252.

VI.   THE SENSE OF *KESELARASAN*

As we have seen in Chapter II.1, *Keselarasan* has its roots in the terminology of the *gamelan* orchestra. The nucleus of the idea of *Keselarasan* formed with the history and remained strong even during the many encounters with Hinduism, Buddhism, Islam and Christianity. In the period of Hinduism, society was influenced by Indian civilization and its thought. The awareness of identity and that everyone has to fight according to his identity, as taught in Bhagavad-Gītā, enriched some aspects of the contents of *Keselarasan*. This idea is not used to preserve the high class of society, but it is applied to the relation with ancestors, mystic experience and society.

The spirit of Buddhism also enriches aspects of self-organization in order to reach self-fulfilment. It maintains practices of self-discipline and ascetical life. The common usage of the Pali word *upāya*[312] in Javanese society points out an influence from Buddhist thought. In Buddhism, the background of *upāya* is an absolute interdependence of things and an idea of "not-self." From this background, *upāya* might be understood as a principle of adaptation. In Javanese thought, the meaning of this word *upāya* developed further. It does not merely mean the capacity of adapting to something but it also includes efforts or struggles in order to solve problems in any human situation.

In addition, the Buddhist teaching about the middle way enriches the Javanese pattern of thought. It is characterized by avoiding a rigorous categorial system of thought as either "black and white." This tendency of the Javanese pattern of thought, manifested in the ideas of *gotong royong,*[313] *musyawarah,*[314] and so on, enables such a middle way to be integrated in their system of thought.

---

[312] The Pali word *upāya* literally means way, means, resource.

[313] *Gotong royong* is mutual cooperation. N. Mulder interprets such a cooperation as a practice of extending mutual aid in communal life. Cf. N. Mulder, *Individual and Society in Java. A Cultural Analysis,* Yogyakarta, 1992, p. 34.

[314] *Musyawarah* is a Javanese term to designate "mutual deliberation". Cf. N. Mulder, *Inside Indonesian Society. An Interpretation of Cultural Change in Java,* Bangkok, 1994, pp. 47, 49.

The image of God as the Almighty and Omnipotent supports the Javanese longing for unification between human beings and the Creator, between the servant and the Lord. Such an assumption leads the Javanese to see human life as a process of returning to its sources. Islamic thought has contributed to Javanese thought an accentuation of the perspective of "surrendering or trusting in God."

The image of paradise, šalōm and the description of the last day of the world is commonly known in Javanese society. The process of interior reflection, as detailed by St. Augustine, has some similarities to the way of reflection in the *Kebatinan*. However, the personal efforts and self-organization of forces through ascetic practices are more dominant in Javanese reflection. The longing for freedom from passions and the consciousness of the possibility of unification of various things which has been experienced throughout a long Javanese history, constitutes a further development of the concept of *Keselarasan*.

Keselarasan itself, of necessity, contains a pluralistic reality. It is defined as a quality of relationship between two things or more, which is animated by the principle of balance, concordance, appropriateness, harmony, avoidance of public conflict and the perception of reality as a composite whole. This quality points out a state of having a particular capacity to unite things.

Keselarasan as a balance consists of a unity derived from two or more very distinct realities. These may even be in contrast with one another, such as day and night, south and north, east and west, black and white, life and death and so on. Even though they are contradictory to one another, there is an energy which unites them. It is like a tension of polarities. This tension unites two very different things. From this tension there is generated a balance that we call *Keselarasan*. This idea is coloured by the dynamic aspect of the quality of relationship.

The tension between the different things is with regard to the other's existence. It is not a mixture of a little reality of one thing and a little reality of another thing in a view of the world from dualism philosophy. It is rather a tension of two polarities, in which the principle of maintaining existence is stressed. In contrast with this, conflict usually

104

has a tendency to exclude the other. Such conflict happens when someone is under the domination of a more powerful one or in a dominated situation. Avoidance of public conflicts manifests an existential form of *neng-nengan*.[315] The *neng-nengan* is a Javanese existential pattern of thought which is a case of the powerless one's conflict against a very strong enemy in a public situation.

Keselarasan as an accordance or *cocok*, is based on different things in good relation or contact. It constitutes a kind of unity in a pluralistic world. This idea is closer to the idea of compatibility. *Keselarasan* here can be described as an analogy, namely a relationship between two or more things, based on similarities. In other words *Keselarasan* includes proportional analogy and attributive analogy as in Western thought. *Keselarasan* in this sense underlines good relationships with regard to the identity of two or more things.

The other perspective of *Keselarasan* points to a totalistic view of the world. All things are connected as a whole reality, composing a unique unity. This unity has its basis in the wholeness of things in the togetherness of reality. Thus *Keselarasan* is a quality of relationship which points out a state of concordance, balanced composition, compatibility, avoidance of public conflicts, and totality.

Ethically, *Keselarasan* points to a harmony of personal and social life by means of living in peace (*rukun*) with one another. It is realized by respecting others, having a consciousness of one's own identity and place, and by avoiding every kind of public conflict. Orientation toward others and society constitutes the first step in reflection of a personal identity and a social attitude.

The realization of *Keselarasan* requires a capacity of self-control and regulation of human forces, coming both from the interior of a human person and from exterior. This aspect points to the concept of

---

[315] *Neng-nengan* is a Javanese attitude in dealing with conflicts in which one does not speak to the other or one does not address the other. Such an attitude contains an assumption that someone treats the other as if the other does not exist. Accordingly, one does not consider the existence or presence of the other, even they are in a same room or meeting.

humanity in Javanese thought. We further speak about this when we speak about the anthropological approach of the *Keselarasan*.

The social perspective colours almost the entire concept of *Keselarasan*. It is a necessary element in this concept, because the essence of *Keselarasan* necessarily contains the existence of others. There is no *Keselarasan* without the existence of other things or realities. A human being will better understand one's identity and place when one faces other things or when one is face to face with other realities.

Consequently, individuality is found as an interdependent reality of a human being. Individualization is nothing else than the process of self-integration based on the values from outside. This process underlines the introverted character of the Javanese method of thinking. And so, the aspect of adaptation and interior reflection becomes a kind of deep psychological reflection.

Finally, it must be noted that *Keselarasan* constitutes the pattern of thought which manifests itself in language, self-integration or adaptation, possibility of tolerance, and co-existence of differences. We will further analyse this comprehensive concept of *Keselarasan* in the next chapter.

106

CHAPTER III

ANALYSIS OF THE CONCEPT OF *KESELARASAN*

I.   THE JAVANESE VIEW OF THE WORLD
   IN *KESELARASAN*

Prevailing throughout Javanese history, *Keselarasan* has arrived as a very rich concept which includes ideas of the universe, human life, ethics and language. We will analyze *Keselarasan* from the perspective of the Javanese view of the world, anthropology, ethics and linguistics, with regard to unity and diversity. To begin with, we will examine *Keselarasan* from the perspective of cosmology.

Javanese thought does not explain its cosmology in a systematic way as does Western philosophy. Here, cosmology is not intended in the rigorous scientific sense, but rather as a view of the world such as that typically expressed in Javanese thought. By the way of overall comparison, Western thought which is more analytical and rational, while Javanese thinking is more global and intuitive; it is thought in which reflection on feelings, and mythical expression have remarkable roles. For this reason, we have to speak about myth in order to understand the Javanese view of the world.

A.   Myth

Keselarasan has a close relation with myth, because myth embraces a wide possibility of realities beyond reason. Besides, mythical thinking is in concord with Javanese thought which we have already described as intuitive, global and reflective. We find mythical expressions in both *Wédhatama* and *Wayang*.

In *Wédhatama*, for example, we find the name of *Kangjeng Ratu*

Kidul[316] or the *Queen of the South,* which indicates a queen who reigns over the southern ocean of Java. According to tradition, the kingdom of *Kangjeng Ratu Kidul* lay under the sea in the southern ocean of Java. She, the Queen, is powerful and mysterious; nevertheless she recognises the authority of Panembahan Senopati.[317] If she recognises the authority of Panembahan Senopati, it means that Panembahan Senopati has a greater authority and has reached the deepest knowledge of Javanese wisdom. The greatness of Panembahan Senopati is not only expressed by the Queen's recognition, but further, his capability of gathering the forces of the universe is also symbolically expressed in his marriage with her.[318] Consequently, the Javanese see him as the figure of the perfect man who gatheres the forces of the universe.

The existence of myth in *Wayang* appears in Javanese belief in spirits and ancestors who can disturb human life. Their image of the world is connected to the idea of the world as a big world and a small world, with three places for creatures, namely the human world, an upper world and an underworld. The spirits and ancestors live in the upper world or world below depending upon their good or bad character. Concerning the myth of spirits, C. Geertz attests: "After *slametan* the local spirits will not bother you, will not make you ill, unhappy or confused. The goals are negative and psychological-absence of aggressive feeling toward others, absence of emotional disturbance."[319] The *Wayang* performance is held in order to fulfill promises or to participate in a *slametan* ceremony which is dedicated to a special theme,[320] thereby

---

[316] *Wédhatama*, canto *Sinom* 4. Cf. S. Robson, *The Wédhatama. An English Translation* (with original text), Leiden, 1990, p. 26; Sartono Kartodirdjo, *Modern Indonesia. Tradition & Transformation*, Yogyakarta, 1988, p. 219.

[317] Panembahan Senopati is a king of Mataram, Yogyakarta from 1586 to 1601. According to the Javanese traditional story, he was biologically the eldest son of Adiwijaya. Cf. W. Fruin-Mees, *Sedjarah Tanah Djawa* (translated by S.M. Latif), Weltevreden, 1922, pp. 32-36; G. Moedjanto, *The Concept of Power in Javanese Culture*, Yogyakarta, 1990, pp. 17-18.

[318] G. Moedjanto, *The Concept of Power in Javanese Culture*, Yogyakarta, 1990, p. 24.

[319] C. Geertz, *The Religion of Java*, Chicago and London, 1976, p. 14.

[320] When a parent has only one child, they have to make the ceremony of *slametan*, traditionally called *Ruwatan*. In this ceremony, the *dalang* uses the theme in which the child is saved from the menace of the spirits, especially called *Bathara Kala*.

expressing the belief in spirits.

Mythical thinking is also used to express Javanese respect for the tombs of the ancestors. These tombs have a special symbolic and magical significance. The Javanese often tend to regard these dead "saints" as peculiarly their own. Accordingly, it is readily understandable that the Javanese make pilgrimages to the tombs (*nyadran*) and to such holy places (*punden*), in order to seek blessings.[321] Besides, the Javanese have sacred heirlooms called *pusakas*. They are the objects inherited from previous generations. These objects connect them to magic power (*kasekten*) and sometimes become a kind of legitimization for the rulers. "The gamelan of Majapahit," for example, is regarded as a sign of continuation of power and a kind of historical testimony.[322] Such mythical thinking is evident throughout Javanese history and receives its form according to the circumstances of the time.

One of the most popular myths, in which we might find philosophical ideas, is the myth of *Déwa Ruci*.[323] This story speaks about Bhima who was looking for the water of life, the essence of reality. Bhima asked Drona a question about the water of life. Drona sent him to the ocean. His family and relatives tried to block his intention, but Bhima did not change his mind. On the way to his goal he faced various difficulties. He had to fight against Naga, the big serpent in the ocean. He defeated Naga, and in a state of life-and-death he met *Déwa Ruci*, the image of himself in a very small form. Acting on the advice of *Déwa Ruci*, he experienced incredible things and he could see the world and himself. He could speak in a noble language and understand the reality

---

[321] Sartono Kartodirjo, *Agrarian Radicalism in Java: Its Setting and Development*, in: C. Holt, (ed.), *Culture and Politics in Indonesia*, Ithaca, 1972, p. 80.

[322] Cf. Inge Skog, *North Borneo Gongs and Javanese Gamelan*, Stockholm, 1993, pp. 141-142.

[323] The story of *Déwa Ruci* was probably written in the eighteenth or nineteenth century. Pigeaud gives us information that a *Déwa Ruci* text was published already in 1873 in Semarang. According to Soebardi, a fragment of the story of *Déwa Ruci* was found in the book *Pěsinden Bědaya* in 1796. This book, written by Yasadipura I, then, is considered as the oldest *Déwa Ruci* text. The story of *Déwa Ruci* is also used as a theme in the *Wayang* performance. Cf. Th. Pigeaud, *Literature of Java*, Vol. I, The Hague, 1967, pp. 241-242; v. also S. Soebardi, *The Book of Cabolèk*, The Hague, 1975, p. 22.

110

of human life and the world.

Bhima's meeting with *Déwa Ruci* in the ocean was considered an account of a philosophical reflection and a profound religious mystery. Bhima was conscious of the essence of human life. In the state of life-and-death he had found the water of life, namely, the source of life. Bhima found the source of life inside himself, in the form of *Déwa Ruci*, who was similar to himself but in diminutive form. In other words, the source of life was the coming together of the human identity and the identity of the world through inner reflection upon human life and self.

Such a myth as this, expresses the adventure of understanding the reality of self. The capacity to go beyond obstacles, described as the bondage of relatives and passions (fighting with Naga) brings about success in seeing the reality of self. Ultimately, this reflection underlines the significance of mind or heart, in which the Javanese find the accumulation of feelings.

In the writing of Ki Ageng Suryomentaram, the philosophy of feeling has a close relationship with the will which has fundamental characteristics such as "being diffused" (*mulur*) and "being integrated" (*mengkeret*). He also maintains that the essence of human life is the will.[324] This will contains the feelings and consciousness accumulated throughout human life. It can embrace every reality so that even the world can enter into the human will in our heart. Thus God, the human self and the world can be found in the human heart. Things come into the human heart in the form of shadow or, in Western expression, "idea".

From the example of *Déwa Ruci*, it can be seen that mythical thinking contains philosophical ideas; nevertheless it is a particular way of thinking that has no sharp dividing line in clarifying what is real and what is not. In other words, Javanese myths might be understood as old stories believed to be guidelines for human life and attitudes which preserve high values from generation to generation.[325] Accordingly, they

---

[324] Cf. Grangsang Suryomentaram, *Kawruh Jiwa. Wejanganipun Ki Ageng Suryomentaram* (Knowledge of Psyche. Ki Ageng Suryomentaram's Teaching), Vol. I, Jakarta, 1989, p. 14.
[325] Cf. Sri Mulyono, *Simbolisme dan Mistikisme dalam Wayang. Sebuah Tinjauan filososofis*

symbolically tell of heroes and their adventures which may carry them to the land of human wisdom, or they may confront goodness and evil, life and death, or they may climb to a summit from which they may clearly view the world, or they may symply be exemplars of customs.

Myth, therefore, has a threefold function in Javanese society: 1) The use of myth brings about a consciousness in its human listeners so that they can participate in and live the mysterious power of the universe; 2) Myth actualizes the events in the old stories so that it becomes a guarantee that gives protection.[326] The myth is considered to prevent danger in the future; and 3) Myth has the function of explaining the universe, cosmology and cosmogony in its own unique way, using the story of *deva* and so on, which is evident in the *Wayang*.[327] Now let us see further the function of myth in the *Keselarasan* in comparison with myth as embedded in Western philosophy.

In Greek philosophy, especially in the Pre-Socratic period, myth or *muthos* which was used in contrast to *logos*. Myth, to the ancients, was thought purified in reason. Plato's writings imply that myth is a story in order to express the similarity of ideal truth which is beyond reason. It includes human imagination and fantasy. In Plato's philosophy, reason is subordinated to myth. On the contrary, to Aristotle, myth is subordinate to reason which is the basis of scientific research.

In the modern period, myth has been seen in various ways. Francis Bacon (1561-1626) defined myth as an allegory, -the clarification by narrative description of one subject under guise of another suggestively similar thing.[328] Philosophical truth and religious mystery are placed in

---

(Simbolism and Mysticism in *Wayang*. A Philosophical Review), Jakarta, 1989, p. 28.

[326] In the Javanese rite of *ruwatan*, the shadow play uses themes of the *ruwatan* story, such as *Bhārata Yudha* or the tragic war of *Mahābhārata*. The word *ruwatan* and the verb *ngruwat* derive from the Javanese word *luwar*, meaning "be free from", "be freed". Thus *ruwatan* is a kind of ceremony with shadow play, held in order to free someone from dangers, assumed to be in the future.

[327] Cf. Sri Mulyono, *Simbolisme dan Mistikisme dalam Wayang. Sebuah Tinjauan Filosofis* (Symbolism and Mysticism in *Wayang*. A Philosophical Review), Jakarta, 1989, p. 29.

[328] Francis Bacon revolts against Aristotelianism and proposes the use of the inductive method to discover truth and the secrets of nature. Accordingly, myth is based on data, empirical

myth and treated symbolically in allegory and parable. In other words, they create a myth as a description of reality by using other things which are similar. G. Vico(1668-1744) interpreted myth as human creativity in the pre-logic stage, characterized as infantile imagination.[329] Lévy-Bruhl (1857-1939) interprets myth as primitive mentality within which there is no distinction between invisible reality and sensible objects.[330] There is a participation of the subject in the object as something living. Ernst Cassirer (1874-1945) said that the method of mythical thought is a fact of symbolical nature on which reason is based. For Cassirer, myth is a symbolic form which is a fundamental form of the objective spirit, an independent mode of spiritual formation. Cassirer saw that all other symbolic forms originate in mythical consciousness. Myth sometimes is connected to religion. It is a general notion which is akin to religion. In contrast with this, Lévi-Strauss (1908-...) states that myth is a phenomenon of socio-anthropology.[331] The meaning of a myth is found behind the narrative surface which is close to the individual incidents and items in the narrative. In addition, myth is also an expression used to judge the customs and culture of a society, but it is not always a sacred narrative.

In the Javanese tradition, a myth is an account of the deeds of a god or supernatural being, which is used to explain the relation between man and the universe, customs, the peculiarities of an environment, the existence of some social organization and the like.[332] Myth describes the various and sometimes dramatic breakthrough of the sacred into the

---

observation, experiment, and the importance of induction. Cf. Bertrand Russell, *History of Western Philosophy*, London, 1991, pp. 527-528; P. Edwards, (ed.), *The Encyclopedia of Philosophy*, Vol. I, London, 1967, pp. 235-241.

[329] G. Vico maintains the importance of memory and fantasy in the human mind. The criterium of truth is "in the making" (Verum ipsum factum). This is applied to history which is man-made.

[330] As a historian of philosophy and ethnologist, he proposed the definition of "primitive mentality" as a mystic which considers the tangible world and the invisible as a unique reality, depending on instances of invisible power.

[331] Lévi-Strauss, a French ethnologist, uses his structural method to analyse myth and ritual masks. He maintains that myth is the manifestation of the structure of unconscious mentality which constitutes a formal structure as a mental condition of human life.

[332] Cf. Lewis Spence, *Introduction to Mythology*, Delhi, 1990, p. 11.

world, and is this sudden breakthrough that really establishes the world and makes it what it is today. Furthermore, it is a result of the intervention of Supernatural Beings that man himself is what he is today, a mortal, sexed, and cultural being.[333] Moreover, myth is regarded as a sacred story, and hence "true story," because it always deals with realities. The cosmogonic is "true" because the existence of the world has to have an origin. Myth, in summary, reveals the reality of the world, and of human life. The world and life have a supernatural origin and history, and this history is significant, precious, and exemplary.[334] The myth of the origin of death is equally true because man's mortality proves it.

The sacred story narrated by myth constitutes esoteric "knowledge," as it is accompanied by a magical religious power and performed in a sacred way. The story of the world reveals the world that one knows and in which one lives. In a variety of cultures, people believe that the world must be annually renewed. This renewal is brought about by following the model of the cosmogony or the origin myth that plays a significant role in esoteric knowledge.[335]

Myth, as we have mentioned, gives meaning to the world and human life. For this reason, its role in the constitution of mankind is immense. The ideas of reality, value and transcendence slowly dawn through the myth so that the world can be comprehended as a perfectly articulated, intelligible, and significant cosmos.

Myth teaches mankind primordial "stories" that constitute humans existentially. Everything which is connected with one's existence and legitimate mode of existence in the cosmos concerns humanity directly. Myth is essential not only because it provides the individual with an explanation of the world and one's own mode of being in the world, but above all because, by recollecting and re-enacting the myths, a society is able to repeat what the gods, the heroes and the ancestors did at the beginning. To know the myths is to learn the secret of the origin of

---

[333] M. Eliade, *Myth and Reality*, London, 1975, p. 6.

[334] Cf. M. Eliade, *Myth and Reality*, London, 1975, p. 19.

[335] Cf. M. Eliade, *Myth and Reality*, London, 1975, p. 57.

things. In other words, one learns not only how things came into existence but also where we are able to find them and how to make them reappear when they disappear.[336]

In general it can be said that myth, as experienced by archaic societies, constitutes the history of the act of the supernatural. This history is considered to be absolutely true. Accordingly, myth is always related to a "creation." It tells how something came into existence, or how a pattern of behaviour, an institution, a manner of working were established. For this reason, a myth constitutes a paradigm for all significant human acts. By knowing the myth one not only knows the origin of things, but hence can control and manipulate them at will. Therefore myth is not an "external," "abstract" knowledge but a knowledge that one experiences ritually, either by ceremonially recounting the myth or by performing the ritual for which it is the justification. One lives the myth in the sense that one is seized by the sacred, exalting poem of the events recollected or re-enacted.[337]

B.   Image of the World

We have seen mythical thinking used to express the reality of the world, customs and human life. Besides this, we find in myth a clear expression of the image of the world, such as the place of human life, the place of fragile things, a temporary halting place for human life. This concept of the world is like a process of human history. This is the image of the world which is the common image in Javanese society.

Further, the Javanese conception of the world is one of a universal harmony. This world view centers on the universe, the unity and harmony of microcosm (*Jagad cilik*) and macrocosm (*Jagad gedhé*), with their two dimensions of the "visible" and "invisible."[338] For the Javanese, reality is

---

[336] Cf. M. Eliade, *Myth and Reality*, London, 1975, pp. 13-14.

[337] Cf. M. Eliade, *Myth and Reality*, London, 1975, pp. 18-19.

[338] Cf. A. Nunuk Murniati and I. Kuntara Wiryamartana, *An Indonesian Contribution to a Spirituality of Liberation: Two Perspectives. An Approach from the Javanese World View*, in: V. Fabella, P.K.H. Lee, D. Kwang-sun Suh, *Asian Christian Spirituality. Reclaiming Traditions*, Maryknoll, 1992, p. 44.

not divided into separated categories without connection to each other, but reality is composed of a unification of the whole.[339] In addition, everything has its own place, function and value in the universe. This image of the world is found both in literature and in Court tradition. This view of the world is also maintained in Inge Skog's analysis of *gamelan*, when he says:

> The basic tenet in the Javanese conception of the world is the idea of universal harmony. In central Java, the human realm was constructed to mirror this cosmic balance, because 'humanity is constantly under the influence of forces emanating from the directions of the compass and from stars and planets."[340]

The world consists of elements which have similarity with human elements. Those elements are water, air, fire and matter.[341] Because of this similarity, the Javanese refer to the universe as *jagad gedhé* (big world) and to human life as *jagad cilik* (small world). *Serat Wédhatama* also deals with the idea of "big world" and "small world."[342] Besides these, the *Wédhatama* implies the existence of three kinds of worlds in canto *pucung,* verse 2, and in canto *gambuh,* verse 18, by the use of the term *triloka*.[343] The *Wédhatama* does not give any further explanation of the term *triloka*. Perhaps such idea of *triloka* comes from Hindu terms which indicate the division of three worlds. In general these three worlds are heaven, earth and the nether regions. Rgveda calls them *Yamaloka, Svarloka* and *Brahmaloka*.[344] *Yamaloka* denotes the world of the dead; *Svarloka* is the supraterrestrial sphere or world; and *Brahmaloka* denotes the abode of Brahmā. From the Hindu influence, the term *triloka* in *Wédhatama* comes to denote the Javanese traditional conception of three worlds, namely, the human world, the underworld, and the upper world.

---

[339] Cf. Franz Magnis-Suseno, *Etika Jawa. Sebuah Analisa Falsafi tentang Kebijaksanaan Hidup Jawa (Javanese Ethic. A Philosophical Analysis on the Javanese Wisdom of Life)*, Jakarta, 1984, p. 82.

[340] Inge Skog, *North Borneo Gongs and Javanese Gamelan*, Stockholm, 1993, p. 143.

[341] Cf. Muhammad Subuh Sumohadiwidjoyo, *Susila Budhi Dharma*, Jakarta, 1989, p. 276.

[342] Cf. Endang Daruni, et al., *Konsep Manusia dalam Wedhatama. Laporan Penelitian* (The Concept of Man in *Wédhatama*. A Report of Research), Yogyakarta, 1984, p. 5.

[343] Cf. S. Robson, *The Wédhatama. An English Translation* (with original text), Leiden, 1990, pp. 34, 44.

[344] Cf. Ralph, T.H., *Hymns of the Rgveda*, Vol. II, Delhi, 1987, p. 430.

116

These three are always in connection with one another. A broken relationship disturbs the harmony of the world and human life, and calls for a reconciliation, which is traditionally performed in ceremonies such as *slametan, Wayang,* "cleansing the tombs," and so forth.

The cosmos, including human life, things and events in the world, constitutes a coordination, a unity of existence of all spiritual and material phenomena.[345] Human sensibility responds to the cosmos with its contents, which is kept in the individual's unconsciousness. And so, the universe also exists in human beings, even though it is only in the form of a shadow.[346] Herein, Javanese cosmology is also tinged with *Keselarasan* which is sometimes expressed in a mythical way.

From the discussion of the conception of the world, we can extricate some important characteristics which closely align with the concept of *Keselarasan*: 1) The unification of the world as a whole; 2) The connection of events to the world; and 3) The reciprocal relationship between one's image of the world and the adaptation pragmatic values to obtain a silent, peaceful heart and a balanced mind. All these points, taken together, constitute a harmonious expression of reality and human life without rigorous distinction between religion, society, the world and culture.

Javanese thought emphasizes a cosmos that includes the total of existence, which is animated by Life (with a capital letter). Life is perceived as a mysterious energy which sustains the whole reality of Being. The Javanese view of the world points to an essential balance of the totality of forces and the conflicting currents between the macrocosm and microcosm.[347] Life, therefore, must be the essential existence and

---

[345] Cf. Franz Magnis-Suseno, *Etika Jawa. Sebuah Analisa Falsafi tentang Kebijaksanaan Hidup Jawa* (Javanese Ethic. A Philosophical Analysis on the Javanese Wisdom of Life), Jakarta, 1984, p. 86; N. Mulder, *Mysticim and Everyday Life in Contemporary Java. Cultural Persistence and Change,* Singapore, 1978, p. 17.

[346] S. Haryanto, *Bayang-bayang Adhiluhung.. Filsafat, Simbolis dan Mistik dalam Wayang* (Beautiful and Noble Shadows. Philosophy, Symbol and Mystique in *Wayang*), Semarang, 1992, p. 130.

[347] Cf. J. Wanandi, *Socio Political Development in Indonesia,* in: Institute of Asian Affairs, (ed.), *Indonesia Seminar, Hamburg November 22-23, 1976,* Hamburg, 1977, p. 48.

secret that penetrates this order of the world. Accordingly, in such a view of the world, Life sustains the unity of existence, order, and the individual being's capacity to arrive at a harmonious relationship with the whole.

The reality of the world is seen from two perspectives, namely, *lair* (outer side) and *batin* (inner side). The outer side (*lair*) is not the essence of the reality, but is a shadow of the reality. An Individual has to train oneself to reach an understanding of one's essence and the essence of the world through self-discipline and meditation. Meditation is a kind of reflection which takes one from the exterior world to the interior self and whereby one comes to a recognition of human identity, and to a consciousness of the identification of the universe or cosmic mind. The consciousness of human unison with the world reveals an inner core which becomes a source of integrity in the world.

It should be kept in mind that for the Javanese, human beings are part of the whole of creation, and every human being has an inner core through which he can potentially share in the essence of the whole of existence. In addition, the universe is perceived as an organic whole with the web of relations knitting together each and every part of it. Nature and the human are not viewed as antagonistic to each other, but as chords in a universal symphony.[348]

The Javanese idea of the world cannot be separated from a consideration of the image of God in the Javanese cult.[349] God sometimes has other names such as *Hyang Murbeing Dumadi* meaning "The First exists," *Allah, Hyang Widhi*[350] meaning "supreme ruler, Orderer of

---

[348] G. B. Rosales and C.G. Arévalo, *For All the People of Asia. Federation of Asian Bishops' Conferences Documents from 1970 to 1991,* Quezon City, 1992, p. 9. In the Asian Bishops' conference at Sukabumi, Indonesia 1-7 July 1988, Asian Bishops discussed the resources from the Asian tradition, including the Javanese traditional view of the world, in order to improve the dialogue of interreligious affairs. Further reflection is found in Asian Bishops' conference at Bandung in Indonesia on 27 July 1990. Cf. G.B. Rosales and C.G. Arevalo, *For All the People of Asia Federation of Asian Bishops' Conferences Documents form 1970 to 1991*, Quezon City, 1992, pp. 273-289.

[349] Cf. L. Fischer, *The Story of Indonesia*, London, 1959, p. 205.

[350] *Wédhatama*, canto 14. Cf. S. Robson, *The Wédhatama. An English Translation* (with

universe or creator," *Bathara gung*[351] meaning "the Lord Most High," *Hyang Manon* meaning "The Most Knowlegeable," *Hyang Wisesa* meaning "the Almighty which is distinguished from others, with its special qualities," *Gusti Kang Akarya Jagad Saisine*[352] meaning "the Lord who made the universe and its contents," *Sangkan Paraning Dumadi* meaning "the origin and destination of being," and many others. It must be noted that the Javanese have no sharp dividing line between the universe and God. They believe that God dwells in heaven, in the world and also in the heart of humankind. Further, the inner world is always connected with the outer world through the all-encompassing God.[353] Consequently, there is no rigorous distinction between the secular and the divine, and once more we see see that all things together have a kind of connection that unites one to the other.

C.   The Understanding of Space and Time

First of all, it must be noted that the Javanese have no systematic philosophy of space and time. Nevertheless, in this section we shall make an effort to clarify what ideas of space and time appear in Javanese thought. In *Wédhatama*[354] we find an expression *Bali ing alaming asuwung,* which is translated by Robson as "he has returned to the realm of Void."[355] *Alaming asuwung* also signifies the realm of emptiness which is sometimes identified as God.[356] This expression describes the reality of

---

original text), Leiden, 1990, p. 24.

[351] *Wédhatama*, canto *Pucung* 12. Cf. S. Robson, *The Wédhatama. An English Translation* (with original text), Leiden, 1990, p. 38.

[352] Sujamto, *Reorientasi dan Revitalisasi Pandangan Hidup Jawa* (Reorientation and Revitalization of the Javanese Way of Life), Semarang, 1992, p. 48.

[353] Cf. J.P. Windyatmadja, *A Spirituality of Liberation: An Indonesian Contribution*, in: V. Fabella, P.K.H. Lee, D. Kwang-sun Suh, *Asian Christian Spirituality. Reclaiming Traditions*, Maryknoll, 1992, p. 50.

[354] *Wédhatama*, canto *Pangkur* 14. Cf. S. Robson, *The Wédhatama. An English Translation* (with original text), Leiden, 1990, p. 24.

[355] Cf. S. Robson, *The Wédhatama. An English Translation* (with original text), Leiden, 1990. p. 25.

[356] Sri Mulyono uses the term *"awang-uwung"* to indicate the same reality as *"Alaming asuwung"* as the realm of emptiness which is identified with the Lord with the title *"Sang Hyang"*.

God as the origin and destination of human beings which is beyond space and time. Accordingly, space and time existed *Gusti Kang Akarya Jagad lan Saisine* (the Lord who made the world and its contents) created the universe.

Space is pictured in *Wayang* through the *pendapa suwung* or the empty hall with a stretched out cloth screen (*kelir*), and leather puppets neatly arranged and placed beneath the screen.[357] On the right side are the leather puppets of the good characters, on the left side are the bad.[358] The hall, which is empty of contents, indicates the space in which events and incidents take place. The space can be understood as an ambient of events and a place which is necessary for existence. A human being that exists in the world needs a space for his self-realization. It is the total surrounding in which a thing or activity exists. Human activities, the incidents of the universe, changes in nature, and so on, take place in such space.

It is said in *Wédhatama* and *Wayang* that human beings come from "nothing" and finally return to "nothing." This assumption brings about the Javanese expression *Sangkan Paraning Dumadi* meaning "the origin and destination of creation."[359] In addition, space is not eternal, but it is for a short time as human life in the world itself is only a temporary stopover. When a human being comes to death, his soul or his *Sukma*[360]

The name or character of empty is *Taya*. In addition, the obscure character is called mystery and the character of one is Tunggal. Consequently, its realm of emptiness has a complete name as *"Sang Hyang Taya"* or *"Sang Hyang Tunggal"*, which is the First exists before anything come to be. Cf. Sri Mulyono, *Simbolisme dan Mistikisme dalam Wayang. Sebuah Tinjauan Filsosfis* (Symbolism and Mysticism in *Wayang*. A Philosophical Review), Jakarta, 1989, p. 100.

[357] Cf. Sri Mulyono, *Simbolisme dan Mistikisme dalam Wayang. Sebuah Tinjauan Filosofis* (Symbolism and Mysticism in *Wayang*. A Philosophical Review), Jakarta, 1989, pp. 104, 111, 119.

[358] Cf. Sunardjo Haditjaroko, *Ramayana. Indonesian Wayang Show,* Jakarta, 1993, p. 1.

[359] Sri Mulyono, *Simbolisme dan Mistikisme dalam Wayang. Sebuah Tinjauan Filosofis* (Symbolism and Mysticism in *Wayang*. A Philosophical Review), Jakarta, 1989 p. 89.

[360] *Sukma* (human soul) is considered as a divine spark in a human being which continues as essential core of human life. Ki Ageng Suryomentaraman calls its essence as *"Karep"* or in English expression "the will"which is eternal and beyond the space. *"Saderengipun jagad raya punika wonten punapa-punapa, karep sampun wonten. Sebab karep mboten gadhah wiwitan lan*

120

is believed to be able to go beyond space and time because it is eternal.

The idea of space cannot be separated from the idea of time which is pictured as a cycle. The Javanese idea of time is different from Aristotle's idea of time as *numerus motus secundum prius et posterius*. Consequently, "time" according to Aristotle is a number of events progressing in a line from a previous event to a successive event. Outside of time, there is of necessity unchanged reality.

In a popular sense, the Javanese understand "time" as moments characterized by fragility, change, and brevity. They use the terms *wingi*, *saiki*, *besuk* in the sense of "past," "present," and "future." They use these terms in understanding the progression of time, such as the past is over, the present is existing and the future is not yet here.

Philosophically, the Javanese perceive "time" as a circle of changes, which is seen from a dynamic perspective. There are some names of "time" that we might mention, such as *wayah, wektu, kala*, and *mangsa.*[361] In *Wédhatama*, the comprehension of "time" can be seen from such an expression as: *"Liring sepuh, sepi hawa-Awas roroning atunggil."*[362] The expression means "Old age is free from passions and understands or sees the unity of the two." According to common usage in Javanese daily life, the word *sepuh* indicates someone who has passed

---

pungkasan, langgeng. Jalaran langgeng sedaya watekipun ugi langgeng. Jalaran saking awang-uwungipun ingkang tanpa wangen punika, sajawinipun boten wonten punapa-punapa". (*"Before anything exists in the universe, the will exists, because the will has no beginning and end; it is eternal. Because of its emptiness or infinite space (*"awang"* means "sky or air" and *"uwung"* means "hollow" or empty), therefore there is not anything outside"). Cf. Grangsang Suryomentaraman, *Kawruh Jiwa.Wejanganipun Ki Ageng Suryomentaram* (The knowledge of Psyche. Ki Ageng Suryomentaram's Teaching), Vol. IV, Jakarta, 1993, p. 6.

[361] The words *wayah, wektu, kala,* and *mangsa* point out the same reality of time, but they have different nuances according to the context where they are used. *Wayah* alludes to Sanskrit word *wayas* which has nuances of vigorous age, periode of age, age or a certain duration of time. *Wektu* alludes to a strict point of time; for example, *wektu iki* means at this moment. *Kala* derives from two kinds of the Sanskrit word *kāla*, meaning time and time as inescapable fate. The word *mangsa* as nuance to the Sanskrit word *māsa* means season, time in general, time of the day and hour.

[362] *Wédhatama*, Canto *Pangkur* 12. Cf. S. Robson, *The Wédhatama. An English Translation* (with original text), Leiden, 1990, p. 24.

121

through many years of life. This difference underlines the speculative reflection of *Wédhatama* upon "time" which is understood in connection with the quality of life. In other words, the significance of time, including days and years, is not the number or quantity of them, but rather a quality, ie., the capacity of integration and freedom from human passions.

Such signification of time comes from the perception of time as cyclic. This understanding is remarkable in Javanese thought. Some describe as the wheel of life which is named *Kālacakra* in Old Javanese, and others call it *Cakra manggilingan* as *Wayang* terminology, which means the "rolling wheel." Such expressions point out the marked changes and development in the perception of time. It is evident that morning, noon, and night always return. The brightness of the day and the darkness of the night continuously come and go. Reflection on the dynamic of time has given rise to the speculative idea of the wheel of time which is characterized by integration and diffusion. Ki Ageng Suryomentaram expresses the same assumption in different terms as *Windu Kencana* and *Windu Ungkul*,[363] which are characterized by integration or peace and diffusion or confusion.

The image of cyclic time is also expressed in the idea of the rolling process of *Jaman emas* (Golden age) and *Jaman edan* (Crazy age).[364] Between those periods, the Javanese use Hindu terminology such as *Tretā Yuga* and *Dvāpara Yuga* (the second period and the third period of the ages of the world, respectively). In this Hindu assumption, therefore, the *Jaman emas* can be identified as *Krta Yuga* and *Jaman edan* can be identified as *Kali Yuga* (the fourth periode of the ages of the world). Suffice it to say that to the Javanese, "time" is the product of a speculative reflection on history or change. In summary, time is considered a cyclic process of history which is characterized by integration and diffusion.

---

[363] *Windu Kencana* is the expression for the time of peace, prosperity, humility and good collaboration with each other. *Windu Kencana* ends the *Wingka Kencana* which is the time of superior feeling which causes competition, the feelings of difference and the confusion. Cf. G. Suryomentaram, *Kawruh Jiwa. Wejanganipun Ki Ageng Suryomentaram* (The Knowledge of Psyche. Ki Ageng Suryamentaram's Teaching), Vol. I, Jakarta, 1989, pp. 48-62.

[364] Cf. R. Tanaya, *Djangka Djajabaja. Sjèch Bakir*, Solo, 1940, p. 16, 24.

The ideas of space and cyclic time have a moral consequence in the Javanese attitude toward life. The view of the world, which includes space and time, are closely connected to morality. If human life is limited in time and space, which is fragile and brief, then human beings must have a guideline for passing through life.

Moral attitudes are placed in the frame of cyclic time since they have one of the positions in the rolling wheel of time. When one exists in the upper position of the wheel of time, they observe the expression *Aja dumeh* meaning "do not be arrogant but have respect for other."[365] Thus in times of integration, success and prosperity, a human being has to be aware of the changes of time. Accordingly, a human being should not treat the poor or the powerless with malevolence.

In contrast to this, is the time when someone exists at the lowest position of the wheel of time. At this moment, circumstances are coloured by diffusion and confusion. Human beings has to have hope and not loose spirit, even though they are dealing with disappointments, suffering and difficulty. At such a moment, Javanese morality applies the expressions *nrima* meaning "acceptance of reality or situation without murmur and protest,"[366] *lega* meaning "released and free from psychological burden," and *rila* meaning "is not bound by possessive feeling and ready to give one's own."[367]

Humans have a duty in life to look for the best ways of moving in accord with the rolling of the wheel of time, so that a human being gains peace of mind in union with God and hopefully can return to God. Self-discipline, austere practices and meditation, therefore, are important elements in Javanese morality. Moral behaviour and self-control have

---

[365] Cf. N. Mulder, *Pribadi Masyarakat Jawa* (Personality of the Javanese Society), Jakarta, 1985, p. 58.

[366] Cf. Franz Magnis-Suseno, *Etika Jawa. Sebuah Analisa Falsafi tentang Kebijaksanaan Hidup Jawa* (Javanese Ethic. A Philosophical Analysis on the Javanese Wisdom of Life), Jakarta, 1984, p. 143.

[367] Cf. Franz Magnis-Suseno, *Etika Jawa. Sebuah Analisa Falsafi tentang Kebijaksanaan Hidup Jawa* (Javanese Ethic. A Philosophical Analysis on the Javanese Wisdom of Life), Jakarta, 1984, p. 143.

significant roles to play for the person who hopes to the state of stable integration which gives peace of mind in the sense of unity between a fragile human being and an unlimited God. The latter aspiration is further improved by Javanese society in the practices of mysticism as in *Kebatinan*'s movements.

Finally, the Javanese view of the world and the ideas of space and time constitute a further reflection on human identity, reality and the mystery of the universe. We shall speak further of the identity of human life and of things which are distinguished from human beings in the succeeding chapter.

II. ANTHROPOLOGICAL REFLECTION
ON *KESELARASAN*

The Javanese perceive human life in the world as a shadow and life as a contemporary journey towards its origin. The existence of human beings in the world, therefore, is always in a framework of space and time. In other words, human life in the world is found in a history which is characterized by developments and changes without excluding continuity. The world seems to be in perpetual flux and undergoing a continuous sequence of ceaseless transformation. However, each human life in the world exists only for a short time. Hence collegated to the sense of permanence and change, there arise the philosophical distinctions of identity and otherness. We will reflect further on these classical themes in the following sections.

A.   Identity in the Concept of *Keselarasan*

The word "identity" derives from the Late Latin word *identitas* which is the equivalent of the Greek *tautotès*.[368] Thus the word "identity" means sameness, or a likeness which implies the sameness of permanent elements and the specific character of a reality. The Javanese use the term *jati diri* to express the sense of identity. In addition, the word *jati* means "true condition," "nature" and "form of existence fixed by birth." The word *diri* means "self." Thus the sense of identity in the Javanese term *jati diri* means "the true condition or the nature of self." The *jati diri* is

---

[368] A. Ernout - A. Meillet, *Dictionnaire Étymologique de La Langue Latine*, Paris-Klincksieck, 1954, p. 545.

found in a reflection on human life and the world, tinged with the contrasting features of permanence and change. On the one hand, a human being finds his existence as a permanent reality, while on the other hand, he experiences the process of change which is going on in his life.[369]

As long as a human being lives in the world, his mind and body experience change and development which will end only in human death. At the moment of death, a human being comes to eternity and constancy which is expressed in *alam suwung*, that is, a realm of void which is both origin and destination. The identity of human beings, therefore, lies in a unity of mind and body which exists in the world that the Javanese call *alam keramaian*[370] or *dunia fana*.[371] Human beings can experience their own identity because they have a consciousness of self, of the world and of change.[372] The problem of change in contemporary things brings forth the question of what is permanent in human life.

The problem of permanence and change is a classical problem of philosophy, which has existed since the ancient period of Greek philosophy. Parmenides (ca. 6th- 5th century B.C.) and Heraclitus (536-470 BC) already contributed significant thoughts on this polemic. Parmenides maintained that there is only one being which really exists without inner differentiation. In brief, his doctrine states that being, the one, is, and that becoming, change, is illusion.[373] He denies change and diversity in the name of the First principle, and unity. Being is an abstract corporeality filling space. The particularity and the plurality of an individual thing is mere appearance and illusion. There is, however, no doubt that Parmenides with his arguments concerning the unchanging One

---

[369] Cf. Y. Boelaars, *Kepribadian Indonesia Modern. Suatu Penelitian Antropologi Budaya* (Personality of Modern Indonesia. A Study on the Anthropology of Culture), Jakarta, 1984, p. 9.

[370] *Alam keramaian* is a terminology used to express the reality of the world which is full of many events and changes in contrast with *alaming asuwung* which is empty, constant and eternal.

[371] *Dunia fana* means the "temporary world" which is perishable, fragile and full of changes.

[372] Cf. Endang Daruni, et al., *Konsep Manusia dalam Wedhatama. Laporan Penelitian* (The Concept of Man in *Wédhatama*. A Report of Research), Yogyakarta, 1984, p. 37.

[373] Cf. F. Copleston, *History of Philosophy*, Vol. I, London, 1976, p. 48.

had an exteremelyimportant influence on Heraclitus.[374] Parmenides' perception of "being" is in contrast to the perception of "becoming" in Heraclitus. According to Heraclitus, all things and the universe as a whole are in constant and ceaseless flux. Nothing exists, because the real is changing and continuously passing away. The statement that all things are in a state of flux, is an important aspect in his philosophy.[375] This assumption is also strong in Buddhist thought and influenced the Javanese, as we have seen in the previous chapter.

Plato proposed the doctrine of dualism as a solution to the problem of permanence and change. For him, there are two kinds of world namely the world of ideas and the sentient world. The world of ideas contains ideas which are eternal, permanent and universal. The sentient world contains the things which are impermanent, changeable and not eternal. In other words, the sentient world is becoming.[376] The realities in the world are an imitation of the eternal reality in the world of ideas. Tangible things are connected to the world of ideas by participation. In other words, tangible things participate in the world of ideas which is eternal, permanent and universal. Consequently, such a view of the world brings about two kinds of knowledge according to Plato. They are the knowledge of ideas called *epistêmê* which is gained by *logos* or the activity of reason, and the knowledge of tangible things called opinion.

There is an objection that Plato's conclusion is dualistic and too idealistic. For an understanding of the dualistic conclusion of Plato we need to return to his doctrine of reminiscence, in which the immortal mind is able to conceive the Ideas. The immortality of the mind emphasizes the pre-existence of the soul and the subordination of the body.[377] The rational mind is not composed with material substance and it contributes to immortality. Therefore it must be distinguished from the

---

[374] Cf. G. Watson, *Greek Philosophy and the Christian Notion of God*, Dublin, 1994, p. 11.

[375] Cf. F. Copleston, *History of Philosophy*, Vol. I, London, 1976, p. 39.

[376] Cf. F. Copleston, *History of Philosophy*, Vol. I, London, 1976, p. 247.

[377] In the *Timaeus* or elsewhere in Plato's writing, the primacy of soul or spirit over matter is undoubted. Cf. Gerard Watson, *Greek Philosophy and the Christian Notion of God*, Dublin, 1994, p. 28.

body[378] because the mind is the principle of change in the body.

The conclusions of Parmenides and Plato are based on the idea that real things have to be permanent and so whatever is real cannot change. This assumption leads to the conclusion that realities which are changing are not real. They are only illusions. The objections to this conclusion brought about the concept of "hylomorphism" in Aristotle (384-322 B.C.) and then had its comprehensive solution in St. Thomas Aquinas (A.D. 1225-1274). Aristotle did not agree with Plato's teaching on "being," because the essence of being is found in the concrete thing that Aristotle called *ousia*. Aristotle taught that the body and mind are two aspects of one substance that he calls *hulê* and *morphê*, matter and form, respectively, which are related as act and potency. Every change, including position, implies the passage from potentiality to actuality. The thing that exists is the concrete one, outside it nothing exists. The universal "being" reveals a being which exists in the concrete and is together with the concrete.[379]

In the works of St. Thomas Aquinas the discussion is more technical; he uses the terms *substantia* and *existentia*. Thus we might say that the problem of change brings about the questions of substance, of ideas and of individuality. Further, Thomas Aquinas assumed that there are timeless divine insights and temporal human beings. The timeless divine insight embraces the totality of all successive events in one act, thereby emphasizing the immutability of God.[380] Thomas Aquinas proposes five ways to explain the existence of the world and to prove the existence of God. For the existence of the world there must be a first unmovable mover which is absolute Being. This absolute mover we call "God." The five ways of Thomas Aquinas are based on different

---

[378] Cf. G. Basti, *Il Rapporto Mente-Corpo nella Filosofia e nella Scienza*, Bologna, 1991, p. 28.

[379] This idea is clear in nominalism of William Ockham. He emphasizes that the general being is only a name, but the real one is the singular concrete thing. For example, the terminology "human being" is only a name, but the one that really exists is John, Bill, and so on. Cf. Alessandro Ghisalberti, *Guglielmo di Ockham, Scritti Filosofici*, Firenze, 1991, p. 18.

[380] Summa Theologiae, I, Quaestio 9. Cf. Sancti Tomae de Aquino, *Summa Theologiae*, Torino, 1988, pp. 38-40.

arguments. The first is based on the argument of movement or change. The second is based on cause. The third is based on necessary Being. The fourth, delineates the gradual level of being which leads our mind to the perfect Being. Finally, he presents the argument of finality of the cosmic order. The identity of God is different from that of human being, for God is the unmovable mover, the ultimate cause, the necessary, the perfect one, and finality of all the orders of the world. The disputes and the discussions involved in the philosophical subject of identity, as we mentioned above, might cast a light on the position of Javanese thought in searching for a philosophical explanation of identity.

The *Wédhatama* perceives the essence of the human realm as a unity of plurality that Endang Daruni and some other experts call "monopluralis."[381] It indicates that human identity consists of many elements which constitute the unity of human reality. The fundamental expressions of the perception of identity are *roroning atunggil* and *jiwangga*.[382] *Roroning atunggil,* meaning the "two in one," indicates a perceived solution to the problem of identity. This solution is also expressed in the term *jiwangga,* which derives from the words *jiwa* and *angga. Jiwa* means "soul" which might be compared to the mind in Western philosophy. The word *angga* means "body" or corpus. There are two reasons why *Wédhatama* uses these words in the one expression *jiwangga.* First, it is the Javanese style of literature to unite some expressions; second, it is used to emphasise the notion of unity in mind and body. I do not think the first reason is contradictory to the second reason, but rather that both reasons demonstrate the emphasis of the notion of unity of mind and body. The word *jiwangga* gets a remarkable emphasis in the usage of *roroning atunggil* (two-in-one). Thus a human being identifies first the unity of mind and body.[383]

The consciousness of this unity comes from the inseparable

---

[381] Cf. Endang Daruni, et al., *Konsep Manusia dalam Wedhatama. Laporan Penelitian* (The Concept of Man in *Wédhatama*. A Report of Research), Yogyakarta, 1984, p. 5.

[382] *Wédhatama,* canto *Pangkur* 12. Cf. S. Robson, *The Wédhatama. An English Translation* (with original text), Leiden, 1990, p. 24.

[383] Cf. N. Mulder, *Pribadi dan Masyarakat di Jawa* (Individu and Society in Java), Jakarta, 1985, p. 20.

reciprocal relationship of mind and body. Thus essentially, a human being is in unity with the world, because we cannot think of a human being apart from the existence of the world. Nevertheless, a human being does not fuse with the world but rather in this relationship a human being finds an identity which is different from that of other things or beings. The true reality of a human being, therefore, is a unity of mind and body which is found in a reciprocal relationship with the world and its elements.

Finally, we can conclude that the identity of a human being is a creation of God, a temporary existence in a journey to its origin and destination, a unity of mind and body, an essence united with the whole existence of the world. The identity of humanity as creation is expressed in the words *dumadi* meaning "becoming" or "being created." And such, the identity of a human being is tinged with passive and active characteristics at the same time. It is the reality of the shape of the body, the place of birth, the parents of a human being, that we receive in a passive way. Nevertheless our further personal identity is an unceasing process of becoming, so that the guidance of *Wédhatama* has its significant role. In arriving at the positive identity of a human being, *Wédhatama* includes the whole perspective of a human being, such as individual and social characteristics, spiritual and material, and so on.

In *Wédhatama,* the discussion regarding human beings shows us that the human being is a subject and at the same time an object of reflection. After human beings understands their identity, the *Wédhatama* leads to a further reflection on how human beings should live in their contemporary world, and how human beings gain virtues and come to human perfection in a life which is characterized by good manners, happiness and a peaceful mind.[384] The process of human perfection includes a reflection on morality and human worship. Human thought is used to gain knowledge; the human feelings, which fulfill the desire for beauty, serve as a fulfillment of human longing to attain goodness.

In the *Wayang,* human beings on the one hand are described as

---

[384] Cf. S. Robson, *The Wédhatama. An English Translation* (with original text), Leiden, 1990, p. 46.

130

puppets which are only shadows and *dalang* or *pramanas* who both have a definitive role in the activities and the fate of a human being. In addition, the theme (lakon) of the wayang is decided by *yang nanggap Wayang*, indicating "the Almighty God."[385] Thus, one of the human characteristics in *Wayang* is the dependence of a human being upon the Creator or God. This identity seems to cause a fatalistic attitude, or *mung saderma nglakoni*.

Sri Mulyono criticises such an interpretation of *mung saderma nglakoni* as fatalistic (*pasrah total*) by maintaining the attitude of *mandiri*. *Mandiri* is a capability to decide one's own way of life as self-determination. In other words, *mandiri* emphasizes a human autonomy in one's life so that a human being does not depend upon others. Accordingly, such an autonomy is seen as the point of God's greatness. The fatalistic interpretation of *"mung saderma nglakoni"* alludes to the domination of Almighty God so that a human being is made to feel weak in front of him. In contrast with this, Sri Mulyono's interpretation maintains that a human life is full of choices and demands. A human being has to make decisions, and even if a human being does not choose anything, that too is a choice. That is why every human being is entangled in the problem of choice, and choice is central in *Wayang*.[386] He says further that a human being has to make constant efforts according to his capability, because his circumstances and way of life become good or bad entirely dependent on human struggle itself. In any case, one has to recognise the human limitation and that even freedom is surrounded by this limitation. For this reason, a human being should see the identity of his life. In other words, when one wants to change his fate and have autonomy, one has to know oneself without fear and anxiety. Accordingly, one has to deepen the deepest reality of oneself; so one is able to know and meet the reality of oneself. This self-knowledge is the basis and the key to happiness and success.[387]

---

[385] Cf. Endang Daruni, et al., *Konsep Manusia dalam Wedhatama. Laporan Penelitian* (The Concept of Man in *Wédhatama*. A Report of Research), Yogyakarta, p. 44.

[386] Sri Mulyono, *Human Character in the Wayang*, Jakarta, 1977, p. 14.

[387] Cf. Sri Mulyono, *Simbolisme dan Mistikisme dalam Wayang. Sebuah Tinjaun Filosofis* (Symbolism and Mysticism in *Wayang*. A Philosophical Review), Jakarta, 1989, p. 143.

Success is the combination of hard efforts and perseverance which are accompanied by deep prayer. Happiness is peace of mind as the culmination of every pleasure, beauty and satisfaction. Happiness is gained when someone has been free from the feeling of anger, irritation or jealousy and then can see the essence and the purpose of every occurrence. That is why the idea *"sangkan paraning dumadi"* is remarkable in *Wayang*. This perfection will guide someone to be wise and tactful. The figure in *Wayang* is described as Bhima. Bhima is considered as someone who has gained perfection and has known the self. Because of this, one is not arrogant or disrespectful toward others, but one's personality is characterized by humility and good intention and one is a gentle person who has a strong will to realize aspirations.[388]

The description of the human identity in *Wayang* with its various figures leads us to see the two kinds of philosophy which are dominant in Javanese thought. They are existentialism and phenomenologism. The elements of existentialism can be seen from *Wayang*'s assumption that the identity of human existence proceeds toward death or nothingness, and so the *jati diri* of human life has to face the problem of death with a peaceful heart. Human life comes from nothing, then it is born in the world to live, and finally dies. That is the true life with which we have to deal.

Such a true life is phenomenologically described by the performance of *Wayang*. The performance of *Wayang* demonstrates the phenomena of life and human existence. From the phenomena that we see, we can learn the essence of things. Consequently, the performance of *Wayang* can help persons in the audience to know their own identity and the identity of others. Oe's identity will be clearer when it is compared to otherness. We shall dealing with this subject in the sucessive part.

---

[388] Cf. Sri Mulyono, *Simbolisme dan Mistikisme dalam Wayang. Sebuah Tinjaun Filosofis* (Symbolism and Mysticism in *Wayang*. A Philosophical Review), Jakarta, 1989, p. 144.

B.   Otherness in the Concept of *Keselarasan*

With regard to questions of human identity as a created being in the world, when human existence is taken together with the existence of other creatures, we find that there are some interesting differences among human beings, between human beings and other living beings, between living beings and inert things. There is physical continuity and discontinuity in a human being. In this part, our concern are discontinuity and otherness.

The identity of a human being as creature necessarily contains the idea of a creator which is distinguished from creation. Consequently, the creator must be greater than human beings. In the *Wédhatama* the creator has many different names. These names allude to the transcendence of God, except the name *Hyang Suksma* which indicates the immanent aspect of God in a human being.

The identity of a human being as a creature, therefore, points to a creator. The creator is different from human beings. This distinction is also pointed out by the term *Sangkan Paraning Dumadi*, meaning the origin and destination of what exists. Thus the creature is not from self but from outside all human beings.

Creation includes the world, animals, plants and matter which are different from human beings. However, the existence of human beings is bound together with different beings or creatures in the world. In other words, otherness expresses an existence of a reciprocal connection among things in comparison. The essence of these things exists in the realm of the human being. Before God, a human being finds himself as very different from God, but at the same time he finds his own deepest and true identity.

In summary, for the Javanese, the existence of a human being is an indication that one is on the way of returning to the origin, a characteristic aspect where a human being is in common with all others in the whole reality of life. From this assumption, we find that the identity of a human life is in relationship with the things and realities which are different from oneself. We discover human existence in the world, which is the place where human life, living creatures, and inert things are found. All these things are considered as one whole reality, everything existing in connection with others but distinct from all. A human being is distinguished from other created beings such as inert objects, plants or animals. A human being is created from nothing, and is born in a place and environment which are distinct from oneself and different from persons around one such as one's mother, father and siblings. Human beings are distinguished from others by consciousness, will and language.

In Aristotle's philosophy, otherness includes the change of quality, of development and of place. However, the change of quality is distinguished from changes of growth and of location. In addition, characteristics such as tall or short and the elements of human appearance differ from one human being to another and they distinguish human beings from other created beings.

Through these differences from others, a human being gradually becomes aware of one's identity and the identity of other persons, recognized as distinguished from oneself. There are other human beings and non-human beings besides oneself; and the former ones have thoughts, feelings and other mental attributes. It is typical of *Wayang* that the elements do not stand apart from one another. The separate elements must be combined and interwoven into a cohesive whole with all the others, and the resulting unity is what gives the classic *Wayang* its greatness and resonance.[389] A human being was created by God to be "monopluralistic." The concept that humans are "monopluralistic" is found in both *Wédhatama* and *Wayang*.

Wédhatama shows us that there are differences between the young and the old generation. It is the purpose of *Wédhatama* to bridge the difference between the young and old generations and to preserve the ancestors' wisdom and values so that they live on in good manners. The words *roroning atunggil* mean the existence of two different realities

---

[389] Sri Mulyono, *The Human Character in the Wayang. The Javanese Shadow Play*, Singapore, 1981, p. 18.

being united in one. Unity does not exclude plurality.

Niels Mulder says that the Javanese tend to be conscious of others. A human being is not alone, but lives together with others. People continually move into and out of one another's space. Such contact is preserved by recognising the presence of others by greeting, or in stopping when walking past someone.[390] In this sense, consciousness of others is not reduced to uniformity but maintains a recognition of the others' existence.

C.   Reciprocal Relationship Between Identity and Otherness

Philosophy tries to pierce the veil of mystery covering reality; thinking radically and inevitably leads to universally applicable conclusions. It cannot be denied that there is a relationship between cause and effect, that systems unite things and that objects exist and have a purpose. Different philosophies try to find the universal truth hidden behind the particularities that surround and confuse us.[391]

A person's distinct identity becomes clear when confronted by something which is different from itself. A man is conscious of a difference from a woman when they are before each other. A servant really becomes a servant in front of his lord. Suffice it to say that human beings find themself or their identity in contrast to others. The identity necessarily contains the self of another or otherness at the same time. Consequently, every action of a human being has to contain oneself and others. Ki Ageng Suryomentaram[392] said:

---

[390] N. Mulder maintains that there is an exchange of politeness which is an almost obligatory ritual that may open the way to further conversation or some questioning; its main point is the mutual acknowledgment of each other's existence. Cf. N. Mulder, *Individual and Society in Java. A Cultural Analysis*, Yogyakarta, 1992, pp. 36-37.

[391] Sri Mulyono, *Human Character in the Wayang. Javanese Shadow Play*, Singapore, 1981, pp. 24-25.

[392] Ki Ageng Suryomentaram was a princely ascetic and influential Javanese philosopher in the period between the world wars. He is best known for his *Kawruh Beja, The Knowledge of Happiness*, a *Kebatinan* doctrine that makes no reference to God or dependence on Him. Cf. N. Mulder, *Inside Indonesian Society. An Interpretation of Cultural Javanese Change in Java*,

Tiyang punika lelawanan kaliyan barang-barang, kaliyan tiyang sanes, lan kaliyan gagasanipun piyambak utawi raosipun piyambak. Tiyang punika mesthi lelawanan lan tiyang kok boten lelawanan punika boten saged. Tiyang anggenipun kraos wonten, punika wonten ing lelawanan. Jalaran raos wonten punika damelipun namung ngraosaken wontenipun punapa-punapa. Dados raos wonten punika lelawanan. Lelawanan punika mesthi ngemot awakipun piyambak lan dede awakipun piyambak. Sarehne raos wonten punika lelawanan, mila saben tindak sejangkah, pangucap sakecap lan krenteg sakedhepan, punika mesthi lelawan lan mesthi isi awakipun piyambak lan dede awakipun piyambak. (A human being is in contrast to matter, other persons, his own ideas or feelings. A human being must be in contrast, and a human being without contrast is impossible. In the feeling of "being," a human being exists in contrast, because the feeling of "being" has the function of feeling the existence of everything else. Thus the feeling of "being" is in contrast. And because the feeling of "being" is in contrast, so every action, word and desire must be in contrast and contain himself and others).[393]

Thus the identity of a human being necessarily contains others' existence. In other words, the consciousness of oneself is always akin to others. This maintains the connection between identity and otherness as a rational distinction, which points out a singular reality within a whole composition.

There is reciprocity in the acknowledgement of another's presence, expressed by different ways of greeting and levels of the language. The relationship with others underlies the powers of individual will, emotions, and self-interest. In this consciousness of others the avoidance of public conflicts and the appearance of *rukun* (peace) is maintained to free the relationship from an annoying situation.

The individual and social characters of the Javanese are evident both in *Wédhatama* and *Wayang*. The relationship between the individual and society has central importance for one's subjective feeling or inner personality which constitutes one's continuity and integrity. For this reason, one should cultivate right relationships that are important for survival in society. One should keep himself at a distance by not

---

Bangkok, 1994, p. 21.

[393] Grangsang Suryomentaram, *Kawruh Jiwa. Wejanganipun Ki Ageng Suryomentaram* (Knowledge of Psyche. Ki Ageng Suryamentaram's Teaching), Vol. II, Jakarta, 1990, p. 41.

involving oneself in others' affairs.[394] The interpersonal distance depends on each other's use for survival, based on the principle of reciprocity, such as an exchange of help and assistance in the consciousness of mutual dependence.

There is a strong tendency toward conformity, elaboration of politeness, the wisdom to move with the flow (*ngèli*). The tendency of the Javanese concept of politeness and wisdom in social reality could offer a hope of reaching a new interpretation of social relationships. Then an awareness of others and interpersonal relations can become distant and impersonal.[395]

Finally it must be noted that differences do not destroy identity. On the contrary, these differences from others' existence even help maintain one's identity. Nevertheless, this rational reciprocity between identity and otherness causes a moral tension between autonomy and heteronomy. In the successive part, we shall see the primacy of consciousness and human will in human identity and otherness.

D. The Primacy of Conscience and Will

The Javanese through their indigenous psychology and anthropology, find a positive way to live in an inner and private self. The true centre of existence is located in the inner self that exists in isolation from society. The *Kebatinan* finds a way for an individual expression of the self; meanwhile social demands sometimes do not respect, or may even suppress, the personal need for self-realization.

In this case, Ki Ageng Suryomentaram has an indigenous psychological and anthropological approach, in which the reflection of conscience and will has significant primacy. He maintains that the essence of human life is the will (*karep*) which is an eternal reality.[396]

---

[394] N. Mulder, *Individual and Society in Java. A Cultural Analysis*, Yogyakarta, 1992, pp. 152-153.

[395] Cf. N. Mulder, *Individual and Society in Java. A Cultural Analysis*, Yogyakarta, 1992, p. 160.

[396] "*Dados karep punika tiyang. Mila tiyang punika langgeng gek bungah gek susah, gek*

When someone comes to know the will, which is characterized by alternating endlessly between glad and sad, that person becomes the seer of their own will. The seer of their own will has the feeling of "I", that of "being". A human being has the feeling of "I"; therefore a human being without the feeling of "I" is impossible. Every feeling of "I" must be a feeling of "being," a feeling of "being" without a feeling of "I" is impossible. The seer is the origin of glad and sad feelings.[397]

The soul or mind cannot be seen, but a human being can feel its existence. Accordingly, the mind has feeling, and someone who knows his own feelings has knowledge of himself.[398] A person who feels, thinks and desires things is formed from many and various feelings throughout his life. The term *Kramadangsa* is used to indicate an accumulation of incidents or events and things throughout one's human history which are stored in one's memory.[399] The orientation of mind or attention has an

---

bungah gek susah. Yen mangertos, yen tiyang punika langgeng, tiyang lajeng luwar saking naraka getun sumelang." (Thus the will constitutes a human being. A human being, therefore, is the eternal change of being happy and sad. If one knows that the will is eternal, he will be free from hell of sorry and anxiety).Gransang Suryomentaram, *Kawruh Jiwa. Wejanganipun Ki Ageng Suryomentaram* (Knowledge of Psyche. Ki Ageng Suryomentaram's Teaching, Vol. I, Jakarta, 1989, p. 23.

[397] "*Ingkang tukang nyawang karepipun piyambak punika raos aku, raos ana. Tiyang punika rak kraos aku, lan tiyang kok boten kraos aku punika boten saged. Saben kraos aku punika mesthi kraos ana, lan kraos aku, kok kraos ora ana, punika boten saged. Ingkang tukang nyawang punika langgeng; jalaran punika barang asal. Barang asal punika boten wonten asalipun ingkang dipun damel, nanging malah dados asal. Inggih punika asaling raos aku bungah, aku susah.*" (The seer of his own will is the feeling of "I," that of "being." A human being, therefore, is the feeling of "I," and a human being without the feeling of "I" is impossible. Every feeling of "I" must be a feeling of "being," and a feeling of "I" without a feeling of "being" is impossible. The seer is eternal, because it is an original matter of the feeling of being glad and sad.). Grangsang Suryomentaram, *Kawruh Jiwa. Wejanganipun Ki Ageng Suryomentaram* (Knowledge of Psyche. Ki Ageng Suryomentramam's Teaching), Vol. I, Jakarta, 1989, p. 31.

[398] Ki Ageng Suryomentaram called the knowledge of human own feeling as *pangawikan pribadi*. Cf. Grangsang Suryomentaram, *Kawruh Jiwa Wejanganipun Ki Ageng Suryomentaram* (Knowledge of Psyche. Ki Ageng Suryomentaram's Teaching), Vol. II, Jakarta, 1990, pp. 41-48.

[399] Grangsang Suryomentaram, *Kawruh Jiwa. Wejanganipun Ki Ageng Suryomentaram*, (Knowledge of Psyche. Ki Ageng Suryomentaram's Teaching), Vol. II, Jakarta, 1990, p. 65. "*Kramadangsa punika kedadosan saking cathetan-cathetan raja-darbe, pakaryan, kehormatan, panguwasa, kaluwarga, grombolan, bangsa, jinis, kasagedan-kesagedan, kepercayaan, raos gesang lan sapanunggalipun.*" (*Kramadangsa* is formed from notes of properties, job, prestige, power,

important role in the *Kramadangsa*,[400] as a feeling of one's own name which is united with all feelings in one's own self. Such a phenomenological analysis is inward-looking; nevertheless it is an empirical attempt to sort out the contingent and the permanent, the human and the divine, within the *batin* (inner mind).[401]

The importance of the will is also found in the kinds of worship according to the *Wédhatama*. These kinds of worship are the worship of the body, of thought, of the soul and that of essence. The *Wédhatama* teaches: "Samengko ingsun tutur - Sembah catur supaya lumuntur - Dhihin raga cipta jiwa rasa kaki...." (Now I shall teach the four kinds of worship, so that you may acquire them: First, that of body, then of thought, of the soul and of the essence, my boy....)[402] It is interesting that thought (*cipta*) is distinguished from soul (*jiwa*); and thought, which is also called heart (*kalbu*),[403] is subordinated to soul. Thought or the heart brings about a certainty of knowledge and the revelation of a higher world (*wenganing alam kinaot*). The latter might be expressed as an experience of the transcendent, reached by inner stillness(*eneng*), clarity (*ening*) and awareness (*eling*).[404] From such a description we might divide the human structure as follows: body, mind (thought or heart), soul, and essence of the core's creation. It is said that the activities of the soul are the culmination of the way; further the essence of the core's creation is a state of being free from anxiety in mind when someone trusts in God's providence.

---

family, group, classification, capabilities, belief, feeling of life, and so forth.). Cf. Grangsang Suryomentaram, *Kawruh Jiwa. Wejanganipun Ki Ageng Suryomentaram* (Knowledge of Psyche. Ki Ageng Suryomentaram's Teaching), Vol. II, Jakarta, 1990, pp. 106-131.

[400] The Javanese use the term *rewes* or *perhatian* for the word "attention". Cf. Grangsang Suryomentaram, *Kawruh Jiwa. Wejanganipun Ki Ageng Suryomentaram* (Knowledge of Psyche. Ki Ageng Suryomentaram's Teaching), Vol. II, Jakarta, 1990, p. 80.

[401] Geertz, C., *The Religion of Java*, Chicago and London, 1976, p. 316.

[402] *Wédhatama*, canto *Gambuh* 1. Cf. S. Robson, *The Wédhatama. An English Translation* (with original text), Leiden, 1990, p. 38.

[403] Cf. *Wédhatama*, canto *Gambuh* 11. S. Robson, *The Wédhatama. An English Translation* (with original text), Leiden, 1990, p. 42.

[404] Cf. S. Robson, *The Wédhatama. An English Translation* (with original text), Leiden, 1990, pp. 42-43.

In other words, the activities of thought lead to the certainty of knowledge; and the activities of the soul give human insight and awareness[405] that one is united with the universe, and the macrocosm comes into the human soul. Both macrocosm and human soul contain and are contained by each other.[406] Such distinctions will be clearer if we compare them to the development of the ideas of "reason" and "intellect" in Western Philosophy.[407] In Javanese thought, the human soul is superior to thought or reason, because a human soul is considered as a divine spark and the human essence becomes a meeting point of the divine and the human. It is the central part of one's inner life, the palace wherein God resides in the individual.[408] The residence of divine life in the centre of human depth does not mean that the essence of God exists in the human self, but the power and the will of God reside in the core of the human heart.[409] That is why the soul has a very important role in a human being.

Finally, we can summarize by saying that identity cannot be separated from otherness. The certainty of identity becomes clear in a comparison with others. That is why both identity and otherness are always in connection with one another. It is like connecting two contrasting things, each of which maintains the identity of the other. Such

---

[405] Cf. *Wédhatama*, canto *Gambuh* 17. Cf. S. Robson, *The Wédhatama. An English Translation* (with original text), Leiden, 1990, pp. 44-45.

[406] Cf. *Wédhatama*, canto *Gambuh* 22. Cf. S. Robson, *The Wédhatama. An English Translation* (with original text), Leiden, 1990, pp. 44-45.

[407] Plato and Aristotle used the terms "intellect" as *nous* and 'reason" as *dianoia*. In Plotinos we find *nous* as intellect and *logos* as reason. (In the Biblical idea, especially the Gospel of John, *logos* is something more than *nous*). Augustine distinguishes inferior reason and superior reason in human mind. Thus "cogitatio" in Augustine is a unison of three elements, intellect, memory, and will. Cf. De Trin. 12, 3; Confessiones X, xi. Sant'Agostino, *Le Confessioni*, (translated by Carlo Vitali), Milano, 1992, p. 465; Saint Augustine, *Confessions*, (translated by H. Chadwick), Oxford, 1992, p. 189.

[408] The meeting point of God and a human being is considered to be the core of the individual, the deep centre of his being. Thus the "heart" in this sense is a kind of spiritual location, the place in the depths of the individual where his true self and the ultimate *rasa* (feeling), which is God, can be found. Cf. Geertz, *The Religion of Java*, Chicago and London, 1976, p. 314.

[409] Cf. Sri Mulyono, *Simbolisme dan Mistikisme dalam Wayang. Sebuah Tinjauan Filosofis* (Symbolism and Mysticism in *Wayang*. A Philosophical Review), Jakarta, 1989, p. 130.

140

a unity is a remarkable characteristic in the concept of *Keselarasan*. In addition, we also find the unity of two contrasting realities in the human heart, namely, the infinite divine reality and the finite human reality.

Understanding the reciprocal relationship between identity and otherness is the fruit of the activity of the will, found through meditation, reflection, self-discipline, and mystical experience. C. Geertz says that a human being must *ngesti*, meaning unify all the powers of the individual and direct them towards a single end, to concentrate one's psychological and physical faculties towards one narrow goal. Such an effort leads a human being to understand the reality of human life. Knowledge of the identity (*jati diri*) of a human person is *pawikan pribadi*.[410]

The understanding of identity, otherness and their reciprocal connection leads to ethical consideration in Javanese thought. For this reason, Javanese ethics is a fundamental manifestation of the concept of *Keselarasan*. We will speak about Javanese ethics in the following section.

---

[410] Cf. Grangsang Suryomentaram, *Kawruh Jiwa. Wejanganipun Ki Ageng Suryomentaram* (Knowledge of Psyche. Ki Ageng Suryomentaram's Teaching), Vol. II, Jakarta, 1990, p. 40-41.

III.   *KESELARASAN* AND JAVANESE ETHICS

Keselarasan has its most expressive manifestation in Javanese ethics, with which I would like to deal in this section. First, I shall consider the place of Javanese ethics under the umbrella of *Keselarasan*, and then continue with an explanation of its principles and an interpretation of virtues.

A.   The Affinity of Javanese Ethics with *Keselarasan*

Some philosophers[411] have a tendency to reduce *Keselarasan* to a principle of ethics. Consequently, the meaning of *Keselarasan* becomes understood merely as a state of peace and harmony in society, wherein everyone has their own proper place and people take care of each other in society, so that conflicts and disturbances are avoided.[412] It is true that *Keselarasan* has a central place as in Javanese ethics. Nevertheless *Keselarasan* extends beyond ethics. It has become a pattern of thought which colours the understanding of human life, the world, language, culture, ethics and so on.

Our perception of *Keselarasan*, therefore, has a wider arena than that of ethics. This comprehension is based on the following considerations. First, the understanding of *Keselarasan* cannot be

---

[411] Toety Heraty Noerhadi and Franz Magnis-Suseno might be in the same current in seeing *Keselarasan* a principle of harmony which pertains solely to ethics. Cf. Franz Magnis-Suseno, *Wayang dan Panggilan Manusia* (Wayang and Vocation of Human Beings) Jakarta, 1991, p. 67.

[412] Cf. Franz Magnis-Suseno, *Wayang dan Panggilan Manusia* (Wayang and Vocation of Human Beings), Jakarta, 1991, pp. 71-72.

separated from its origin in the ambient of Javanese music, *gamelan*. Magnis-Suseno's writings lack this perspective. From its origin in the *gamelan*, *Keselarasan* implies concord, appropriateness and a unified composition of the whole of reality, which include the reality of beauty, the method of thought in mystical reflection, the dynamic melody that accompanies events, and more. Thus it is not merely a requisite of ethics which prescribes peace and the avoidance of public conflict, but rather a method of thought which penetrates the heart of the Javanese culture. Second, *Keselarasan* includes the perception of time as circular. The Javanese do not ordain time as linear progression, but on the contrary, time is considered as a cycle which is characterized by the dynamics of integration and of diffusion. The time of *Krta yuga* is the time of integration in which the principle of *Keselarasan* reaches its fullness. The time of *Kali yuga* is the time of diffusion in which the principle of *Keselarasan* is in distortion, in movement of returning towards its fullness. Between these two poles there is the time of *Tretā yuga* and that of *Dvāpara yuga*. They all constitute the rolling wheel which is animated by the principle of *Keselarasan*.[413] In addition, the positive changes that take place bring back a state of integration, the time of *Krta yuga* which is full of harmony.

Keselarasan has a remarkable significance in Javanese ethics; however, to reiterate, *Keselarasan* is the more comprehensive. *Keselarasan* does not only fall within the sphere of ethics, but on the contrary, Javanese ethics becomes subordinate to *Keselarasan*. We might say that without an understanding of *Keselarasan*, we would fail to understand Javanese ethics. Keeping in mind this comprehension of *Keselarasan* we now look further at Javanese ethics.

Javanese ethics refers to a system of ethics which is akin to the idea of a relationship between an individual and society. This ethics has social and cosmological dimensions in which the world and human existence are considered as interrelated. Before we discuss this relationality, we need to define Javanese ethics.

---

[413] Supra, pp. 121 ff.

Javanese ethics is understood as the norms of attitudes and communal customs which exist in Javanese society. "Norm" here refers to a prescript by which Javanese society translates recognized values. On one hand, the subject of ethics is the Javanese people. On the other hand, the object is the ethical principles. Thus our discourse is one of reflection upon the norms of attitudes and customs as used in the Javanese society. It is necessary, then, when we speak of Javanese ethics, that we take into account how the Javanese use or live these norms and values in their life.

According to Magnis-Suseno, the centre of Javanese ethics is the effort to preserve harmony in society and the universe. Harmony guarantees safety and has value in itself.[414] Such harmony is extant when all the elements of the world, including human beings, are in their proper place. Consequently, the moral duty of a human being is to be conscious of one's own proper place and to behave according to that proper place. From this perspective, Javanese ethics constitutes a step toward, or basis for reaching, happiness.

The Javanese ethics is termed a wisdom ethics, in which arguments are based on the importance of the human person. Humans have the duty to obey the principles which exist in Javanese ethics. Such an ethics emphasizes concrete, individual attitudes toward society. An individual is asked to adapt to the demands and rules of society.[415] One example of this concrete attitude can be seen in *gotong royong*.[416] Koentjaraningrat identifies three kinds of values in *gotong royong*. First, there is a consciousness that human life is dependent upon neighbours, so that human beings have to take care of maintaining a good relationships with their neighbours. Second, human beings should help

---

[414] Cf. Franz Magnis-Suseno, *Etika Jawa. Sebuah Analisa Falsafi tentang Kebijaksanaan Hidup Jawa* (Javanese Ethic. A Philosophical Analysis on the Javanese Wisdom of Life), Jakarta, 1984, p. 196.

[415] Cf. Franz Magnis-Suseno, *Etika Jawa. Sebuah Analisa Falsafati tentang Kebijaksanaan Hidup Jawa* (Javanese Ethic. A Philosophical Analysis on the Javanese Wisdom of Life), Jakarta, 1984, p. 227.

[416] *Gotong royong* is working together of Javanese society in order to help for each other or to do help a public interest. In other words, *Gotong royong* is "mutual cooperation". It takes place when someone builds a house, has feasts or creates a new street for public, and so on.

their neighbours. Third, human beings have to adapt themselves to society in such a way that they do not need to display their own capability over others, but should rather have a common attitude toward society.[417] Consequently, there is a kind of tension between the individual and society which in Javanese ethics.

The Javanese believe that ethics can be taught. This conviction is evident in expressions such as *kurang ajar!* meaning "lack of education," and *durung ngerti* meaning "does not know yet." "Knowing" is not merely an intellectual activity but it includes human attitudes and actions, as *Wédhatama* says *"ngèlmu iku kelakoné kathi laku"* meaning that knowledge is gained through attitudes and actions or goes together with practice.[418] It is for this reason that the *Wédhatama* was written; the purpose of *Wédhatama* is to offer guidance for attaining morality.

Javanese ethics is internalized through acts of politeness, individualization of feelings of *isin* (shame), *sungkan* (a state of uncomfortable feeling in expressing the truth with/about others), and *wedi* (fear).[419] Language and the performance of *Wayang* become the media for the transmission of Javanese ethics. The possibility of teaching ethics is based on the apprenhensibility of knowledge which goes together with practice. With this in mind, we shall identify principles of Javanese ethics in the following section.

B.   Principles of Javanese Ethics

As we have previously mentioned, Javanese ethics necessarily contains some principles as a kind of guideline or moral direction for society. With regard to our concern for *Keselarasan* we define three ethical principles which are the most noteworthy in Javanese ethics.

---

[417] Cf. Koentjaraningrat, *Rintangan-rintangan Mental dalam Pembangunan Ekonomi di Indonesia* (Mental Obstacles in the Economic Development in Indonesia), Jakarta, 1969, p. 35; Franz Magnis-Suseno, *Etika Jawa. Sebuah Analisa Falsafi tentang Kebijaksanaan Hidup Jawa (Javanese Ethic. A Philosophical Analysis on the Javanese Wisdom of Life)*, Jakarta, 1984, p. 51.

[418] *Wédhatama*, canto *Pucung* 1. Cf. S. Robson, *The Wédhatama. An English Translation* (with original text), Leiden, 1990, p. 34.

[419] Infra, p. 147-148.

These are the principles of *hormat* (respect), *rukun* (peace) and *empan papan* (awareness of one's place).

1. The Principle of *Hormat*

Hormat is the principle which pertains to the norm of relationships among people in Javanese society. This principle is defined as that attitude of respect for others whereby every member of society has an obligation to show an attitude of *hormat* to others, especially to their elders and superiors. Such an attitude expresses the recognition of others' positions and feelings. This principle of *hormat*, therefore, indicates a model of Javanese communication which implies a social hierarchy and an inequality of people in the society.

The principle of *hormat* in Javanese society predicates the moral world characterized by mutual obligations. These obligations are not equally distributive, as they provide for the existence of a hierarchy in which there is an obligation for some to guide and lead the others. This is manifested in respect for superior, as Mulders says: "Elders, teachers and especially parents are the subject of extreme reverence, of worship (*pepudhèn*), a place that they deserve because of their care, protection, and teaching."[420]

The high position of parents and elders is based on the Javanese order of family. Parents become representative of life because they connect life to life by marriage and having children. They have a duty to beget and rear the children until the children get married and take on the task of continuing the life line. Consequently, parents become the source of *restu* , "recognition and blessing."[421]

It is morally wrong if children do not respect their parents, do not listen to their advice, or even hurt their feelings. The primacy of parents and elders is the best assurance for preserving the good order of

---

[420] N. Mulder, *Inside Indonesian Society. An Interpretation of Cultural Javanese Change in Java*, Bangkok, 1994, p. 48.

[421] Cf. N. Mulder, *Pribadi dan Masyarakat di Jawa* (Individual and Society in Java), Jakarta, 1985, p. 28.

146

relationships in Javanese society. Hence Javanese ethics gives rise to humility and respect for others' feelings. The children, thus, have to respect and obey their parents or, in Javanese expression, *ngajeni*. When Javanese marry, they receive the name *wis mentas*, meaning that they have become independent from their parents and have become ready to continue life.

The principle of hormat is transmitted through the feelings of *wedi, isin* and *sungkan*. *Wedi* is a feeling of fear toward those who are stronger or menacing. *Isin* is a feeling of shame, which has orientation more toward self so that another's view is directed to one's own feelings. *Sungkan* is a kind of uncomfortable feeling in front of a superior which is a very subtle control of self for reasons of respect for others. Consequently, it might happen that someone does not express the truth because of *sungkan*. Javanese children begin to learn the principle of *hormat* in the family, through forms of politeness and Javanese language, especially when the situation demands that they show an attitude of respect. Consequently, it is not enough to know the principle of *hormat*, but the Javanese have to demonstrate their knowledge of *hormat* to elders and superiors.

The individualization of the principles of *hormat* constitutes a mentality found in state officers, governors, the army and those who are in the middle class. Such a mentality is characterized by a tendency of orientation to the behaviour of the leader. The leaders, such as those who have a higher rank or who are older, must be served and widely respected. The inferiors feel they are respectful when they can give small presents, and those who are in the upper hierarchy (*atasan*) listen to them, protect them and give them moral guidance. Superior take into account the dedication and loyalty of subordinates.[422]

The upper class or elder people are considered as knowing or aware of what the lower class thinks and feels. The figure of *atasan* as protector (*pengayom*) means that the leaders or upper class people listen

---

[422] Cf. Franz Magnis-Suseno, *Etika Jawa. Sebuah Analisa Falsafi tentang Kebijaksanaan Hidup Jawa* (Javanese Ethic. A Philosophical Analysis on the Javanese Wisdom of Life), Jakarta, 1984, p. 66.

to and understand the needs of the lower class. In response, the lower class obeys them and treats them with full respect. The failure of being *pengayom* brings about dissatisfaction, indifference or even disobedience.

An attitude of *hormat,* however, is not a guarantee of obedience. The word "yes" might be an expression of *hormat* which can mean "I do agree," or "perhaps," or "no" in a respectful way. The subordinate has learned that obedience to authority is useful, but it does not mean that one willingly performs the demands of those who are in authority.

The leader becomes a figure like a father (*bapak*) who offers protection and stimulates a feeling of faith and dependence. This person is attentive to the lower class and behaves according to the leadership position. In turn, the lower class will respect their leader. This principle of *hormat* brings about a hierarchical relationship between the leader and follower so that the relationship becomes a relationship of status which is oriented toward the leader. This vertical relationship is considered as contributing stability and continuity, but on the adverse side, it has a strong tendency to creates authoritarian leadership.[423]

There are differences between relationships of intimacy (*keakraban*) and relationships based on *hormat.* A Javanese will feel comfortable and secure when free from the obligation of observing *hormat.* A relationship of closeness, moreover, creates a space in which an individual can live in a relaxed and free state, free from the demands of the order of politeness.

According to Javanese thought, the principle of *hormat* is important for preserving a good and peaceful order. Social life appears as a kind of circumstance in which individuals behave according to their status and rights. Respect and self-esteem tend to be connected to apparent demands. For this reason, it is not impossible that an individual's status is equivalent to one's identity in Javanese society. Accordingly, one shows the dignity of his status or one becomes demanding of respect from others, especially from the lower class.

---

[423] Cf. N. Mulder, *Pribadi dan Masyarakat di Jawa* (Individual and Society in Java), Jakarta, 1985, p. 59.

The principle of *hormat* functions in a framework of hierarchical order in which aspiration, order and protection come from those above to those below.[424] In such an order, position or status is followed by task and duty according to one's position and place in society.[425] Therefore one is never separated from the duties of one's status in the whole hierarchical order in which some have to lead and some have to obey. If all act according to their own place in such an order, the whole order will be well preserved and all persons will be respected according to their status. The transmission of this principle is also supported by language and the hierarchical social structure. That is why this principle is so strong in Javanese society and is an important element in Javanese ethics. However, the existence of a hierarchical order cannot be free from criticism. Javanese society also has experienced changes and improvements resulting from wider communication and the influence of modernization.

2.   Principle of *Rukun*

The principle of *rukun* signifies the Javanese conviction of the importance of a tranquil and peaceful state in society. The word *rukun* implies unity through collaboration, in order to help one another without quarrel or conflict. Such collaboration takes place when all people of society live in peaceful co-existence and when they like to collaborate and to accept one another in a situation of tranquillity and understanding. In families, villages and society, principle of *rukun* is preserved and performed through tradition, customs, and forms of socialization.

This principle of *rukun* can be viewed from two perspectives, namely, imperative and indicative. As an imperative, the principle of *rukun* means that everyone should observe *rukun*, so that all members of society try to avoid the seeds of tension among individuals and groups in a society. In other words, every member of society has an obligation to

---

[424] Cf. N. Mulder, *Pribadi dan Masyarakat di Jawa* (Individual and Society in Java), Jakarta, 1985, p. 159.
[425] Cf. N. Mulder, *Pribadi dan Masyarakat di Jawa* (Individual and Society in Java), Jakarta, 1985, p. 159.

create a good relationship with others and to be involved in a good social life. In this perspective, *rukun* demands continuous efforts to avoid or omit those elements which may cause conflicts and disturbances.[426] Society, therefore, must preserve itself from any disturbance which distorts the principle of *rukun*. In other words, the principle of *rukun* demands attitudes and actions that protect the peace and tranquillity of society.

As indicative, the principle of *rukun* denotes a state of social harmony which has existed for centuries as a norm for organizing the whole of society. Such social harmony must be protected. The emphasis on harmony in society brings about demands of behaving in a general way (*umum*) and an obligation to protect peaceful relationships and togetherness. For this reason everyone in Javanese society becomes a protector of the peace and tranquillity. Consequently, in the application or practice of *rukun* the individuals put aside their own interests and have a preferential option for public interests. An individual is considered unworthy if that individual improves too much beyond the common state of society.

These imperative and indicative perspectives have to be seen as two aspects of the principle of *rukun*. In this principle the individual acts together with society or a group. Accordingly, the individual is considered as bad when he takes initiatives without taking into account the collectivity of society. Society does not easily accept initiatives which are strikingly different from common pursuits. It is an assumption of Javanese people that such initiatives tend to be outside of the public interest which has been integrated in society, and that these new extremes may easily cause quarrels and conflicts.

A solution of conflicts takes place through action according to norms of behaviour and public concessions which protect social harmony from emotional explosions or public conflict. Consequently, Javanese society demands self-reflection (*mawas diri*) and the capacity to controll

---

[426] Cf. Franz Magnis-Suseno, *Etika Jawa. Sebuah Analisa Falsafi tentang Kebijaksanaan Hidup Jawa* (Javanese Ethic. A Philosophical Analysis on the Javanese Wisdom of Life), Jakarta, 1984, p. 39.

emotions and feelings. The figure of a noble person, therefore, can be seen from one's skill of self-control and the capacity to be calm, and to not easily become nervous, confused, or surprised in dealing with anything.

The core of the principle of *rukun* demands the avoidance of any attitude bringing about a public conflict. Hence the result of the state of *rukun* (peace) is social harmony in which everyone lives peacefully with others in society. Further, the principle of *rukun* is like a social mechanism which integrates various interests important for society. Just someone has to put aside his own personal interests, does not mean that in the principle of *rukun,* a Javanese has no personal interests. It does mean that by the preferential option for the public interest, an individual also receives social protection which enables him to have a peaceful mind and life to improve his personal advantage. Nevertheless, someone has acquiesce to compromise and to prevent the disruption of the harmony of social life. It must be noted that the idea of *rukun* contains a balance of positions, statuses, tasks, duties and a mutuality or "give and take," which creates a hierarchical order of life. The hierarchical order of life in society must be respected as a moral demand in itself.

The ideal society is described as a society which is governed by the principle of *rukun*. In such a state, peace becomes characteristic for the vertical and horizontal relationships in Javanese society. Nevertheless, such an ideal society sometimes has to face the fact of conflict and the danger of division. In order to reach the state of peace, it is not right to bring to light personal affairs. In addition, everyone makes an effort to be sensitive to the feelings of others or, in the Javanese expression, *tepa selira*. The content of *tepa selira* is similar to the golden rule: "What is bad if done to yourself, do not do to the others." Thus the ideal Javanese society demands self-control, self-reflection and control of feelings for the sake of others. The negative consequence is that the pressure of environment and society is so strong that there is a tendency for the development of a moral heteronomy. In other words, there is a danger that social considerations and peer pressure can give rise to a tension between moral autonomy and moral heteronomy. This is evident in the hierarchical structure of the Javanese society.

We will deal further with the hierarchical social order of life in the principle of *empan papan*. Here, suffice it to say that the practice of the principle of *rukun* is a constituent part of the structure of the Javanese society, and this is why the principle of *rukun* becomes noteworthy in Javanese ethics. The acquiescence of people in making compromises, public concessions, deliberations and common agreements is stimulated by the power of the principle of *rukun* which is in turn propagated through the structure of society, social tradition and customs.

Politeness, which is called *tata krama* in Javanese, facilitates the observance of *rukun*. This politeness includes the way of speaking, sitting, gesturing and the content of discourse, through which the Javanese train themselves to control their emotions, attitudes and consciousness of others' positions. Accordingly, a person feels that his existence depends upon the unity within society or the group in which one can feels secure, safe and peaceful. Javanese experience social and psychological pressure when they are in confrontation with the common norms of society. They also feel shame and guilt when their attitudes disturb the state of peace in society. In addition, Javanese society also demands the attitude of *rukun* and will punish an unsuitable attitude by isolation or the designation of *ora umum* (uncommon).

Members of Javanese society try to behave according to *rukun* by encouraging good relationships, social forms of give and take, and compromise and the spontaneous sacrifice of one's own interests for the common prosperity and solidarity. Such efforts create peace of heart and the consciousness of dependence on one another. Consequently, the peaceful relationships, mutual respect and understanding, and an adaptable attitude toward society are reasonable, because these duties and established values are appreciated. In addition, the members of society are motivated to take account of others' existence and mutual dependence structured in norms and forms of politeness.

3.   Principle of *Empan Papan* (Awareness of One's Place)

The principle of *empan papan* necessarily contains a consciousness of one's position or place in society. One's place indicates a social status and the existence of a social structure. The context of one's status or position, which is manifested in various kinds of cultures, language and moral behaviour, is this social structure. The principle of *empan papan* will be examined in the light of this hierarchical order in Javanese society.

It is important to note that the hierarchical order is distinctive. Geertz divides Javanese society into three groups: *Abangan, Santri* and *Priyayi. Abangan* is considered as that group of the society which is characterized by an amalgamation of Animism, Hinduism and Islam. The popular tradition of syncretism is the main basis of its civilization. In other words, *Abangan* emphasizes the elements of Animism and syncretism which distinguish the urban inhabitants and farmers. The second that Geertz names, *Santri*, is a group which has an Islamic tradition and also a wide network of trade throughout the whole island of Java. The tradition of *Santri* includes the practice of the Islamic religion such as prayer, fasting and *hajj* (pilgrimage to Mecca). In addition to this, they are also involved in social and political organizations. Most of them are involved in society as Islamic traders. The third distinct group is *Priyayi* which has its roots in the Hindu-Javanese kingdom and has connections with the elements of bureaucracy. They preserve and improve the art, literature, mysticism and etiquette of the kingdom. The elements of Hinduism are outstanding in this group. This group has contributed a view of the world with its ethical and social behaviour which has become the model of the élite class and most of society.[427]

These three groups constitute an interesting comprehension of the structures of Javanese society. Geertz's approach is based upon research during 1953-1954 at Modjokuto, East Java, with its 200,000 inhabitants.[428] In addition, he is rather concerned with accurate data and a systematic analysis of society and culture. However, he lacks an understanding that the *Priyayi* can be also *Santri* at the same time, so that in fact there is no

---

[427] Cf. C. Geertz, *The Religion of Java* (translated by Aswab Mahasin, *Abangan, Santri, Priyayi dalam Masyarakat Jawa*), Jakarta, 1989, pp. 6-9.

[428] Cf. Harsja W. Bachtiar, *The Religion of Java: Sebuah Komentar*, (The religion of Java: A commentary), in: C. Geertz, *The Religion of Java*, (translated in Indonesian by Aswab Mahasin, *Abangan, Santri, Priyayi dalam Masyarakat Jawa*), Jakarta, 1989, p. 521.

behaviour. Or, in other words, virtue can be understood as habits or behaviours which contain good values. Values have significance as far as they contribute others in society.

In addition, Javanese virtue is of value in itself, because the essence of Javanese virtue is the presence of good, which is made manifest through action. Furthermore, something has value depending on its utility or contribution to society, human life or the universe. The values of a virtue are formed and performed in relationship with society and the universe so that cosmological and social aspects are evident in Javanese virtue.

If we understand Javanese virtue in this sense, then the principles of Javanese ethics *hormat, rukun* and *empan papan*, can also be consider as belonging to the category of virtue. *Hormat, rukun* and *empan papan* are said to be the virtues which constitute certain attitudes and habits in Javanese society. We might say that these "principles" of Javanese ethics become or have parallel the primary virtues in Javanese ethics. In addition, there are numerous minor virtues, such as faithfulness (*kesetiaan*), honesty (*kejujuran*), patience (*sabar*), among others.

1. The Virtue of *Hormat*

From the perspective of virtue, *hormat* contains the values which are useful and important in organizing various good relationships in the Javanese society. Everyone uses behaviour and gestures to demonstrate the presence of *hormat* or respect for others. The existence of respect can be seen in one's attitude towards recognition of the position and feelings of others.

The virtue of *hormat* is not an attitude which is demanded only of younger or lower members in society. Elders and the upper class have to show respect for the poor and the powerless in a proportional way. *Hormat* is to be practiced by all, because there is the possibility of status changes. For example, the King must have respect for the poor or for servants, as the relationship can change as illustrated in the theme of *Petruk dadi Ratu* of *Wayang,*where Petruk, the servant, becomes a

156

King.[433] The theme of such a story in *Wayang* is a reminder for the barons, nobles, governments or those who are in the higher positions that they are not superior and free to despise the poor and the smaller. For those who are in the higher positions and prosperous, the motto *aja dumeh*[434] is relevant in underlining the virtues of *hormat*.

The virtue of *hormat* can be taught, so that it is lived by individuals and becomes a habitual way of behaving. Education in this virtue takes place through attaining the knowledge of three feelings, namely, fear (*wedi*), shame (*isin*) and unwillingly saying or doing what is true (*sungkan*). Javanese children learn the virtue of *hormat* in the family, so they will know when situations demand them to observe *hormat* in society. The structure of Javanese society and its social functions psychologically support the demands of the virtue of *hormat*. Somebody who lacks such virtue will be designated as *ora ngerti urmat* which brings about the feeling of being ashamed. The integration of this feeling stimulates the spirit to gain the virtue of *hormat*. The level of virtue of *hormat* indicates the maturity of the Javanese personality. For the Javanese, it is not adequate that they know the virtue of *hormat* and the three feelings above, but they have to demonstrate the virtue of *hormat* toward others.

The objective of education in virtue, therefore, is correct behaviour or action. One gains the knowledge of virtue together with its practice. Consequently, the Javanese perceive an action as the culmination of thinking or in Javanese, *nyambut gawé iku sumèlèhing pikir*. By means of such education, the virtue of *hormat* is transmitted to the next generation as an important element in Javanese ethics.

2.   The Virtue of *Rukun*

Rukun, as a virtue, has its own value as an ideal for society;

---

[433] N. Mulder, *Individual and Society in Java. A Cultural Analysis*, Yogyakarta, 1992, p. 99.

[434] *Aja dumeh* is a motto which reminds everybody not to despise others, especially the small and the poor. Besides, it is also a reminder not to use opportunities and position for personal interests. Cf. N. Mulder, *Pribadi dan Masyarakat di Jawa* (Individual and Society in Java), Jakarta, 1985, pp. 58, 104.

members behave in such a way that they peacefully live together with one another. *Rukun* incorporates is the habit of not making public one's private affairs. The virtue of *rukun* embraces minor virtues such as *ngalah* (acceptance of defeat), *sabar* (patience), *nrima* (acquiescence), and *mengendalikan diri* (self-control). These minor virtues belong to the virtue of *rukun*.

The virtue of *rukun* necessarily infers the capacity of a person to have self-control for the sake of unity. This is why the virtue of *rukun* implies concord in society. The thing that is right and good is that with which it is compatible and concordant in the situation and conditions. Insofar as an attitude or habit does not hurt another's feelings, it does not directly disturb the sense of unity, balance and harmony. Thus concordance means "good," "right," but it must also inhere in right relationships. As a corollary to *rukun*, self-control is one of the important minor virtues in Javanese ethics which plays a primary role in attaining *rukun*, and in turn, the realization of unity or togetherness.

3.   The Virtue of *Empan Papan*

The virtue of *empan papan* necessarily presupposes two basic Javanese postures, that is, an awareness of the ambience which constitutes a certain social order and an awareness of one's identity accompanied by self-control. These also influence the way Javanese behave when they deal with others. The virtue of *empan papan* has its basis in the relationships among the people of society as structured in the hierarchical order.

Javanese perceive life as an ordered and coordinated whole which people must accept and to which they should adapt themselves. With such a perception, Javanese count among their rights and duties the moral duty to respect life's order.[435] Life's order is implicit in the relationships between parents and children which becomea model with rules for their

---

[435] Cf. N. Mulder, *Individual and Society in Jawa. A Cultural Analysis*, Yogyakarta, 1992, p. 11.

158

hierarchical society.[436] The hierarchical society then can extend to the moral world which is animated by the social principles of solidarity and inequality.[437]

Such a structure of society demands the capacity of each individual to place himself properly. We hve already noted, in this context, that a Javanese individual reaches maturity when this capacity is attained; it is to be accompanied by politeness and correal behaviour, the latter of which returns, cycclically, to the necessity of knowledge or consciousness of one's proper place.

This consciousness of place is internalized in an individual through the social order[438] and the levels in Javanese language such as *krama* (high levels) and *ngoko* (low level).[439] Through the usage of Javanese language, the structure of the Javanese society and the awareness of one's place are internalized in an individual from the very beginning as a child learns to speak and realte with the family. Sartono Kartodirdjo says that the behavior and the feelings of the child have to be patterned according to the social values. All these values have to be internalized in order to transform the child into a social personality.[440]

---

[436] "The ensuing relationships between parents and children are highly elaborated and stand as the exemplary model for the rules of hierarchical model". N. Mulder, *Individual and Society in Java. A Cultural Analysis*, Yogyakarta, 1992, p. 23.

[437] Cf. N. Mulder, *Inside Indonesian Society. An Interpretation of Cultural Javanese Change in Java*, Bangkok, 1994, p. 49.

[438] According to C. Geertz, there are three levels of the Javanese society, namely *Abangan* which consists of the farmers who are influenced by Animism, *Santri* consists of Muslims with its syncretism and they are connected with merchants and traders, *Priyayi* which consist of those who are more bureaucratic and influenced by Hindu elements. Cf. C. Geertz, *The Religion of Java*, (translated in Indonesian by Aswab Mahasin, *Abangan, Santri, Priyayi dalam Masyarakat Jawa*), Jakarta, 1989, pp. 6-9.

[439] The level of *ngoko* is considered as rough level which is used in a situation of intimacy or for those who are speaking to the younger or to those who have lower social status than the speaker. The level of *krama* is used for those who are speaking to the older or to the unfamiliar person. Thus *krama* is considered as level of honour and respect. Someone who lacks of knowledge on such rules of language will be considered as *"ora ngerti unggah ungguh"* (he does not know the norms of politeness). Cf. G. Moedjanto, *The Concept of Javanese Power*, Yogyakarta, 1990, p. 55.

[440] Cf. Sartono Kartodirdjo, *Modern Indonesia. Tradition and Transformation*, Yogyakarta,

The Javanese family emphasizes positions in the form of obligations in order to keep social life well ordered and peaceful. Accordingly, social life is perceived as being fixed and each element has to be put in its proper place so that harmony and stability can be maintained. Further, the inner life of the family should be protected by the maintenance of its order and the willingness to cultivate mutual, harmonious relationships. An awareness of one's place reflects the interdependency among societal elements. *Empan papan*, therefore, becomes a moral virtue in order to maintain social order in the family and society.

The virtue of *empan papan* should be practised by every Javanese person so that it becomes a permanent quality of a person which contributes a wide tolerance and spirit of compromise in the face of the various moral and religious views.[441] Such virtue also offers a way to mastery of the outside world which simultaneously, is conducive to one's inner calm, such as the half-social, half-psychological state of peace (*tentrem*) and the deep personal feeling of quiet contentment (*ayem*). For this reason, one should also learn to master the emotions while moving with the social flow (*ngeli*), and to cultivate endurance (*sabar*), humility (*andhap asor*), and the capacity to accept reality and one's situation, in the hope of experiencing a better tomorrow (*nrima*).[442]

In order to arrived at a greater understanding of Javanese virtue, a comparison with the cardinal virtues of Plato is useful. Our concern in this comparative study is the Platonic meaning of virtue, the differences and similarities of the cardinal virtues of Plato and those of Javanese ethics, and finally, the conclusive justification of such an effort.

The word "virtue" derives from the Greek word *aretê* meaning "excellence" or "goodness of any kind." Perhaps it is an abstract noun

---

1988, pp. 188-189.

[441] Cf. Franz Magnis-Suseno, *Etika Jawa. Sebuah Analisa Falsafi tentang Kebijaksanaan Hidup Jawa (Javanese Ethic. A Philosophical Analysis on the Javanese Wisdom of Life)*, Jakarta, 1984, p. 159.

[442] Cf. N. Mulder, *Individual and Society in Java. A Cultural Analysis*, Yogyakarta, 1992, pp. 60-61.

160

which is connected with the Greek word *aristos* meaning "excellent." *Aretê* is commonly translated "virtue" which is a transliteration of the Latin *virtus*. Virtue indicates a particular capacity or a condition for perfection and quality of excellence.[443]

In Platonic philosophy, virtue is expressed as the capacity to govern men,[444] desiring fine things and being able to acquire them,[445] and concord of soul.[446] These various senses have to be seen in the context of Plato's ethics which is eudaemonistic, in the sense that ethics is directed towards the attainment of man's highest good and happiness.[447] Accordingly, man's good is a condition of soul primarily, and it is only the truly virtuous man who is a truly good man and a truly happy man.[448] Furthermore, Plato also described virtue as an attribute of the spirit and something advantageous which is a sort of wisdom, in his Meno:

> If then virtue is an attribute of the spirit, and one which cannot fail to be beneficial, it must be wisdom, for all spiritual qualities in and by themselves are neither advantageous nor harmful, but become advantageous or harmful by the presence with them of wisdom or folly. If we accept this argument, then virtue, to be something advantageous, must be a sort of Wisdom.[449]

From such a philosophy of virtue, we may say that in general Plato accepted that virtue is a knowledge.[450] It is made clear in Meno that if virtue is knowledge, it can be taught, and yet it is shown in the Republic that it is only the philosopher who has true knowledge of the

---

[443] Cf. A. Carlini, *Virtù*, in *Enciclopedia Filosofica*, Firenze, 1982, pp. 705-715; F. Compagni, G. Piana, S. Privitera, (ed.), *Nuovo Dizionario di Teologia Morale*, Milano, 1990, p. 1450.

[444] Meno 73.

[445] "It seems to me then, Socrates, that virtue is, in the words of the poet, 'to rejoice in the fine and have power', and I define it as desiring fine things and being able to acquire them" (Meno 77b). Cf. Plato, *The Collected Dialogues*, (edited by Edith Hamilton - Huntington Cairns), Princeton, 1989, p. 360.

[446] "....these feelings are in concord with understanding, thanks to early discipline in appropriate habits - this concord, regarded as a whole, is virtue" (Laws II, 653b). Cf. Plato, *The Collected Dialogues*, (edited by Edith Hamilton - Huntington Cairns), Princeton, 1989, p. 1250.

[447] Cf. F. Copleston, *History of Philosophy*, Vol. I, London, 1976, p. 216.

[448] F. Copleston, *History of Philosophy*, Vol. I, London, 1976, p. 218.

[449] Meno 88 c, d. Plato, *The Collected Dialogues*, (edited by Edith Hamilton - Huntington Cairns), Princeton, 1989, p. 373.

[450] Cf. F. Copleston, *History of Philosophy*, Vol. I, London, 1976, p. 218

good for man.[451] Furthermore, the world will never be justly ruled until the rulers are philosophers, that is, until they are themselves ruled by the idea of the good, which is divine perfection and brings about justice, which is human perfection.[452]

According to Plato, the cardinal virtues are courage, prudence, temperance and justice.[453] Courage is a state of conservation of right and lawful belief and that of response toward those who make one fearful.[454] The virtue of prudence is a state of having wisdom which inspires advices.[455] The virtue of temperance is a state of equilibrium and self-dominion. In addition, it is also a kind of beautiful order and a continence in regard to certain pleasures and appetites, making one "master of oneself."[456] The virtue of justice is a state of using reason to convey proper and true rights. Plato further says that justice is the principle of doing one's own business and the unification after we have found the virtue of courage, prudence and temperance.[457] Consequently, prudence is a virtue of the rational part of the soul, and courage is of the spirited part, while temperance consists in the union of the spirited and appetitive parts under the rule of reason.[458]

This brief exposition of the cardinal virtues in Plato's writings should be seen as helpful in order to reach a further clarification of the philosophy Javanese of virtue. As with the ideas of identity and otherness, we shall contrast the idea of virtue with western thought in order to perceive precisely the richness of Javanese thought regarding virtue. The comparison of cardinal virtues of Plato with the Javanese virtues follows:

---

[451] F. Copleston, *History of Philosophy*, Vol. I, London, 1976, p. 219; Cf. Plato, *The Collected Dialogues*, (edited by Edith Hamilton - Huntington Cairns), Princeton, 1989, p. 353.

[452] Cf. Plato, *The Collected Dialogues*, (edited by Edith Hamilton - Huntington Cairns), Princeton, 1989, p. 576.

[453] Meno 73e-74a; Rep. IV, 427-428a.

[454] Rep. IV, 429-430c.

[455] Rep. 428b-429a.

[456] Rep. 430e.

[457] Rep. IV, 433b.

[458] Cf. F. Copleston, *History of Philosophy*, Vol. I, London, 1976, p. 220.

162

The Cardinal Virtues of Plato	The Javanese Virtues

Virtue:
 	
    knowledge, capacity to govern men, concord of soul, desiring fine things and able to acquire them, an attribute of the spirit.[459]
	Virtue :
	
	    habit or behaviour contains good value.

Kinds of virtue :
 	
  1. Courage
  2. Prudence
  3. Temperance
  4. Justice
	Kinds of virtue :
	
	  1. *Hormat* (respect)
	  2. *Rukun* (peace)
	  3. *Empan papan* (consciousness of one's place)
	  (4).*Keselarasan* (quality of relationship characterized by concordance, quilibrium, harmony,a ppropriateness and unified composition of the whole of reality)

From the comparison we make above, the differences between the cardinal virtues of Plato and the virtues in Javanese ethics are evident. Virtue in Plato's works, has various meanings which imply that it can be be both an attribute of spirit and an intellectual process. That is why orientation toward the attainment of man's highest good is quite strong. In Plato, there is no one, definitive sense of virtue. Later, in Aristotle's writings, virtue is understood as *habitus,* a stable disposition of the soul and permanent habit to do good.[460] In contrast with Plato's multi-faceted comprehension of virtue, the Javanese virtue give a certain singular meaning to the virtue, i.e., a habit or behaviour which has a high value

---

[459] Supra 161.
[460] Cf. Nichomachean Ethic I, 13,1103a 9-10.

for self or society. The root of the word *virtu* in both Indonesian and Javanese comes form the Sanskrit *uttama* which means uppermost, highest, chief, best and excellent. Virtue as a habit or behaviour contains, for the Javanese, a permanent will to act morally.[461] There is a strong emphasis on an orientation toward others, so that virtue as a good, moral habit has to do with society.

The cardinal virtues according to Plato, can be learned by intellectual process.[462] The word "process," as an intellectual activity is accentuated. A synopsis of Plato's reasoning goes like this: Knowledge can be taught; if virtue is knowledge then it also can be taught. According to Plato, learning is understood as a process of recollection of ideas that are permanent and unchanged. This process takes place through questions and responses or in other words "dialogue." Javanese ethics underlines the possibility of teaching the virtues through the feelings of *wedi, isin* and *sungkan*.[463] Further, as we have previously mentioned, *sungkan* also brings about the unwilling telling of the truth to/about superior. Consequently, emphasis on social pressure and surroundings has a significant role in learning the virtues and values.

For Plato, the virtue of justice includes the virtues of courage, prudence and temperance.[464] Justice in Plato's works is both one of the cardinal virtues and the crown of the other three cardinal virtues. In Javanese ethics, the virtue of justice, which indicates the same sense as *ambeg paramarta,* belongs to the minor virtues. *Keselarasan* does not belong to the virtues, but is beyond the category of virtue. On one hand, *Keselarasan* is the scope and the end of the other three principal virtues in Javanese ethics. On the other hand, *Keselarasan* is the basis of happiness on which Javanese virtues are based. Finally, the fulfillment of a human being, who is always in contact with others or in a relational state, is relegated to beatitude.

---

[461] Cf. Franz Magnis-Suseno, *Etika Jawa. Sebuah Analisa Falsafi tentang Kebijaksanaan Hidup Jawa (Javanese Ethic. A Philosophical Analysis on the Javanese Wisdom of Life)*, Jakarta, 1984, p. 204.

[462] Cf. Meno 89c.

[463] Supra. pp. 147-148.

[464] Rep. IV, 427e, 433-434.

To conclude the discourse on Javanese virtue, I would like to stress the meaning of Javanese ethics as a norm of behaviour in a pluralistic society. Their conception and election of the different virtues developed in parallel with their long history. The emphasis on an orientation toward others, society, and the cosmos accentuates the value of the existence of others. This existence of others, who are different, is appreciated; the valuation of others enriches the identity of the individual self. Inter-dependence is the basis for co-existence, but this is coupled with a tension between the prescribed societal role of the individual and full liberty.

The virtues of *hormat, rukun* and *empan papan* have a primary role in the concrete realization of social harmony for human beings, in the cosmos and in the world of the spirits. Accordingly, the virtues, with their value in se, must become habitual so that human beings may be able to reach their human fullness within puralistic society.

IV.   COMMUNICATION: AN EXAMINATION
OF THE CONCEPT OF *KESELARASAN*

The concept of *Keselarasan* as that quality of relationships among two or more beings which is characterized by concordance, avoidance of public conflict, appropriateness, and the unified composite of the whole of reality, emphasizes the importance of inter-relationships. Communication is a concept of interpersonal relationship which is based upon spiritual participation with others. Such an interpersonal relationship contains a transmission from a communicator to a receiver. From the perspectives of the content of transmission, human communication can be declarative, imperative or interrogatory. Furthermore, declarative communication is a transmission of information; an imperative communication transmits an order, demands or command; and interrogatory communication is the transmission of a question. These transmissions are comprehended as an interaction between human persons which creates social and interpersonal relationships.

Furthermore, communication is also a system of signification, in which one person sends a code, and a partner receives it and understands its message. Communication, therefore, demands of necessity the existence of at least one sender and one others-the receiver. The process of communication can be rationally distinguished as two parts of one reality. The first is the message being communicated and the second is the message being received. In the moment of transmission the communicator is active in sending the message and the partner is passive in receiving the message. Then the roles are reversed, and the partner becomes active in sending the response that he has received the message, and the first communicator becomes passive in receiving the response from the partner. Such a dynamic process creates a reciprocal relationship between communicator and receiver which takes place at the moment of communication.

The action of the communicator not only demands intentionality on his part, but is also a stimulation for a comprehension or action on the part of the receiver.[465] For example, someone says: "Give me the book, please." This is not only a sentence to be understood, but also a stimulation of the receiver to perform a certain action. In this light, the statement of *Wédhatama* that *ngelmu kelakone kanthi laku* or "the knowledge goes together with practice"[466] can be better understood. Practice and action, furthermore, are also understood as manifestation of thought (*nyambut gawé iku sumèlèhing pikir*). Thus in Javanese communication, there is a reciprocal connection between language, activities of thought, and action.

Communication, then, is understood as the relationship and interaction among human persons which is inevitable in human existence. In addition, human existence in its togetherness constitutes a society in which communication can take place. No human society can exist without communication. Speech, art, mythology, knowledge, religious practices, family, social systems and governments have a direct communication dimension which means that these cannot exist without communication and their respective communicative networks.[467]

Concerning society, on one side, society is perceived as hierarchically ordered relationships. This vertical order demands a certain kind of communication between the elder and the younger, the upper and the lower. Such communication is characterized by *kekeluargaan*,[468] as a

---

[465] Cf. Sante Babolin, *Sulla Funzione Communicativa del Simbolo*, Rome, 1989, p. 164.

[466] *Wédhatama* canto *Pucung* 1. Cf. S. Robson, *The Wédhatama. An English Translation* (with original text), Leiden, 1990, pp. 34-35.

[467] Cf. Franz-Josef Eilers, *Communicating Between Cultures. An Introduction to Intercultural Communication*, Rome, 1990, p. 21.

[468] *Kekeluargaan* means the relationship which is based on the pattern of relationship between parents and child or relationship which is based upon blood kinship. Such relationships also maintain the principle of *rukun* in which the Javanese are taught that wrong treatment of siblings, especially the elder, causes punishment from supernatural forces. That is why the elder is *malati*

unique model of communication. On the other side, societies are formed by the inter-relationship and the inter-connection of communal life, and this underlines horizontal communication.

In communications using the Javanese language, speakers take into account such an important fact as the social relationship between themselves and the persons to whom they speak. When one is addressing a person of a higher social position, one generally avoids rude words and colloquial expressions. A spekaer expresses thought more fully and carefully, and sometimes uses long sentences in situations, where instead, a single word would suffice among intimate friends or family.[469] Such an event indicates Javanese society which is relational, as Mulder explains:

> The ideal of communal life is to experience harmonious community, or *rukun*. Such *rukun* does not come as a gift or matter of course, but is the result of the active willingness to respect and adjust to each other. That willingness is grounded in the recognition that one is neither alone nor self-sufficient and that one needs others to pursue the business of life. Consequently one needs to mind each other's existence, to be aware of reciprocal expectations, to treat all people with tolerance and respect, and to observe mutuality in dealing with each other as conscious efforts to keep everybody approachable.[470]

The ideal communal life necessarily contains communication, because the word "communal" indicates the existence of others as a necessity.

The social character of communication is also evident in the *Wédhatama*. The contents of *Wédhatama* include all aspects of human life, such as creature of God, unity of spirit and body, individual and social being,[471] and the very purpose of *Wédhatama* is communication - the transmission of the moral values of the ancestors to the young. Communication and society are reciprocally dependent as good relationships are conducive to peaceful existence so that positive inter-

---

meaning the state of a person that will cause supernatural punishment if an injustice is done to him. Cf. Koentjaraningrat, *Javanese Culture*, Singapore, 1990, p. 111; Franz Magnis-Suseno, *Etika Jawa. Sebuah Analisa Falsafi tentang Kebijaksanaan Hidup Jawa* (*Javanese Ethic. A Philosophical Analysis on the Javanese Wisdom of Life*), Jakarta, 1984, pp. 49, 61.

[469] Cf. E.M. Uhlenbeck, *Studies in Javanese Morphology*, The Hague, 1978, p. 295.

[470] N. Mulder, *Individual and Society in Java. A Cultural Analysis*, Yogyakarta, 1992, p. 40.

[471] Cf. Endang Daruni, et al., *Konsep Manusia dalam Wedhatama. Laporan Penelitian*, (The Concept of Man in *Wédhatama*. A Report of Reseach), Yogyakarta, 1984, p. 4.

relationships with their messages and responses, serve the purpose of self-maintenance in a well-defined order.

We have already affirmed that neither society nor communication can exist without language. In other words, they are sustained and facilitated by its use. The Javanese language is well known in Javanese society, and is not only useful for communicating the moral traditional values as we found in *Wédhatama*, but it also preserves and maintains the structure of the Javanese society and the pattern of Javanese thought. It is interesting to see further the richness of communication in the Javanese language which contains various levels of speech.[472]

The Javanese language belongs to the elements of Javanese culture in which the Javanese symbolic system finds its most expressive manifestation.[473] The symbolic system of the Javanese is considered in two categories which are connected to the idea of contrast or antagonism, for example; the notion of contrast between people and things that have high positions and those that have low positions, the notion of contrast between refined (*alus*) and crude (*kasar*); the notion of contrast between people or things that are unfamiliar, remote and formal (*tebih*), and those that are familiar, close and informal (*celak*).[474] The notion of contrast is also evident in the usage of speech levels in the Javanese language such as *krama* (high level) and *ngoko* (low level).[475]

The aspect of contrast also encompassed in *Keselarasan* in which everything contrast has its place with regard to its own existence so that all contrast and differences, taken together, comprise a whole reality, which is in communication. The Javanese preserve contrast through *krama* and *ngoko*, the use of which creates a unique communication in society.

This unique communication can be seen in the Javanese term *krama* which is used in Javanese grammar to designate those substitutes

---

[472] Cf. G. Moedjanto, *The Concept of Power in Javanese Culture*, Yogyakarta, 1990, p. 10.
[473] Cf. Koentjaraningrat, *Javanese Culture*, Singapore, 1990, p. 446.
[474] Cf. Koentjaraningrat, *Javanese Culture*, Singapore, 1990, p. 446.
[475] Cf. G. Moedjanto, *The Concept of Power in Javanese Culture*, Yogyakarta, 1990, p. 1.

for a number of words when the speaker addresses someone who, according to Javanese norms, is his social superior. The term *ngoko* is used in Javanese for those words which correspond to their *krama*-counterpart.[476] *Krama* and *ngoko* are in semantic opposition to each other. The direction of the communication determines the grammar or the level of speech, namely, *krama* or *ngoko*, which will be used in communication.

The development of the *krama* elements has its basis in *ngoko*-morphemes. For example, the *ngoko* term *wedi* (afraid) which constitutes a unique pair with *ajrih* in the standard language, has a dialectical *krama*-equivalent, *wedos*, formed in accordance with a long series of pairs of the type *"dadi: dados"*.[477] It must be noted that the Javanese language not only consists of the objective system of phonemes, morphemes, words, word groups, intonation and synthetic constructions, but also of all the subtle nuances of tone whereby the speaker reveals his own mood, his feelings towards the addressee, and even his attitude toward the subject of his utterance.[478]

In communication, an understanding sometimes is perceived as a meeting of ideas from both the communicator and the partner. The word is the medium for the ideas which can create an image in human thought. In the process of communication by language, the word stimulates the intellect of the partner so that the partner can see and grasp the same idea. For this reason, communication and language, which are characteristic of human existence, are the fundamental media for unity.

In Javanese communication, it is not only the word which can stimulate certain ideas in the partner's thought, but tone and changes of grammar can also modify meanings and their nuances. Pamanahan's challenge to Arja Penangsang in the book *Babad Tanah Djawi*[479]

---

[476] Cf. E.M. Uhlenbeck, *Studies in Javanese Morphology*, The Hague, 1978, p. 280.

[477] The Javanese words *dadi* and *dados* mean become. Cf. E.M. Uhlenbeck, *Studies in Javanese Morphology*, The Hague, 1978, p. 289.

[478] Cf. E.M. Uhlenbeck, *Studies in Javanese Morphology*, The Hague, 1978, p. 295.

[479] *Babad Tanah Djawi* is an antique story of the land of Java which contains the chronicle of Java as it is published by J.H. Meinsna (ed.), *Babad Tanah Djawi* (Chronicle of the Land of

illustrates an example of this. His letter of challenge is written as follows:

> Pènget! Lajang-ingsoen kangdjeng Soeltan Padjang toemekaa marang Arja Panangsang. Lir ing lajang: jèn sira njata wong lanang sarta kendel, pajo, prang idjen, adja nggawa bala, njabranga marang sakoelon bengawan iki. Soen-entèni ing kono. (Attention! This is the letter from me, the Sultan of Pajang, to Arja Panangsang. The content of the letter is as follows: if you are really a man and a man of courage, let us fight face to face. Come alone without your people. Cross to the west of this lake. I am waiting for you there).[480]

This letter of challenge is written in the level of *ngoko* because Pamanahan is angry. In a normal situation, Pamanahan would write this letter with its same meaning and intention in the level of *krama* as follows:

> Pènget! Serat kulo kanjeng Sultan Pajang dhumateng panjenanganipun (kakang) Arya Panangsang. Wosing serat: yen panjenengan saestu piyantun kakung sarta kendel, suwawi prang ijen, sampun ngasta bala, kula aturi nyabrang ing sakilening benawi punika, kulo entosi wonten ing ngriku.[481]

When one is angry, a letter is never written in *krama,* but the *krama* level of speech is changed to *ngoko*. Seen against the background of Javanese culture, a change of grammar from *krama* to *ngoko* brings out the strong nuance of anger. Accordingly, the anger in such a communication becomes stronger and tougher according to Javanese feeling. The rule of the game in the Javanese language, therefore, is to stimulate consciousness and certain feelings in the receiver so that sensitivity to the changes, circumstances and context influence the communication.

The words and structure of language and its usage, therefore, function as symbols which can sharpen the meaning of the word and make for stronger communication. The same comprehension is gained when both the communicator and the receiver or partner have the same background in Javanese culture. A different cultural background frequently leads to a misunderstanding of a Javanese communication, just

---

Java), 's-Gravenhage, 1941.

[480] J.H. Meinsna (ed.), *Babad Tanah Djawi* (Chronicle of the Land of Java),'s-Gravenhage, 1941, p. 56; Cf. G. Moedjanto, *The Concept of Power in Javanese Culture,* Yogyakarta, 1990, p. 70.

[481] Cf. G. Moedjanto, *The Concept of Power in Javanese Culture,* Yogyakarta, 1990, p. 71.

171

as in communication in any other language.

The appearance of the social aspect in Javanese communication brings out the communal sense of social life or, on the contrary, it can cause the introversion of society. In other words, Javanese communication in the Javanese language contains a paradigm for unity in diversity. Communication in the Javanese language, on one hand, can unify the various human persons and different structures in society into one whole community, in which everyone is conscious of his own place and position. However, we must admit that, on the other hand, such communication also contains a potential for misuse, for the superior or elder can use it to dominate their subordinates by preserving the feelings of inferiority which are facilitated by the structure of the Javanese language. Nevertheless, the Javanese language plays a remarkable part in relationship and communication, whithout which there would be no possibility for integration and diffusion, for unity and diversity, or for *Keselarasan*.

CONCLUSION

are *gotong royong* (mutual cooperation), *kekeluargaan* (familiarity), and *Bhinneka Tunggal Ika* (unity in plurality).[492]

The characteristics of *dwitunggal*, two in one, plurality in unity or unity in diversity are evident. Rachmat Subagya calls such a reality by various names, such as monistic dualism, mutual symbiosis, cosmic relationship, cosmic feeling of oneness, and mono-dualistic.[493] These expressions show that there is a longing of human beings for balance, peace and harmony without losing one's own personality.[494] We have spoken of such a strong desire as found in *Wédhatama* in the expression *roroning atunggil*.[495] Participation in the higher reality leads to unification.

All the tribes and people of Indonesia are bound together by unity. This unity derives from the common basic elements of their civilization.[496] Civilization here would be understood as everything which is created for the advancement of human life. For example, language and mass-media which are a part of culture belong to such a civilization. Moreover, culture is understood as the complex whole of the expressions of human thought and sentiment performed by individuals or groups in society.

Keselarasan, which is characterized by balance, concordance, avoidance of public conflict and the unified composite of the whole of reality, presupposes unity in diversity. The two complementary ideas of unity and diversity characterize one single reality in Indonesia, which indicates not only the fact, but also the problem and the aspiration. This

---

Realm of Original Spirituality in Indonesia), Jakarta, 1979, p. 52.

[492] Cf. A.M.W. Pranarka, *Sejarah Pemikiran Pancasila* (History of Thought on Pancasila), Jakarta, 1985, p. 29; Rachmat Subagya, *Agama dan Alam Kerohanian Asli di Indonesia* (Religion and the Realm of Original Spirituality in Indonesia), Jakarta, 1979, p. 56.

[493] Cf. Rachmat Subagya, *Agama dan Alam Kerohanian Asli di Indonesia* (Religion and the Realm of Original Spirituality in Indonesia), Jakarta, 1979, pp. 99-100.

[494] Cf. Rachmat Subagya, *Agama dan Alam Kerohanian Asli di Indonesia* (Religion and the Realm of Original Spirituality in Indonesia), Jakarta, 1979, p. 99.

[495] Supra, pp. 34, 37 ff.

[496] Cf. Eka Darmaputera, *Pancasila and the Search for Identity and Modernity in Indonesian Society*, Leiden, 1988, p. 32.

is why a dynamic of balance and tension, and of integration and disintegration is very real and is an original and indigenous feature of the society. This dynamic has become part of society from its origination in the very beginning of Indonesian history and from the base of its culture. Consequently, both compromise and consensus are only possible when they are solidly based on such complementariety.[497]

A similar expression can also be seen in *Wayang* in which the *dalang* and the puppets are complementary to one another, and both of them form a two-part unity, a *Bhinneka Tunggal Ika;* consequently, the one cannot exist without the other.[498] It is obvious that this is in line with the Javanese world view which is totalistic. Such a world view sees all things, visible and invisible[499] as parts and aspects or emanations of one wholeness, called "God" who is *Sang Hyang Tunggal* (The One). All things come from and will return to the One. The Javanese call this *Sangkan-paran*, meaning the origin and destiny of everything.

Furthermore, God sometimes is considered as all and in all which brings out the importance of unity and harmony. Such a notion implies the tradition of *Slametan* in which the reality that all live within one community and that each person is part of the totality is maintained. In concrete manifestation of this tenet, everyone is granted the same participation in meals and blessings. Here is required an awareness of a sense of community which surpasses individual differences. In addition is demanded that everybody keep all differences private as what really matters is being part of the whole.

Concordance or *cocok* implies relationship and one's place in the existing system and order. It presupposes the existence of new or foreign elements, adaptation, and encounter with other cultures. Therefore,

---

[497] Cf. Eka Darmaputera, *Pancasila and the Search for Identity and Modernity in Indonesian Society*, Leiden, 1988, p. 41.

[498] Cf. Eka Darmaputera, *Pancasila and the Search for Identity and Modernity in Indonesian Society*, Leiden, 1988, p. 96.

[499] Gods, ghosts and ancestors are considered as the guardians of the established order, reflected in sacrosanct customary law. Cf. M.P.M Muskens, *Partner in Nation Building. The Catholic Church in Indonesia*, Achen, 1979, p. 49.

harmony must continually be restored and things have to be made concordant with one another again and again. Changes and revolution, likewise, are considered as disturbances of social harmony. Nevertheless, Javanese realize that things change over time. There are things which were *cocok* in the past but are not concordant at the present time. Changes, however, should be made in a gradual way, for abrupt change is not desirable. In other words, the life that the Javanese want is orderly and undergoes smooth developments, which are maintained by a process of adaptation.

The individual members of society are seen as parts of the whole. They are interconnected with one another in a totally interdependent system. The whole society takes priority and the individual member's activities must conform to this. The task of each member in society is to contribute to the internal harmony and order of the society.[500]

The balance and avoidance of public conflicts prevent tension from arising as a result of differences. Discernment of human acts as appropriate (*pantes*) or inappropriate (*ora pantes*) and an emphasis on the social order maintains this equilibrium. Furthermore, unity in diversity as *Bhinneka Tunggal Ika* contains elements of the concept of *Keselarasan* which is manifested, sustained and guarded by Pancasila, the country's national ideology and the philosophy of the Indonesian state. We shall speaks about Pancasila in the following section.

2.   PANCASILA

Etymologically, Pancasila derives from the words *Panca* meaning "five," and *Sila* meaning "basis" or "principles."[501] This name was used for the first time by Soekarno on the 1st of June 1945; it contains a deep background of the culture and history of Indonesia.[502] Pancasila,

---

[500] Eka Darmaputera, *Pancasila and the Search for Identity and Modernity in Indonesian Society*, Leiden, 1988, p. 137.

[501] Cf. National Committee for commemoration of the Birth of Pantja Sila 1 June 1945 - 1 June 1964, *Pantja Sila. The Basis of the State of the Republic of Indonesia*, Jakarta, 1964, p. 34.

[502] The symbolism of number is important in the cultural background, since the fundamental obligations of Islam are five in number, the fingers are five, human senses are five (*panca indera*),

furthermore, is intended to designate the five principles as they are found in the Preamble of the 1945 Constitution,[503] namely, *Ketuhanan yang Maha Esa* (One Lordship), *Kemanusiaan yang adil dan beradab* (Just and civilized humanity), *Persatuan Indonesia* (Unity of Indonesia), *Kerakyatan yang dipimpin oleh hikmat kebijakasanaan dalam permuyawaratan/perwakilan* (Peoplehood which is guided by the Spirit of Wisdom in Deliberation/ Representation), and *Keadilan sosial bagi seluruh rakyat Indonesia* (Social Justice).[504]

These five principles of Pancasila were accepted and legitimized as the foundation of the Republic of Indonesia on the 18th of August 1945. Accordingly, the decree of MPRS, No. XX/MPRS/1966 maintains that the Preamble of the 1945 Constitution is the one set by the proclamation of independence on the 17th of August 1945. For this reason nobody can change it, not even the general electorate nor the

---

the *Pāndavas* are five persons i.e. Yudhisthira, Bima, Arjuna, Nakula and Sadéwa. Cf. National Committee of Commemoration of the Birth of Pantja Sila 1 June 1945 - 1 June 1964, *Pantja Sila. The Basis of the State of the Republic of Indonesia*, Jakarta, 1964, p. 34.

[503] The English translation of the principles of the Pancasila in this study tries to be as faithful as possible to the original Indonesian text as it is in the Preamble of the 1945 Constitution. The official English translation of the five principles of Pancasila is as follows: (1) Belief in the One and only God, (2) Just and civilised Humanity, (3) The Unity of Indonesia, (4) Democracy guided by inner wisdom in the unanimity arising out of deliberations among representatives, (5) Social Justice for the whole of the people of Indonesia. Cf. H. Johardin, et al., (eds.), *Indonesia 1988, An Official Handbook*, Jakarta, 1988, p. 12. For further consideration of translation see also some books as follows: Ki Hadjar Dewantara, *Pantjasila*, Jogjakarta, 1950; Mohammad Hatta, *Pengertian Pancasila* (Comprehension of Pancasila), Jakarta, 1978; Notonagoro, *Pancasila secara Ilmiah Populer* (Pancasila in Popular and Scientific Way), Jakarta, 1975; Notonagoro, *Pancasila Dasar Falsafah Negara* (Pancasila the Basis of the State's Philosophy), Jakarta, 1974; Roeslan Abdul Gani, *Pengembangan Pancasila di Indonesia* (The improvement of Pancasila in Indonesia) Jakarta, 1976; Soediman Kartohadiprodjo, *Pancasila dan/dalam Undang-Undang Dasar 1945* (Pancasila and/in the 1945 Constitution), Jakarta, 1976; Dardji Darmodihardjo, *Orientasi Singkat Pancasila* (Brief Orientation of Pancasila), Malang, 1978; National Committee of Commemoration of The Birth of Pantja Sila 1 June 1945 - 1 June 1964, *Pantja Sila. The Basis of the State of the Republic of Indonesia*, Jakarta, 1964; A.M.W. Pranarka, *Sejarah Pemikiran Pancasila* (History of Thought on Pancasila), Jakarta, 1985.

[504] Cf. *Pembukaan Undang-Undang Dasar Negara Republik Indonesia*, (Preamble of the 1945 Constitution), in: Krissantono, (ed.), *Pandangan Presiden Soeharto tentang Pancasila* (President Soeharto's View on Pancasila), Jakarta, 1977, p. xvii; Eka Darmaputera, *Pancasila and the Search for Identity and Modernity in Indonesian Society*, Leiden, 1988, p. 155.

representatives of the people's conference, because a modification of the content of the Preamble of 1945 Constitution would mean modifying the country.[505] Thus Pancasila is a wise choice taken by Indonesian leaders, since in such a pluralistic society Pancasila fulfills a need. Besides, the principles of Pancasila are broad and general enough to include as many groups as possible within its embrace.[506]

From a historical perspective, Pancasila is a compromise based on a socio-cultural inheritance for the unification of various differences, as Soekarno said:

> I therefore hope, Sisters and Brothers, that when I have discoursed on Pancasila you will always remember the background I have given you this evening, that we need unity and that Pancasila, apart from being *Weltanschauung* is an instrument of unification belonging to the people of Indonesia in all their variety.[507]

Consequently, Pancasila is a guarantee for preserving unity without losing particularity or variety.

The necessity of unity has its background in the Indonesian fight for independence and her struggle as a new state and nation. This dates back to the founding of the organization of *Budi Utomo* on the 20th of May 1908, which is nationally commemorated as the *Hari Kebangkitan Nasional* or, the "National Day of awakening." *Budi Utomo* is characterized as a national movement which is organised in modern fashion. Previous organizations carried out struggles and efforts on a regional basis, for example: Diponegoro in central Java; Teuku Umar in Aceh; Panglima Polim in Sumatra; Pattimmura in Moluccas; and others.[508] The Pledge of the Youth on the 28th of October 1928 contains the striving of one country, one nation of Indonesia and one language,

---

[505] Cf. Krissantono, (ed.), *Pandangan Presiden Soeharto tentang Pancasila* (President Soeharto's View on Pancasila), Jakarta, 1977, p. 3.

[506] Cf. Eka Darmaputera, *Pancasila and the Search for Identity and Modernity in Indonesian Society*, Leiden, 1988, p. 178.

[507] National Committee of Commemoration of The Birth of Pantja Sila 1 June 1945 - 1 June 1964, *Pantja Sila. The Basis of the State of the Republic of Indonesia*, Jakarta, 1964, p. 74.

[508] Cf. Eka Darmaputera, *Pancasila and the Search for Identity and Modernity in Indonesian Society*, Leiden, 1988, p. 147.

which is Indonesian. Such a pledge strengthened the desire for an independent Indonesia. At the end of the Second World War, the Japanese, who needed all the support they could muster to slow down the progress of the Allied Forces on the Pacific Front, and by so concentrating on this efforts, they in effect allowed more freedom for the Indonesians' struggle. On the 9th of September 1944, the Indonesian anthem and flag were permitted to be used again.[509] On the 1st of March 1945, the Japanese extended a goodwill gesture in a convincing promise of independence by establishing the committee of *Badan untuk Menyelidiki Usaha-Usaha Persiapan Indonesia Merdeka* (The Investigating Body for the Preparation for an Independent Indonesia).[510] The chairman of this committee was Dr. Rajiman Wedioningrat who was a former chairman of *Budi Utomo*. There were two plenary meetings of this committee which were held from the 27th of May to the 1st of June 1945 and from the 10th to the 17th of July, 1945.

In the first meeting, the committee discussed the Constitution. There were three opinions expressed in regard to the Constitution of the country: 1) the intervention of Muh Yamin, 2) the intervention of Supomo, 3) the intervention of Soekarno. Muh Yamin's speech on the 29th of May, suggested the division of the Constitution into five parts as follows: (i) *Peri Kebangsaan* (Nationalism); (ii) *Peri kemanusiaan* (Humanitarianism); (iii) *Peri Ketuhanan* (Lordship); (iv) *Peri kerakyatan* (Peoplehood); and (v) *Kesejahteraan rakyat* (People's welfare).[511] Supomo spoke about the former problem of the form of the country and the relationship between country and religion. He also mentioned characteristics of Indonesian culture such as unity of life, balance of the

---

[509] Cf. Panitia Lima, *Uraian Pancasila* (The Exposition of Pancasila), Jakarta, 1977, p. 29; Eka Darmaputera, *Pancasila and the Search for Identity and Modernity in Indonesian Society*, Leiden, 1988, p. 148.

[510] Cf. McT. George Kahin, *Nationalism and Revolution in Indonesia*, Ithaca, 1952, p. 121; Eka Darmaputera, *Pancasila and the Search for Identity and Modernity in Indonesian Society*, Leiden, 1988, p. 148; A.M.W. Pranarka, *Sejarah Pemikiran tentang Pancasila* (History of Thought on Pancasila), Jakarta, 1985, p.25; Dardji Darmodihardjo, *Orientasi Singkat Pancasila* (Brief orientation of Pancasila), Malang, 1978, p. 28.

[511] Cf. A.M.W. Pranarka, *Sejarah Pemikiran Pancasila* (History of Thought on Pancasila), Jakarta, 1985, p. 26.

material and spiritual, the leader who is united with the spirit of the people, deliberation, a spirit of mutual cooperation (*gotong royong*) and the spirit of familiarity (*kekeluargaan*).[512] On the 1st of June 1945, Soekarno's talk proposed a foundation of the country called Pancasila. The principles of Pancasila in Soekarno's speech were as follows: (i) *Kebangsaan Indonesia* (Indonesian nationhood or Indonesian nationalism); (ii) *Internasionalisme/Perikemanusiaan* (Internationalism/Humanitarianism); (iii) *Mufakat/Demokrasi* (Unanimous consensus/Democracy); (iv) *Kesejahteraan Sosial* (Social Welfare); and (v) *Ketuhanan Yang Maha Esa* (The One Lordship).[513] The first meeting of the committee was coloured by the problem which was at stake, that is, the plurality of Indonesia. For this reason, they set up *Panitia Kecil*[514] (small committee), with Soekarno as its chairman, to facilitate the work of preparing for an independent Indonesia.

In the second meeting, Soekarno reported the result of the *Panitia Kecil* in collecting the members' opinions and proposals, and he spoke about the efforts of the *Panitia Kecil* to reach a compromise between Muslim groups and the nationalistic group.[515] The result of the *Panitia Kecil* was a proposal for a preamble to the Constitution known as *Piagam Jakarta*. On the 11th of July 1945, *Piagam Jakarta* was discussed further, because Latuharharry, Wongsonagoro and Djajadiningrat raised objections

---

[512] The talk of Supomo points out sharp issues on those who proposed Islam and those who proposed secular as the form for *Indonesia Merdeka*. Supomo emphasized the integralistic form of the country in which the country and the whole people were in unity beyond all groups in any area. Cf. A.M.W. Pranarka, *Sejarah Pemikiran Pancasila* (History of Thought on Pancasila), Jakarta, 1985, pp. 28-30.

[513] Cf. National Committee of Commemoration of The Birth of Pantja Sila 1 June 1945 - 1 June 1964, *Pantja Sila. The Basis of the State of the Republic of Indonesia*, Jakarta, 1964, pp. 22-34; Eka Darmaputera, *Pancasila and the Search for Identity and Modernity in Indonesian Society*, Leiden, 1988, p. 150.

[514] This members of *Panitia Kecil* are Ir. Soekarno, Drs. Mohammad Hatta, Mr. A.A. Maramis, Abikoesno Tjokrosoejoso, Abdulkahar Muzakar, H.A. Salim, Mr. Achmad Subardjo, Wachid Hasjim, Mr. Muhammad Jamin. Cf. Dardji Darmodihardjo, *Orientasi Singkat Pancasila* (Brief Orientation of Pancasila), Malang, 1978, p. 32; Eka Darmaputera, *Pancasila and the Search for Identity and Modernity in Indonesian Society*, Leiden, 1988, p. 151.

[515] Cf. A.M.W. Pranarka, *Sejarah Pemikiran Pancasila* (History of Thought on Pancasila), Jakarta, 1985, p. 34.

concerning the phrase *"berdasar atas ke-Tuhanan, dengan kewajiban melakukan sjari'at buat pemeluk-pemeluknja"* (One Lordship, with the obligation for Muslims to carry out the Islamic shari°a). They stated that such a phrase "may become cause of fanaticism," because it seems to enforce the carrying out the shari°a by Islamic adherents.[516] The aspired Indonesia is not theocratic or secular country, but rather an Independent Indonesia, which place all religions in special way with great respect. Thus there was a sharp discussion with regard to the order of Pancasila and the formulation of the principles.[517]

On the 7th of August 1945, Japanese authority established the *Panitia Persiapan Kemerdekaan Indonesia* (Preparatory Committee for the Independence of Indonesia) with Soekarno as chairman, and Mohammad Hatta as his vice chairman. To this committee, the Japanese promised independence would be granted on the 29th of August 1945. At the decisive moment when the Japanese surrendered to the Allied Forces, Sutan Sjahrir held a meeting with Mohammad Hatta. It was the 14th of August 1945. Sutan Sjahrir and the younger groups demanded independence whithout interference from the Japanese. In that crucial moment, the Indonesians declared themselves free, and following, on the 17th of August 1945 the people of Indonesia declared their own independence to the world.[518] The day after the proclamation of independence, on the 18th of August 1945, the Preparatory Committee had a meeting in which the *Piagam Jakarta*, Preamble, was ratified by Supomo's working committee who began preparing the draft of the Constitution. In order to preserve the unity and the harmonious totality of entire Indonesia, the phrase "with the obligation to carry out the Islamic shari°a for its adherents" was omitted from the Preamble of the

---

[516] Cf. A.M.W. Pranarka, *Sejarah Pemikiran Pancasila* (History of Thought on Pancasila), Jakarta, 1985, p. 37.

[517] Cf. Eka Darmaputera, *Pancasila and the Search for Identity and Modernity in Indonesian Society*, Leiden, 1988, p. 151.

[518] A.M.W. Pranarka, *Sejarah Pemikiran Pancasila* (History of Thought on Pancasila), Jakarta, 1985, pp. 51-52; Eka Darmaputera, *Pancasila and the Search for Identity and Modernity in Indonesian Society*, Leiden, 1988, p. 154.

1945 Constitution.[519] The definitive result was the Constitution of the Indonesian Republic, popularly known as the 1945 Constitution. The principles of Pancasila as they are definitively formulated in the Preamble of the 1945 Constitution are as follows: (i) *Ketuhanan Yang Maha Esa* (The One Lordship); (ii) *Kemanusiaan yang adil dan beradab* (Just and Civilized Humanity); (iii) *Persatuan Indonesia* (Unity of Indonesia); (iv) *Kerakyatan yang dipimpin oleh Hikmat Kebijaksanaan dalam Permusyawaratan/Perwakilan* (Peoplehood which is guided by the spirit of Wisdom in Deliberation/Representation); and (v) *Keadilan Social* (Social Justice).

Such an historical Pancasila becomes a history of a noble consensus and compromise of various opinions and ideologies, in which the influences of secular ideology, Islamic ideology and nationalistic ideology are prominent.[520] Pancasila, therefore, is the best solution for the basic reality that Indonesia epitomizes unity and diversity.[521] Furthermore, Pancasila plays a role in the way of life, the philosophical basis of the state of Indonesia and the source of every law in Indonesia in which the spirit of the nation, its identity (*kepribadian*) and the noble aspirations of the nation are manifested and developed.[522] Likewise, the inheritance of the concept of *Keselarasan* is also manifested in the process of noble compromise found in Pancasila. In other words, aspects of the unification of different groups, harmonious totality, and avoidance of public conflict or disintegration, are evident in the history of Pancasila.

The concept of *Keselarasan* is also manifested in the method of understanding Pancasila in which the principles of Pancasila have to be

---

[519] Cf. Eka Darmaputera, *Pancasila and the Search for Identity and Modernity in Indonesian Society*, Leiden, 1988, p. 155. A.M.W. Pranarka, *Sejarah Pemikiran Pancasila* (History of Thought on Pancasila), Jakarta, 1985, pp. 56-60.

[520] Cf. A.M.W. Pranarka, *Sejarah Pemikiran Pancasila* (History of Thought on Pancasila), Jakarta, 1985, p. 53.

[521] Cf. Eka Darmaputera, *Pancasila and the Search for Identity and Modernity in Indonesian Society*, Leiden, 1988, pp. 146-194.

[522] Cf. Dardji Darmodihardjo, *Orientasi Singkat Pancasila* (Brief Orientation of Pancasila), Malang, 1978, pp.16-22.

184

seen as a unified composite.[523] Therefore, every principle of Pancasila has to be seen together with the other principles in Pancasila. For instance, the first principle of the One Lordship cannot be separated from the principles such as "just and civilized humanity," "unity of Indonesia," "Peoplehood guided by the spirit of Wisdom in the deliberation/representation," and "social justice". The unity of the principles of Pancasila is a noble value which has become the identity or personality (*keperibadian*) of the nation. Pancasila unites all levels and groups of society.[524] Such a method of thought is similar to that of the characteristics of *Keselarasan* which itself is a composite whole of all of its elements as one reality. This similarity can be understood since Pancasila has its root in the history and the spirit of the entire Indonesian people, which includes the Javanese.[525]

One of the characteristics of Pancasila is that it allows different kinds of approaches and interpretations. According to Eka Darmaputera, a sole, official interpretation of Pancasila is contradictory to the very character of Pancasila itself.[526] The various approaches and interpretations are not only allowed but are necessary, insofar as they do not depart from the spirit and framework of Pancasila itself. Accordingly, the principles of Pancasila are implemented and put into practice so that each group of society maintains its own identity, and directly or indirectly engages in continuous dialogue with others so that through different approaches and interpretations everyone can learn, at least theoretically, the universal values in Pancasila in order to maintain unity or co-existence, mutual cooperation (*gotong royong*), and humanism.

The word "theoretically" is intended to acknowledge the existence

---

[523] Cf. Krissantono, (ed.), *Pandangan Presiden Soeharto tentang Pancasila* (President Soeharto's View on Pancasila), Jakarta, 1977, p. 3.

[524] Cf. Krissantono, (ed.),*Pandangan Presiden Soeharto tentang Pancasila* (President Soeharto's view on Pancasila), Jakarta, 1977, p. 12.

[525] This idea is said in Soeharto's talk in the commemoration of the birth of Pancasila on 1st June 1968. Cf. Krissantono, (ed.), *Pandangan Presiden Soeharto tentang Pancasila* (President Soeharto's View on Pancasila), 1977, p. 11.

[526] Eka Darmaputera, *Pancasila and the Search for Identity and Modernity in Indonesian Society*, Leiden, 1988, p. 176.

of the distance between theory and reality which is found in practice. This shortcoming can be used as a starting point for constructive criticism in order to see the philosophical aspect of the concept of *Keselarasan*.

3. CRITICISM AND PROSPECT OF *KESELARASAN* : TOWARDS A PHILOSOPHICAL BASIS FOR DIALOGUE AND HUMAN COEXISTENCE

A. Tendency Towards Feudalism

Keselarasan, which maintains concord and balance, unifies diverse elements, and does not allow public conflict, is a potential force in alleviating conflicts. However, it contains only general principles which sometimes cannot grasp the precise core of a particular problem. Essentially, *Keselarasan* presupposes the existence of self-control on the part of each different group for the sake of common interests. Deviation might come from the social structure which preserves the importance of certain groups or class domination. Feudalism in the sense of a social system based on inequality and privileged position in social, moral and economical areas is very powerful in Javanese society. To maintain tranquillity, the younger ones and the lower class have to observe and manifest the principle of *hormat* and *empan papan* to the superiors and the elders. In case a superior or an elder loses their self-control, the ideal of tranquillity and the principles of *Keselarasan* such as *rukun, hormat* and *empan papan* might be used to preserve domination, which is protected or reinforced by the strength of the social structure. In other words, the concept of *Keselarasan* is power that can be used as an instrument by the superior or elder to rule and dominate the younger and the lower.

Such a tendency demands a capacity of self-control and consciousness of interdependence upon one another. The principles of the concept of *Keselarasan* presuppose a good example on the part of the elders and superiors for the common interest, and the obedience of the lower class with regard to the importance of the whole. Consequently, the

186

orientation from top to bottom should be complemented by balance and composition of the whole in reciprocal communication so that everyone becomes involved in participatory decision making which then creates a feeling of *duweni* (feeling of having responsibility for preserving and taking part in a thing). The absence of such elements brings about a reduction of *Keselarasan* to a *stability* in the sense that *Keselarasan* loses its dynamic aspect and becomes simple uniformity. In dealing with strong waves of modern communication, improvements through science and modernity, the concept of *Keselarasan* can still survive since it accentuates a wide area of dynamic action and because of its orientation towards awareness of interdependency and mutual cooperation.

B.   Potential Danger of Uniformity

The concept of *Keselarasan* necessarily contains a dynamic of unity which is made clear in the ideas of integration and disintegration. In the ethical area, it becomes the motive for avoidance of public conflict. Danger arises when unity is identified with uniformity, which is contradictory to the essence of *Bhinneka Tunggal Ika* and the spirit of Pancasila. Uniformity presupposes enforcement of a single form which does not allow for diversity and the realization of self-identity. Consequently, uniformity alludes to the existence of domination by one side, and lost identity for the other side. Unity, finally, should be based on the rediscovery of the concept of the human being and appreciation of the existence of all beings. The concept of *Keselarasan* can contribute to such unity since it is distinct and separate from uniformity.

Unity, in the concept of *Keselarasan*, creates a space for movement from one's surrounding environment to a point or event which enables the possibility of self-realization of particular beings. Accordingly, unity exists in a world of diversity as a relationship and cannot exist without the possibility or existence of diversity. Suffice it to say that the core of dynamic unity in the concept of *Keselarasan* is a quality of relationship based on the process of integration and diffusion

187

which is essential in the comprehension of Javanese philosophy.[527]

C.   Religiosity

The concept of *Keselarasan* contains a certain religiosity which cannot be separated from the characteristics of balance, concordance, avoidance of public conflict and the unified composite of the whole of reality. Such religiosity is based on the principle of humanism, in which beings, especially human beings, have their origin and destination (*Sangkan Paraning Dumadi*). Human existence in the world is a brief journey of returning to one's origin and destination which is believed to be God.

Keselarasan necessarily contains a basic attitude or orientation and openness for transcendency. In *Wédhatama,* in the canto *Gambuh,*[528] such religiosity has its expression in four kinds of worship: worship of body, of thought, of the soul and the worship of essence. These different kinds of worship are a process of basic orientation toward the mystery of transcendence. In my opinion, such transcendency is universal so that it can be a philosophical basis for dialogue among religions.

Religiosity in the concept of *Keselarasan* emphasizes the basic attitude of living human transcendency. It does not depend upon the mechanism of religious institutions, so that religiosity includes all peoples and transcends formal religion. Such religiosity presupposes that universal humanism which is directed toward the mystery of transcendency. The most important thing in such religiosity is not "having religion," but rather living a basic orientation of openness towards the transcendency which unites various religions.

From a human perspective, the reality behind transcendence is incomprehensible. The Javanese perceive the mystery of transcendence as *tan kena kinaya apa* (it cannot be described) and *adoh tanpa wangenan, celak tanpa sengolan* (it is far, far away and yet very close). If such

---

[527] Supra, pp. 131, 135-136.
[528] S. Robson, *The Wédhatama. An English Translation* (with original text), Leiden, 1990, pp. 38-47.

religiosity is universal it must be intelligible in its connection with other religions. In the various religious traditions, the mystery of transcendency has various names. In Buddhism we find expressions such as *sunyāta,* in Hinduism *Trimūrti* or the expressions of Atman and Brahman. Islam affirms the absolute trancendence of the One God; in Christianity, believers adore the mystery of God as revealed in Jesus Christ. In other words, revelation in the various religions does not exclude anyone from the universality of the mystery of human transcendentality. In addition, human comprehension of the revelation behind the mysterious transcendence in religion is always comprehension in a limited way so that when one speaks of God, one speaks always by analogy.

Thus religiosity in the concept of *Keselarasan* is akin to a basic attitude of surrender, hope and faith[529] which includes and unites everyone. In this case, religiosity goes beyond the formal religions which sometimes exclude other groups. This is our a point of departure for further dialogue and union of religions which should advance by the rediscovery of human existence and its religiosity. Such religiosity enlarges the possibility for communicative dialogue so that every adherent of any religion can peacefully live together with the members of other religions and all can reciprocally learn from one another how to enrich the values, teachings, knowledge, progress and fulfillment of human existence, facing life in this world, in its fullest sense-unity in diversity.

---

[529] Faith should be understood in two perspectives, namely as a subjective attitude toward the transcendence and secondly, the content of conviction or belief. The religiosity in the concept of *Keselarasan* indicates the subjective attitude toward the mystery of the transcendency.

GLOSSARY

advaita (Skr.)	Hindu term meaning non dual, not two
aitareya Upaniṣad (Skr.)	name of an Upaniṣad
akal (Jav.)	human reason
alam keraméan (Jav.)	the world which is full of events and changes
alam suwung (Jav.)	realm of nothing, without content
alus (Jav.)	Refine
ambeg para marta (Jav.)	just attitude; full of justice
anattā (Skr.)	Buddhist doctrine of non ego; not self
andhap asor (Jav.)	humble
anicca (P.)	impermanence
apuruseya (P.)	without human authorship
arété (Gk.)	excellence, goodness, virtue
atas (I.)	upper, high, superior
Ātman (Skr.)	the essence or principle of life
ayem (Jav.)	feeling of quite contentment
bali ing alaming asuwung (Jav.)	return to the realm of void
bapak (Jav.)	father
bātin (Arab.)	inward; inner mind, secret
bathara gung (Jav.)	great god

190

Bhagavad-Gītā (Skr.)	the song of the Lord, one of the Hindu Scriptures
bhakti yoga (Skr.)	Hindu system of discipline through love; re-integration through love and unswerving devotion
bodhisattva (Skr.)	one whose being is *bodhi*, the wisdom resulting from direct perception of truth
brahma jñāna (Skr.)	final emancipation by knowledge of the ultimate reality
brahmaloka (Skr.)	the eternal Brahmā-world consisting of infinite truth
Brahmā (Skr. masculine)	creator, the ultimate reality
brahman (Skr. neuter)	All-pervading, self-existent power
Bṛhad-Āraṇyaka Upaniṣad (Skr.)	name of an Upaniṣad
Buddha (Skr.)	enlightened or awakened one; a title given Gautama, the founder of historical Buddhism
budi luhur (Jav.)	noble thought
bhinneka Tunggal Ika (Jav.)	various yet one; one yet various, unity in diversity
Chāndogya Upaniṣad (Skr.)	name of an Upaniṣad
celak (Jav.)	close, familiar
cipta (Jav.)	thought
cocok (Jav.)	concord, compatible, appropriate
dalang (Jav.)	puppeteer
darśana (Skr.)	viewing, demonstration; the views of the six orthodox Hindu priestly schools
dharma (Skr.)/ *dhamma* (P.)	moral and religious duty; truth; law and cosmic order
dukkha (P.)	suffering, ill
dumadi (Jav.)	Being, being created, becoming

191

dunia fana (I.)	the fragile and perishable world
duweni (Jav.)	feling of possessing; having responsibility
Dvāpara yuga (Skr.)	the third period in the ages of the world
empan papan (Jav.)	consciousness of one's own place
eling (Jav.)	remember, awareness
eneng (Jav.)	stillness
ening (Jav.)	clarity
existentia (L.)	existence
Gambuh (Jav.)	metre of Javanese poem or song
gamelan (Jav.)	set of Javanese musical instruments or Javanese orchestra
gotong royong (Jav.)	mutual cooperation, work together
gunungan (Jav.)	a stiff buffalo leather in a form similar at a mountain which is used in shadow play
guru (Skr.)	teacher
Gusti kang akarya jagad saisine (Jav.)	Lord who created the world and its contents
habitus (L.)	Stable disposition of the soul and permanent dispostion toward acting
harta, wirya, winasis (Jav.)	Property, position and knowledge
hormat (I.)	respect for others
Hyang murbeng dumadi (Jav.)	origin of beings
Hyang Widhi (Jav.)	creator; supreme ruler
Hyang Manon (Jav.)	the most knowledgeable
Hyang Suksma (Jav.)	God in the core of human heart
Hyang Wisesa (Jav.)	the most high, the omnipotent
hyle (Gk.)	matter
Iša (Skr.)	name of the shortest of the

192

	principal Upaniṣads
isin (Jav.)	shameful
jagad cilik (Jav.)	the small world, microcosm, human life
jagad gedhé (Jav.)	macrocosm, universe
jati ḍiri (Jav.)	identity, true condition, the nature of self
jiwa (Jav.)/ *jīva* (Skr.)	the principle of life, individual soul
jiwangga (Jav.)	one reality of body and soul, mind and body
Jñāna yoga (Skr.)	re-integration through knowledge
jumbuhing kawula-Gusti/ pamoring kawula-Gusti/ manunggaling kawula-Gusti (Jav.)	union or encounter between servant and Lord
kakawin (Jav.)	old Javanese poem
kali yuga (Skr.)	the fourth period of the ages of the world
karma yoga (Skr.)	re-integration through action and the performance of religious duties
kasekten (Jav.)	an extraordinary capacity of a human person, gained through self-discipline, fasting and esoteric practices
kasunyatan (Jav.)	reality, truth
kasunyatan jati (Jav.)	the true reality, ultimate truth
Katha Upaniṣad (Skr.)	name of an Upaniṣad
Kāthaka (Skr.)	name of an Upaniṣad
kebatinan (Jav.)	religious movement which concentrates the practices of managing peace of mind, feelings

kebijaksanaan (I.)	prudence, wisdom
kehendak (I.) / *karep* (Jav.)	will
kejujuran (Jav.)	honesty
kekeluargaan (I.)	familiarity, the relationship which is based on the pattern of relationship in the family
kepribadian (I.)	personality, identity
kasar (Jav.)	crude
Keselarasan (Jav.)	a quality of relationship characterized by balance, concordance, appropriateness, avoidance of public conflicts and the composite whole of reality
kesetiaan (I.)	faithfullness
keutamaan (I.)/ *kautaman* (Jav.)	virtue (see utama)
krama (Jav.)	"high Javanese", one of the two basic forms of modern Javanese (see *ngoko*)
kramadangsa (Jav.)	accumulation of incidents, events, things which are stored in one's memory
Kṛta yuga (Skr.)	the first period of the ages of the world
kurang ajar (Jav.)	uneducated, impolite
lair (Jav.)	born, outward appearance
laku/ patrap/ sirikan (Jav.)	Javanese practice of discipline avoiding something to eat, or to do
laras (Jav.)	fine, beautiful, concord, balance, aesthetic sense of contemplation
lega (Jav.)	released, free from psychological burden
lila ora gegetun (Jav.)	acquiescence

194

macapat (Jav.)	name of Javanese poem or song consisting of various kind of metre such as Gambuh, Sinom, Pucung and so on
mandiri (Jav.)	autonomy; self-decision
manekunging tyas (Jav.)	bow in one's own heart
Mahābhārata (Jav.)	the great war of Bhārata; the great epic poem of the Hindus, probably the longest in the world
Mahāyāna (Skr.)	great vehicle; one of the main Buddhist schools emphasizing universal salvation
Mahā-Nārāyana Upaniṣad (Skr.)	name of an Upaniṣad
Māṇḍūkya (Skr.)	name of an Upaniṣad
mati jroning ngaurip (Jav.)	"dead while still living", a state of being dead to the actractions of the world, human appetites and passion, but alive
mawas diri (Jav.)	self-reflection
mengendalikan diri (I.)	self-control
mengkeret (Jav.)	being integrated, become small form
morphē (Gk.)	form
mulur (Jav.)	being diffused
Muṇḍaka (Skr.)	name of an Upaniṣad
musyawarah (I.)	deliberation
neng-nengan (Jav.)	no speaking nor addressing as a refined conflict in Javanese
neti neti (Skr.)	not this, nor that
ngalah (Jav.)	acceptance of defeat
ngeli (Jav.)	going with flow
ngèlmu (Jav.)	esoteric knowledge

ngèlmu iku kelakone kanthi laku (Jav.)	knowledge which goes together with practice
ngoko (Jav.)	low level in Javanese language (see *krama*)
nibbāna (P.)/ *nirvāṇa* (Skr.)	release from the limitations of existence; the supreme goal of Buddhist endeavour
nirguṇa (Skr.)	beyond qualities or attributes; without good qualities, worthless, insignificant
Nītiśāstra (Skr.)	science or a work on political ethics
nityā (Skr.)	eternal, perpetual
nrima (Jav.)	receive the reality without murmur and protest, acquiescnce
nyadran (Jav.)	pilgrimage and cleansing the tombs of the ancestors
nyambut gawe iku sumelehing pikir (Jav.)	working or action as the place and manifestation of thinking
nyawiji, manunggal (Jav.)	united in one towards one's own heart
olah rasa (Jav.)	manage or organise the feelings
ousia (Gk.)	nature, essence, substance, being
ora umum (Jav.)	uncommon, odd, strange
ora urmat (Jav.)	no respect; no appreciation
ora ngerti unggah-ungguh (Jav.)	does not know the norms of politeness
Pancasila (I.)	name of the five principles of Indonesian state's philosophy
panentheism	doctrine which teaches that God is found in everything

196

Pangkur (Jav.)	metre of Javanese poem or song
pantes (Jav.)	appropriate, worthy
pawikan pribadi (Jav.)	knowledge of identity of human person
paradeisos (Gk.)	garden, park
pepunden (Jav.)	ancestor, the object of worship (see *punden*)
piwulang (Jav.)	daily Javanese teachings or instructions on right behaviour and morality
Prajñā-pāramitā (Skr.)	the wisdom which has gone beyond; transcendent knowledge or inspiration
pramāṇa (Skr.)	right measure, clear perception, controlling power
Pucung (Jav.)	metre of Javanese poem, meaning bottle, glass container
Punakawan (Jav.)	servants accompanying the five *Pāndavas* in the Javanese *Wayang*
punden (Jav.)	holy place
Puruṣa (Skr.)	man, male; spirit in man, the supreme Being or soul of the universe
pusaka (Jav.)	heirloom
rame ing gawe (Jav.)	shaping life actively, busy with working
relatio rationis (L.)	mental relation of reason
religio naturalis (L.)	natural religion
Ṛgveda (Skr.)	collection of hymns; the 'Veda of praise'.
rila (Jav.)	not bounded by possessive feeling; ready to give one's own possesion

rasa (Skr.)	feeling, taste, sap; opinion, intention
ratu Kidul (Jav.)	a goddess of the South Sea in Javanese legend
roroning atunggil (Jav.)	two in one, two become one
Ṛta (Skr.)	right order, truth, divine law; immanent dynamic order of the cosmic manifestations
rukun (Jav.)	peace, cooperation without quarrell, harmonious relation
sabar (Jav.)	patient, cultivated endurance
samadi (Jav.)	meditation, pray
Sāmaveda (Skr.)	the Veda of sacred songs
Sāmkhya (Skr.)	one of the philosophical schools in India
samsāra (Skr.)	bondage of life, death and rebirth; a term which refers to the notion of going through one life after another
sangkan paran (Jav.)	origin and destination
sangkan paraning dumadi (Jav.)	the origin and destination of being
sharīʿa (Arab.)	conical Law of Islam
sensus communis (L.)	general interior sense
sepi ing pamrih (Jav.)	without self-interests
Serat Centini (Jav.)	name of a Javanese work on mysticism
sepi ing pamrih (Jav.)	without motives of one's own personal interest
Sinom (Jav.)	metre of Javanese poem or song
slametan (Jav.)	communal socio-religious meal, in which neighbours along with relatives and friends participate

198

smṛti (Skr.)	remembered, recall; human tradition; writings done by human authors
śruti (Skr.)	hearing; divine revelation
substantia (L.)	substance
sūkṣma (Skr.)	intangible, subtle, invisible, immaterial; secret
sūñyatā (Skr.)	emptiness, term in Buddhist philosophy to denote the emptiness of ultimate reality
sungkan (Jav.)	state of uncomfortable in expressing the truth to/about others
svarloka (Skr.)	Superterrestial world
Śvetāśvatara Upaniṣad (Skr.)	name of an Upaniṣad
tat tvam asi (Skr.)	Thou art thou
Taittirīya (Skr.)	name of the collections (*samhitas*) in Yajurveda
tanhā (P.)	desire, thirst for sentient existence
tapa/ tapa brata (J.)	esoteric practice by going into solitude
taṣawwuf wujudīah (Arab.)	mystical doctrine that everything which has a form is the manifestation of God
tata krama (Jav.)	order of politeness
tentrem (Jav.)	peace of mind, undisturbed continuity
tepa selira (Jav.)	sensitive to the feelings of others
tretā yuga (Skr.)	the second period in the ages of the world
triloka (Skr.)	threefold world consisting of heaven, earth and the underworld

Triratna (Skr.)	three jewels; Buddha, Dharma and Sangha
upāya (P.)	way; means; resource; creative efforts of wisdom
urip iku mung mampir ngombe (Jav.)	life is like a stop on the road where someone pauses to have a drink
utama (Jav.)/ *uttama* (Skr.)	uppermost, highest, chief, principal, best, excellent
Veda (Skr.)	knowledge; one of Hindu Scriptures
Vedānta (Skr.)	the end of veda; complete knowledge of Veda; name of one of the Hindu scriptures
viveka (Skr.)	detachment as living in solitude, or mentally detached from being affected by an object of sense
walī (Arab.)	saint; semi legendary apostle of Islam in Java
wayang (Jav.)	Shadow play; Javanese puppet theatre
Wédhatama (Jav.)	highest Wisdom; title of KGPAA Mangkunagara IV's work considered as one of the culminations of Javanese literatures
wedi (Jav.)	afraid, fearful
wenganing alam kinaot (Jav.)	revelation of the higher world
windu kencana (Jav.)	time of peace, prosperity, humility and good cooperation, time of integration

windu ungkul (Jav.)	time of confusion and diffusion
Wulang Reh (Jav.)	name of Pakubuwono IV's writing on government
Yajurveda (Skr.)	formulation and liturgical form for the performance of sacrifices
yamaloka (Skr.)	the world of death; the realm of the dead

201

BIBLIOGRAPHY

I. THE MAIN SOURCES

Alisjahbana, S.T., *Indonesia. Social and Cultural Revolution*, Oxford, 1960.

——————— *Values as Integrating Forces in Personality, Society and Culture*, Kualalumpur, 1974.

Amir Mertosedono, *Sejarah Wayang: Asal-usul, Jenis dan Cirinya*, (History of Wayang: Origins, Variety and its Characteristic), Semarang,1986.

Anderson, Benedict R.O'G., *Mythology and the Tolerance of Javanese*, Ithaca, 1965.

——————— *The Idea of Power in Javanese Culture*, in: C. Holt, *Culture and Politics in Indonesia*, Ithaca and London, 1972, pp. 1-69.

Anna Ranasinghe, et al., *Wayang Sedunia. Puppetry of the World*, Yogyakarta (Microfilm), 1993.

Atmasaputro, Suranto and Hatch, M.F., "Serat Wedhatama: A Translation", *Indonesia* 14 (1972), pp. 157-181.

Bakker, J.W.M., *Diagnose Situasi Islam. Masalah Aliran Kepercayaan dan GBHN 1978* (Diagnosis of Islamic Situation. The Problem of the Movement of *Kepercayaan* dan GBHN 1978), Yogyakarta, 1979.

Bambang Murtiyoso, *Studi tentang Repertoar Lakon Wayang yang Beredar 5 Tahun Terakhir di Daerah Surakarta* (Study on the Repertory Play of *Wayang* Spreading in the Last Five Years in Surakarta Area), Bandung, 1990.

Becker, Judith, *Gamelan Stories: Tantrism, Islam and Aesthetics in Central Java*, Cop, 1993.

Bonnef, M., "Ki Ageng Suryomentaram. Javanese Prince and Philosopher (1892-1962)", *Indonesia* 57 (1993), pp. 49-69.

Budi Moehanto, Marwanto, *Apresiasi Wayang* (Appraisal of *Wayang*), Pemalang, 1989.

Choy, Lee khoon, *Indonesia between Myth and Reality*, London, 1976.

Darusuprapto, *Wedhatama dan Wedhatama Lanjutan*, in: Sulastin Sutrisno, Darusuprapto and Sudaryanto (Eds.), *Bahasa Sastra Budaya; Ratna Manikam Untaian Persembahan Kepada Prof. Dr. P.J. Zoetmulder*, Yogyakarta, 1985, pp. 100-130.

Denison Stange, P., *The Sumarah Movement in Javanese Mysticism*, Ann Arbor, 1982.

Drewes, G.W., "The Struggle between Javanism and Islam as illustrated by Serat Darmagandul", *BKI*, 122 (3), (1965), pp. 309-365.

——————— *Indonesia, Mysticism and Activism*, in: *Unity and Variety in Muslim Civilization*, Chicago, 1963, pp. 284-310.

——————— *The Admonitions of Seh Bari*, The Hague, 1969.

Eka Darmaputera, *Pancasila and the Search for Identity and Modernity in Indonesian Society*, Leiden, 1988.

Endang Daruni, et al., *Gambaran Manusia dalam Wedhatama. Laporan Penelitian* (The Concept of Man in *Wédhatama*. A Report of Research), Yogyakarta, 1984.

Geertz, C., *Agricultural Involution. The Process of Ecological Change in Indonesia*, Berkeley and Los Angeles, 1963.

_____ *Indonesian Cultures and Communities*, in: Ruth T. McVey, (ed.), *Indonesia*, New Haven, 1967, pp. 24-96.

_____ *Islam Observed*, New Haven, 1968.

_____ *Peddlers and Princes. Social Change and Economic Modernization in Two Indonesian Towns*, Chicago, 1968.

_____ *The Interpretation of Culture*, London, 1975.

_____ *The Religion of Java*, London, 1976.

_____ *The Social History of Indonesian Town*, Cambridge, 1965.

_____ *Modernization in a Muslim Society: The Indonesian Case*, in: R. Bellalh (ed.), *Religion and Progress in Modern Asia*, New York, 1965.

Geertz, Hildred, *The Javanese Family: A study of Kinship and Socialization*, New York, 1961.

Poedjosoedarmo, Gloria Risser , *Role Structure in Javanese*, Jakarta, 1986.

Gransang Suryomentaram, *Kawruh Jiwa. Wejanganipun Ki Ageng Suryomentaram* (Kowledge of Psyche. Ki Ageng Suryomentaram's Teaching), Vol. I, Jakarta, 1989.

_____ *Kawruh Jiwa. Wejanganipun Ki Ageng Suryomentaram* (Kowledge of Psyche. Ki Ageng Suryomentaram's Teaching), Vol. II, Jakarta, 1990.

_____ *Kawruh Jiwa. Wejanganipun Ki Ageng Suryomentaram* (K o w l e d g e   o f   P s y c h e .   K i   A g e n g Suryomentaram's Teaching), Vol. III., Jakarta, 1991.

_____ *Kawruh Jiwa. Wejanganipun Ki Ageng Suryomentaram* (Kowledge of Psyche. Ki Ageng Suryomentaram's Teaching), Vol. IV, Jakarta, 1993.

204

Groenendael, V.M.C. van, *Wayang Theatre in Indonesia. An Annotated Bibliography*, Dordrecht, 1987.

_____ *The Dalang behind the Wayang*, Dordrecht, 1985.

Guinness, P., *Harmony and Hierarchy in a Javanese Kampung*, Singapore, 1986.

_____ "Local Society and Culture", edited by Hal Hill, Indonesia's New Order, St. Leonard, 1994.

Harjaka Hardjamardjaja, A., *Javanese Popular Belief in the Coming of Ratu Adil, a Righteous Prince*, Rome, 1962.

Harun Hadiwijono, *Man in the Present Javanese Mysticism*, Amsterdam, 1967.

_____ *Konsepsi Manusia dalam Kebatinan Jawa* (The Concept of Man in Javanese *Kebatinan*), Jakarta, 1983.

_____ *Agama Hindu dan Buddha* (The Religion of Hindu and Buddha), Jakarta, 1987.

Haryanto, S., *Bayang-bayang Adiluhung. Filsafat, Simbolis dan Mistik dalam Wayang* (Beautiful and Noble Shadows. Mystic, Symbol and Philosophy in Wayang), Semarang, 1992.

Hatch, Martin Fellows, Jr, *Lagu, Laras, Layang; Rethinking Melody in Javanese Music*, Dissertation, Ithaca, 1980.

Heins, Ernst, "Power in Structure: Gamelan Pakurmatan in Contemporary Java", *Muziek & Wetenschap* 3 (1993), pp. 127-150.

Hoffman, S.B., "Epistemology and Music: A Javanese Example", *Ethnomusicology* 12 (1978), pp. 69-88

I Wahjudi Pantja Sunjata, *Serat Wisnumaya (Tinjauan Struktur Cerita Pewayangan)* (Letter of Wisnumaya. A Structural Review on the Story of *Pewayangan*), Yogyakarta, 1987.

Jong, S. de, *Salah Satu Hidup Orang Jawa* (One of the Javanese Attitudes of Life), Yogyakarta, 1976.

Kartodirdjo Sartono, (ed.), *Agrarian Radicalism in Java: Its Setting and Development*, in: C. Holt, *Culture and Politics in Indonesia*, Ithaca, 1972.

————— (ed.), *Protest Movements in Rural Java: A Study of Agrarian Unrest 19th and Early 20th Century*, Singapore, 1973.

————— (ed.), *Elite Dalam Perspektif Sejarah* (Elite in the Historical Perspective), Jakarta, 1981.

————— *Modern Indonesia. Tradition and Tranformation*, Yogyakarta, 1988.

————— et al., *Sejarah Nasional Indonesia V* (National History of Indonesia V), Jakarta, 1977.

————— (ed.), *Kepemimpinan dalam Dimensi Sosial* (Leadership in Social Dimension), Jakarta, 1984.

————— *Ungkapan-ungkapan Filsafat Sejarah Barat dan Timur* (Philosophical Expressions of Western and Eastern History), Jakarta, 1986.

Kaufmann, Walter, *Selected Musical Terms of Non Western culture: A Notebook-Glossary*, Michigan, 1990.

Koentjaraningrat, *Anthropology in Indonesia*, 's-Gravenhage, 1975.

————— *Javanese Culture, Singapore, 1990.*

————— Javanese Terms for God and Supernatural Beings and the Idea of Power, in: Schefold, R., Schoorl, J.W., and Tennekes, J., (eds.), *Man, Meaning and History*, Leiden, 1980, pp. 126-139.

————— *Rintangan-Rintangan Mental dalam Pembangunan Ekonomi di Indonesia* (Mental Obstacles in the Economical Development in Indonesia), Jakarta, 1969.

Krause G.H. and Krause S.E, *Indonesia*, Oxford, 1994.

Kumar, A., *Royal Myth and Ritual, and Rice. Another View of Java's Affinities*, in: Houben, V.J.H., Maier, H.M.J. and der Molen, W. van, *Looking in Odd Mirrors: the Java Sea*, Leiden, 1992, pp. 258-288.

Kunst, Jaap, *Hindu-Javanese Instruments*, The Hague, 1968.

Lindsay Jennifer, *Javanese Gamelan: Traditional Orchestra of Indonesia*, Singapore, 1992.

Long, Roger, *Javanese Shadow Theatre: Movement and Characterization in Ngayogyakarta Wayang Kulit*, Ann Arbor, c.1982.

Magnis-Suseno, Franz, *Etika Jawa. Sebuah Analisa Falsafi tentang Kebijaksanaan Hidup Jawa* (Javanese Ethic. A Philosophical Analysis on the Javanese Wisdom of Life), Jakarta, 1984.

_____ *Wayang dan Panggilan Manusia* (*Wayang* and Vocation of Human Beings), Jakarta, 1991.

Mangkunagara IV, KGPAA, *Serat Wédhatama*, Semarang, 1989.

_____ *Wedha-Tama dan Terjemahannya* (The Wédha-Tama and its Translation), Jakarta, 1984.

_____ *Pakem Ringgit Madya* (Handbook of *Ringgit Madya)*, Surakarta Hadiningrat, 1992.

_____ *Pilihan Anggitanipun KGPAA Mangkunagara IV* (Selected Writings of KGPAA Mangkunagara IV), (Transliterated by Kamajaya), Yogyakarta, 1992.

Mangkunagara VII of Surakarta, *On the Wayang Kulit (Purwa) and its Symbolic and Mystical Elements*, (translated by C. Holt), Ithaca, 1957.

Martopangrawit, *Sulukan Pathetan dan Nada-Nada Laras Pelog dan Slendro*, (Sulukan *Pathetan* and the Tones of *Laras Pelog* and *Slendro*), Surakarta, 1980.

207

Meinsna, J.H., (ed.), *Babad Tanah Djawi*, (History of the Land of Java), 's-Gravenhage, 1941.

Miyazaki, Koji, *Javanese Classification Systems; the Problem of "Maximal Correspondence"*, Leiden, 1980.

Moedjanto, G., *The concept of Power in Javanese Culture*, Yogyakarta, 1990.

Mulder, Niels, *Mysticism and Everyday Life in Contemporary Java. Cultural Persistence and Change*, Singapore, 1978.

_____ *Mysticism and Daily Life in Contemporary Java. A Cultural Analysis of Javanese World View and Ethic as Embodied in Kebatinan and Everyday Experience*, Amsterdam, 1975.

_____ *Kepribadian Jawa dan Pembangunan Nasional* (Javanese Personality and National Development), Yogyakarta, 1984.

_____ *Pribadi dan Masyarakat di Jawa* (Individual and Society in Java), Jakarta, 1985.

_____ *Individual and Society in Java. A Cultural Analysis*, Yogyakarta, 1992.

_____ *Pribadi Masyarakat Jawa* (Personality of the Javanese Society), Jakarta, 1985.

_____ *Inside Indonesian Society. An Interpretation of Cultural Change in Java*, Bangkok, 1994.

Panitia Penyelenggara Pekan Wayang Indonesia 1993, *Kumpulan Makalah Sarasehan Wayang Indonesia, Jakarta, 19 dan 21 Juli 1993* (Collection of the Papers of *Sarasehan* on Indonesian *Wayang*, Jakarta, 19 and 21 July 1993), Jakarta, 1993.

Pigeaud, G. Th, *Literature of Java*, Vol. I, The Hague, 1967.

_____ *Literature of Java*, Vol. II, The Hague, 1968.

Pigeaud, G. Th, *Literature of Java*, Vol. III, The Hague, 1970.

_____ "KGPAA Mangkunagara als dichter", *Djawa* 7 (1927), pp. 238-244.

_____ *Java in the 14th Century: A Study in Cultural History,* The Hague, 1960-3.

Priadi Dwi Hardjito, *Hypothetical Contemplation Abstract Laras Slendro as Absolute Pattern of World Musical Framework* (Paper presented at the Simposium Gamelan Malaysia, 4-6 September 1980 at Bangi), Bangi, 1980.

Pustokomardowo, R.B., *Sastra Laras dalam Kerawitan* (Literature of *Laras* in *Kerawitan*), Yogyakarta, 1984.

Rahmat Subagya, *Agama dan Alam Kerohanian Asli di Indonesia* (Religion and Realm of Original Spirituality in Indonesia), Jakarta, 1979.

_____ *Kepercayaan -Kebatinan, Kerohanian, Kejiwaan- dan Agama* (Belief -*Kebatinan*, Spirituality and *Kejiwaan*- and Religion), Yogyakarta, 1976.

RAS, J.J, *The Social Function and Cultural Significance of the Javanese Wayang Purwa Theatre*, London, 1979.

_____ *The Shadow of the Ivory Tree. Language, Literature and History in Nusantara*, Leiden, 1992.

_____ *Java and Nusantara*, in: Hoben, V.J.H., Maier, H.M.J. and der Molen, W. van, *Looking in Odd Mirrors: the Java Sea*, Leiden, 1992, pp. 146-162.

_____ "The Panji Romance and W.H. Rassers' Analysis of its Theme", *BKI* 129/4 (1973), pp. 411-456.

Rassers, W. H., *Panji The Culture Hero. A Structural Study of Religion in Java*, The Hague, 1958.

Robson, S.O., *The Wédhatama. An English Translation* (with Original Text), Leiden, 1990.

——————— *Pattern of Variation in Colloquial Javanese*, Clayton, 1991.

——————— *Javanese Grammar for Students*, Clayton, 1992.

——————— "Note on the Early Kidung Literature", *BKI* 135 (1979), pp. 300-322.

Sidik Gondowarsito, M., *Peranan KGPAA Mangkunegara IV dalam pelestarian Wayang* (The Role of KGPAA Mangkunegara IV in the preservation of *Wayang*), Surakarta, 1992.

Skog, Inge, *North Borneo Gongs and the Javanese Gamelan*, Stockholm, 1993.

Soebardi, S., *The Book of Cabolèk*, The Hague, 1975.

Soewito Santosa, *Sutasoma*, New Delhi, 1975.

——————— *Babad Tanah Jawi (Galuh Mataram)*, (History of the Land of Java (Galuh Mataram)), Sala, 1970.

——————— *The Javanese Shadow Play*, Surakarta, 1974.

Sri Mulyono, *Human Character in the Wayang. Javanese Shadow Play*, Singapore, 1981.

——————— *Simbolisme dan Mistikisme dalam Wayang. Sebuah Tinjauan Filosofis* (Symbolism and Mysticism in Wayang. A Philosophical Review), Jakarta, 1989.

——————— *Human Character in the Wayang*, (translated by Medeiros), Jakarta, 1977.

Subandi Djajengwasito, *Javanese Style: A Multiple Discriminant Analysis of Social Constraints*, Ann Arbor, 1981.

210

Sudaryanto, *Bahasa Jawa: Prospeknya dalam Tegangan antara Pesimisme dan Optimisme* (Javanese Language: Its Prospect in Tension between Pesimism and Optimism), Semarang, 1991.

––––––––– *Bahasa Jawa: Apanya yang Dapat Disumbangkan bagi Pengembangan Kebuadyaan Nasional?* (Javanese Language: Which aspects can be contributed to the Improvement of National Culture?), Yogyakarta (Microfilm), 1988.

––––––––– (ed.), *Tatabahasa Baku Bahasa-Jawa* (Basic Grammar of Javanese Language), Yogyakarta, 1991.

Suhardjo Hatmosuprobo; Kartodirdjo, Sartono; and Sudewa A., *Beberapa Segi Etika dan Etiket Jawa* (Some Ethical Dimensions and Javanese Etiquette), Yogyakarta, 1987-1988.

Sunardjo Haditjaroko, *Ramayana. Indonesian Wayang Show*, (8th edition), Jakarta, 1993.

Sutton, R. Anderson, *Traditions of Gamelan Music in Java: Musical Pluralism and Regional Identity*, Cambridge, 1991.

––––––––– *The Javanese Gambang and its Music*, (Master's Thesis), Hawaii, 1975.

––––––––– "Concept and Treatment in Javanese Gamelan Music, with Reference to the Gambang", *Asian Music* 9:2 (1979), pp. 59-79.

––––––––– "Musical Pluralism in Java: Three Local Traditions", *Ethnomusicology* 29/1 (1985), pp. 56-85.

––––––––– *Variation in Central Javanese Gamelan Music. Dynamics of a Steady State*, Illinois, 1993.

Suyamto, *Wayang dan Budaya Jawa* (Wayang and Javanese Culture), Semarang, 1992.

Tanojo, R., *Weddha Tama Djinarwa*, Surakarta, 1963.

──────── *Djangka Djajabaja. Sjech Bakir*, Solo, 1940.

Uhlenbeck, E.M., *Javanese Linguistics. A Retrospect and Some Prospects*, Dordrecht, 1983.

──────── *Studies in Javanese Morphology*, The Hague, 1978.

Ulbricht, H., *Wayang Purwa. Shadows of the Past*, Kualalumpur, 1970.

Wasisto Suryodiningrat, *Gamelan Sepanjang Jaman* (Gamelan throughout the Ages), Yogyakarta, 1988.

Wessing, R., *Cosmology and Social Behaviour in a West Javanese Settlement*, (Dissertation), Illinois, 1974.

Woodward, M.R., "The Slametan: Textual Knowledge and Ritual Performance in Central Javanese Islam", *History of Religion* 28 (1988-89), pp. 54-89.

Zoetmulder, P.J., *Manunggaling Kawula Gusti* (translated by Dick Hartoko), Jakarta, 1991.

──────── *Pantheism and Monism in Javanese Suluk Literature. Islamic and Indian Mysticism in an Indonesian Setting* (edited and translated by M.C. Ricklefs), Leiden, 1995.

──────── *Kalangwan. A Survey of Old Javanese Literature*, The Hague, 1974.

II. SECONDARY SOURCES

AAVV, *Babonign Kitab Primbon. Bundelan 10 Kitab Primbon Pusaka Sumber Ilmu Kejawen Taksih Asli dening Pra Pujonggo Jawi* (Motherbook of *Primbon*. Collection of 10 Primbon's Heirloom Books. Sources of the *Kejawen* Knowledge derived from Javanese authors), Solo, 1946.

212

Abdul Munir Malkhan, *Kebatinan dan Dakwah kepada Orang Jawa* (*Kebatinan* and *Dakwah* to Javanese People), Yogyakarta, 1984.

Abd Mutholib Ilyas - Abd Ghofur Imam, *Aliran Kepercayaan dan Kebatinan* (Currents of Belief and Kebatinan), Surabaya, 1988.

Abdulgani, R., *In Search of an Indonesian Identity*, Jakarta, 1958.

Abe., M., *Dynamic Unity in Religious Pluralism: A Proposal from the Buddhist Point of View*, in: John Hick - Ashkari Hasan (eds.), *The Experience of Religious Diversity*, Aldershot, Hants, and Brookfield, 1983, pp. 163-190.

Achadiati, Y.S, *Zaman Taruma Negara dan Sunda*, (Time of Taruma Negara and Sunda), Jakarta, 1988.

——————— *Zaman Kutai Purba*, (Time of Ancient Kutai), Jakarta, 1987.

——————— *Zaman Majapahit*, (Time of Majapahit), Jakarta, 1988.

Adham, D., *Salasilah Kutai* (Genealogy of Kutai), Jakarta, 1981.

Ahmad, A., *Two Approaches to Islamic History. A Critique of ShibliNu'mani and Syed Ameer Ali's Interpretation of History*, (Dissertation), Philadelphia, 1970-80.

Aivanhov, O.M., *Harmony*, Englewood Cliffs, 1989.

Al-Faruqi, Ismail, *Rights of Non-Muslims under Islam: Social and Cultural Aspects*, in: *Journal of Institute of Muslim Minority Affairs*, Vol. I, No.1 (1979), pp. 90-102.

Ali Murtopo, *Strategi Kebudayaan* (Strategy of Culture), Jakarta, 1978.

Ali, Yusuf A., *The Qur'ān. Text, Translation and Commentary*, Leicester (UK), 1975.

Alles, G.D., "Wach, Eliade, and the Critique from Totality", *Numen* 35 (1988), pp. 108-138.

Anand, S., "The Experience of Wholeness and God-Equivalents in Hinduism" *Dialogue & Alliance* 5/1 (1991-1992), pp. 144-154.

Angelika Malinar, "God, Gods and Divinity in Hindu Tradition of the Pāncarātra", *Concilium* 2 (1995), pp.11-22).

Antlöv, H. and Cederroth, S., (eds.), *Leadership on Java. Gentle Hints, Authoritarian Rule*, Surrey, 1994.

Anwar Soetoen, *Kutai. Masa Lampau, Kini dan Esok* (Kutai. The Past, Present and the Future), Jakarta, 1979.

Aristotle, *The Complete Works of Aristotle*, Vol. I., (edited by Barnes, J.), Princeton, 1984.

——————— *The Complete Works of Aristotle*, Vol. II., (edited by Barnes, J.), Princeton, 1984.

Augsburger, D. W., *Conflict Mediation Across Cultures. Pathways and Patterns*, Louisville, 1992.

Augustine of Hippo, *Le Confessioni*, (translated C. Vitali), Milano, 1992.

——————— *Confessions*, (translated by H. Chadwick), Oxford, 1992.

Babolin, Sante, *Sulla Funzione Communicativa del Simbolo*, Rome, 1989.

Bambang Sumadio, (ed.), *Sejarah Nasional Indonesia II. Jaman Kuno*, (National History of Indonesia II. Ancient Age), Jakarta, 1976.

Banawiratma, J. B., *Yesus Sang Guru. Pertemuan Kejawen dengan Injil* (Jesus the Teacher. Encounter of *Kejawen* and the Gospel), Yogyakarta, 1977.

Barnes, R.H., *Kedang: A Study of the Collective of an Eastern Indonesian People*, Oxford, 1974.

Barua,A.A., "Re-Examination of the Nature of Religion", *Journal of Dharma* 15 (1990), pp. 212-222.

Basti, G., *Il Rapporto Mente-Corpo nella Filosofia e nella Scienza*, Bologna, 1991.

Baxter C., *Harmony of the World*, Lewis Hall, 1984.

Beg, M.A., *Universal Humanism and One World Order*, New York, 1983.

Benda, H., *The Continuity and Change in Indonesia Islam*, New Haven, 1965.

Benda, H.J. - Larkin, J.A., *The World of South Asia. Selected Historical Readings*, New York, 1967.

Berg, C., *The Javanese Picture of the Past*, in: Soedjatmoko, (ed.), *Introduction to Indonesian Historiography*, Ithaca, 1965, pp. 87-118.

Bernet Kempers, A.J., *Ancient Indonesian Art*, Amsterdam, 1959.

Biro Pusat Stastistik, *Statistic Indonesia 1992. Statistical Yearbook of Indonesia 1992*, Jakarta, 1993.

Blaedel, N., *Harmony and Unity*, Berlin, 1988.

Blagden, C.O., *An Introduction of Indonesian Linguistic*, London, 1916.

Blain, Sean Martin, *The Java Man*, London, 1995.

Boellaars, *Kepribadian Indonesia Modern. Suatu Penelitian Antropologi Budaya* (Modern Indonesian Personality. A Study on Anthropology of Culture), Jakarta, 1984.

Bohm David, *Wholeness and Implicate Order*, London, 1979.

Boisselier, J., *Majapahit*, Paris, c. 1990.

Border, F., *The Old Stone Age*, London, 1968.

Bormans, M., "Pluralism and Limits in the Qur'an and the Bible", *Islamochristiana* 17 (1991), pp. 1-14.

Bosch, F.D.K, *Problems of the Hindu Colonization of Indonesia*, in: *Selected Studies in Indonesian Archaeology*, The Hague, 1961.

_____ "C.C. Berg and Ancient Javanese History", *BKI* 112 (1956).

_____ *Selected Studies in Indonesian Archaeology*, The Hague, 1961.

Brockington, J. L., *The Sacred Thread. Hinduism in its Continuity and Diversity,* Edinburgh, 1981.

Brooks, P., *People of Concord*, Conn, 1990.

Brown, R. E., *The Gospel according to John XII-XXI*, Vol. XXIXA, Garden City, 1970.

Brown, S.E., "A First Step in a Dialogue on Spirituality: Impressions of a Conference", *Islamochristiana* 12 (1986), 169-176.

Bruck, Michael von, *Unity of Reality. God, God-Experience, and Meditation in the Hindu-Christian Dialogue*, New York, 1990.

Bruner, E.M., "The Expression of Ethnicity in Indonesia", *Asia Monography 12 Urban Ethnicity*, London, 1974, pp. 251-280.

Budiono Herusatoto, *Simbolisme dalam Budaya Jawa* (Symbolism in Javanese Culture), Yogyakarta, 1984.

Bühlmann, W., *Discussions Between Muslims and Christians in Indonesia*, in: Bühlmann, W., *The Search for God. An Encounter with the Peoples and Religions of Asia*, Maryknoll, 1980.

Caldwell, Malcolm, *Indonesia: An Alternative History*, Sydney, 1979.

Caroko, H., "The Concept of Man according to Pancasila", *The Indonesian Quarterly* XV/4 (1987), pp. 610-619.

216

Chatterjee, An Raj , *History of Indonesia. Early and Medieval,* Meerut (etc), 1967.

Chethimattam, J.B., *The Pre-Aryan Roots of Sankara's Advaita,* in: Thomas Mampra, (ed.), *Religious Experience. Its Unity and Diversity,* Bangalore, 1981.

Chidester, D., "Being Human: Symbolical Orientation in the New Religious Movements", *Journal of Dharma* 7 (1982), pp. 430-451.

Clarke, A., *Clarke's Commentary Genesis-Esther. A Classical Help to a Better Understanding of the Bible,* Vol. I., Nashville, 1828.

Coedes, Gorge., *The Indianized States of Southeast Asia,* Kualalumpur, 1968.

Coedes, George, and Damais, Louis-Charles, *Sriwijaya:History, Religion & Language of an Early Malay Polity,* Kualalumpur, 1992.

Collier, W.L. and Soentoro, *Rural Development and Decline of Traditional Village Welfare Institutions in Java,* Canberra, 1980.

Collins, S., *Selfless Person,* Cambridge, 1982.

Coomaraswamy, A., *History of Indian and Indonesian Art,* New York, 1927.

Copleston, F., *A History of Philosophy,* Vol. I , London, 1966.

_____ *A History of Philosophy,* Vol. II, London, 1966.

Corby, Raymond and Leerssen, Joep (eds.), *Alterity, Identity and Image: Self, Others in Society and Scholarship,* Amsterdam, 1991.

Coward, H. G., *Modern Indian Response to Religious Pluralism,* Albany, 1987.

Cullmann, O., *Unity through Diversity,* Philadelphia, 1988.

D'Aquili, E.G., *The Regulation of Physical and Mental Systems*, New York, 1990.

Dardji Darmodihardjo, *Orientasi Singkat Pancasila* (Brief Orientation of Pancasila), Malang, 1978.

Da Silva, P., *Religious Pluralism: A Buddhist Perspective*, in: Hick.J., and Ashkari, H., (eds.), *The Experience of Religious Diversity*, 1983, pp. 131-143.

Dahm, B., *History of Indonesia in the Twentieth Century,* (translated by P.S. Falla), London, 1971.

Dananjaya, J., *An Annotated Bibliography of Javanese Folklore*, Berkeley, 1972.

Dandekar, R. N., *Insights into Hinduism*, Delhi, 1979.

Danto, Arthur C, *Mysticism and Morality Oriental Thought and Moral Philosophy*, New York / London,1972.

Darminta, J., *"Mawas diri" (Self Examination). A Dialogal Encounter of the Self-Examination of Ki Ageng Suryomentaram in the Perspective of the Javanese Religious Life with the Ignatian Examination*, (Dissertation), Rome, 1987.

Dhavamony, M., *Classical Hinduism*, Rome, 1982.

———— *"Vedantic Philosophy of Religion"*, *International Philosophy Quarterly* 21 (1981), pp. 51-59.

———— *Phenomenology of Religion*, Rome, 1973.

De Pregeand, T.H.G., and Graaf, H.J., *Kerajaan-Kerajaan Islam di Jawa. Peralihan Majapahit ke Mataram* (Islamic Kingdoms in Java. Transition from Majapahit to Mataram), Jakarta, 1974.

De Smet, R., *"Hinduism versus the Plurality of Religious Traditions"*, *Indian Theological Studies* 23 (1986), pp. 22-36.

Deliar Noer, *The Modernist Muslim Movement in Indonesia 1900-1942*, Singapore, 1973.

_____ *Gerakan Moderen Islam di Indonesia 1900-1942* (The Islamic Modern Movement in Indonesia 1900-1942), Jakarta, 1980.

Departemen Pendidikan dan Kebudayaan, *Kutai Perbendaharaan Kebudyaan Kalimantan Timur*, (Kutai, Property of the Eastern Kalimantan Culture), Jakarta, 1979.

De Wit, "The Contemplative Contribution to Interreligious Perspective", *Studies in Interreligious Dialogue* 1 (1991), pp.146-162.

Dipoyudo, Kirdi, "Pancasila the State Basis and View of Life of the Indonesian People", *The Indonesian Quarterly* XV, No. 4 (1987), pp. 537-553.

_____ *Pancasila: Arti dan PelakasanaanNya* (Pancasila: Its Meaning and implementation), Yogyakarta, 1980.

Dister, S.N., *Pengalaman dan Motivasi Beragama* (The experience and Motive of Religion), Yogyakarta, 1982.

Djajadingingrat, R.H., *The Sejarah Banten*, Haarlem, 1913.

Dobby, E.H.G., *South-East Asia*, London, 1967.

Donald, E.S., (ed.), *South Asian Politic and Religion*, New Jersey, 1966.

Drijarkara, N., *Pancasila dan Religi: Mencari Kepribadian Nasional* (Pancasila and Religions: Searching for National Personality), Djakarta, 1972.

_____ *Drijarkara tentang Negara dan Bangsa* (Drijarkara on Country and Nation), Yogyakarta, 1980.

_____ *Drijarkara tentang Kebudayaan* (Drijarkara on Culture), Yogyakarta, 1980.

Duerlinger, J., "Religious Diversity and Possibility of a Single Transcendent Reality", *Dialogue & Alliance* 5 (1991-1992), pp. 18-30.

Dutta, B., *The Javanese Brahmana Purana*, Madura, 1970.

Edi Sedyawati, *Sejarah Kebudayaan Jawa* (History of the Javanese Culture), 1993.

Eilers, Franz-Josef, *Communicating between Cultures. An Introduction to Intercultural Communication*, Rome, 1990.

Eknath Easwaran, *The Upanishads*, London, 1988.

——————— *Bhagavad Gita*, London, 1986.

Eliade, M., *Myth and Reality*, London, 1975.

Eliot, C., *Hinduism and Buddhism. A Historical Sketch*, London, 1962.

Ellwood, R.S., Jr., *Many Peoples, Many faiths: An Introduction to the Religious Life of Humankind*, Prince Hall, 1987.

Emmerson, D., *Indonesia's Elite, Political Culture and Cultural Politics*, Ithaca, 1976.

Ensink, Jacob, *Siva - Buddhism in Java and Bali*, in: Heinze Bechert (ed.), *Buddhism in Ceylon and Studies on Religious Syncretism in Buddhist Countries*, Göttingen, 1978, pp. 178-198

Farquhar, N., and Grisword, H.D., *The Religious Quest of India*, Oxford, 1920.

Fazlur Rahman, *Islam*, Garden City, 1968.

Fernandes, A., "Dialogue in the Context of Asian Realities", *East Asian Pastoral Review* 27 (1990), pp. 202-222.

Fischer, E.A., *South Asia, Social Economic and Political Geography*, London, 1966.

Fischer, L., *The Story of Indonesia*, London, 1959.

Fox, J.J., *The Flow of Life. Essays on Eastern Indonesia*, Havard, 1980.

Frachry Ali, *Agama, Islam dan Pembangunan* (Religion, Islam and Development), Yogyakarta, 1985.

Fruin-Mees, W., *Sedjarah Tanah Djawa* (History of The Land of Java), (translated by Latif, S.M.), Weltevreden, 1921.

Gell, A., *The Anthropology of Time: Culture Constructions of Temporal Maps and Images*, Berg, 1992.

Gerbrandy, P.S., *Indonesia,* London, 1950

Ghisalberti, A., *Guglielmo di Ockham. Scritti Filosofici*, Firenze, 1991.

Gibb, H.A.R., *Mohammedanism* (Indonesian translation by Abusalamah), Jakarta, 1983

Gomes, Luis, and Hiran, W.Woolwurd, Jr., *Borobudur, History and Significance of a Buddist Monument*, Berkeley, 1981.

Gonda, J., *The Presence of Hinduism in Indonesia: Aspect and Problems*, in: *India's Contribution to World Thought and Culture*, Madras, 1970, pp. 535-554.

Goodman, F.D., *Ecstasy, Ritual, and Alternate Reality: Religion in a Pluralistic World*, Bloomington, 1988.

Goudriaan, T., *Sanscrit Texts and Indian Religion in Bali*, in: *India's Contribution to World Thought and Culture*, Madras, 1970, pp. 555-564.

Green, M., *Indonesia. Crisis and Transformation 1965-1968*, Washington, 1990.

Griffith, Bede, *The Golden String*, London, 1954.

_____ *Cosmic Revelation*, Illinois, 1983.

_____ *The Marriage of East and West*, London, 1982.

221

Griffith, Bede, *A New Vision of Reality*, London, 1992.

Groenevelt, W.P., *Historical Notes on Indonesia & Malaya. Compiled from Chinese Sources*, Jakarta, 1960.

Grunebaum, Gustave E. von, *Unity and Variety in Muslim Civilization*, (translated by E. N. Yahya), Jakarta, 1983.

Gunawan Setiardjo, A., *Hak-Hak Asasi Manusia Berdasarkan Ideologi Pancasila* (Human Rights Based on the Ideology of Pancasila), Yogyakarta, 1993.

Hall, D.G.E., *A History of South-East Asia,* New York, 1981.

Harsja W. Bachtiar, *The Religion of Java: Sebuah Komentar* (The Religion of Java: A Commentary), in: C. Geertz, *The Religion of Java* (translated in Indonesian by Aswab Mahasin, *Abangan, Santri, Priyayi dalam Masyarkat Jawa*), Jakarta,1989.

Hatta, Mohammad, *Pengertian Pancasila* (Comprehension of Pancasila), Jakarta, 1978.

——————— *The Co-operative Movement in Indonesia*, (edited by McT Kahin), Ithaca, 1957.

Haven, Wilhelm, and Hood, Mantel, *The Evolution of Javanese Gamelan*, New York, 1988.

Haward, Palwfrey Jones, *Indonesia: The Possible Dreams*, Singapore, 1980.

Hefner, R.W., *Identity and Cultural Reproduction among Tengger Javanese*, Machican, 1982.

——————— *Hindu Javanese. Tengger Tradition and Islam*, New Jersey, 1989.

Heekeren, H.R. van, *The Stone Age of Indonesia*, The Hague, 1972.

Helfritz, H., *Indonesien. Ein Reisebegleiter: Java, Sumatra, Bali und Sulawesi (Celebes)*, Köln, 1988.

Herman, H., *Peace Anyone?*, (translated by F. Rudiyanto), Jakarta, 1970.

Hick, John., *God and the Universe of Faith*, London, 1973.

_____ *Interpretation of Religion*, London, 1991.

Hirschman, C.; Hutterer, K.; Keyes, C.F., (eds.), *Southeast Asian Studies in the Balance: Reflection from America*, Ann Arbor, 1992.

Hofsteede, W., *Decision Making Processes in Four West Javanese Villages,* Nijmegen, 1971.

Holt, C., *Art in Indonesia, Continuity and Change*, Ithaca, 1967.

Hood, Mantel, Javanese Music in the World - Gamelan Djawa Dilihat dari Segi Dunia Musik, (translated by H. Susilo), Yogyakarta, 1958.

I-Tsing, *A Record of the Religion as Practised in India and the Malay Archipelago*, Oxford, 1896.

Ina, E. S., *Cultural Strategis for Survival: The Plight of the Javanese*, Rotterdam, 1982.

Institute of Asian Affairs, (ed.), *Indonesia Seminar, Hamburg 22-23, 1976,* Hamburg, 1977.

Iskandar, T., *The Hikayat Atjeh* (The History of Atjeh), The Hague, 1959.

Jay, R., *Javanese Villagers*, Cambridge, 1969.

_____ *Religion and Politic in Rural Central Java*, Yale, 1969.

Johardin, H., et al., (eds.), *Indonesia. An Official Handbook*, Jakarta, 1988.

Jones, Z., *Rural Leadership in Indonesia*, Jogja, 1959.

Jonnes, A.H., *Indonesian Studies in Australia*, Canberra, 1964.

Judge, W.Q., and Crosbie, R., *Commentari su La Bhagavad-Gītā*, Torino, 1980.

Juergensmeyer, M., *Religion as Social Vision. The Movement against Untouchability in 20th Century Punjab*, Berkeley, 1982.

Kadankavil, K. T., *Gita and the Synthesis of Hindu Religious* in: Thomas Mampra, (ed.), *Religious Experience. Its Unity and Diversity*, Bangalore, 1981.

Kadir Tisna Sjana, *Babad Majapahit* (History of Majapahit), Jakarta, 1988.

Kahin, George McT., *Nationalism and Revolution in Indonesia*, Ithaca, 1952.

Kalm, J. S., *Ideology and Social Structure in Indonesia*, in: Taylor, J.G. and Turton, A., (eds.), *Sociology of the "Developing Societies" South Asia*, Basingstoke, 1988.

Karanggayam, *Serat Nitisruti*, Semarang, 1994.

Khairuddin, H., *Filsafat Kota Yogyakarta* (Philosophy of the City of Yogyakarta), Yogyakarta, 1995.

Kennedy, R., *Bibliography of Indonesian People and Cultures*, New Haven, 1955.

Ki Hajar Dewantara, *Pantjasila*, Jogjakarta, 1950.

Kimball, C., *Striving Together: A Way forward in Christian-Muslim Relations*, Maryknoll, 1991.

Kitagawa, J. M., *Dimensions of the Asian Religious Universe*, in: *History of Religion* 31 (1991-92), pp. 181-209.

_____ *The Quest for Human Unity*, Minneapolis, 1990.

_____ *Villages in Indonesia*, Ithaca, 1967.

Kodiron, *Serat Tuntunan Suluk: Ngewrat Sulukan-Sulukan Laras Slendro Djangkep* (Guideline of *Suluk:* containing complete *Sulukans Laras Slendro*), Surakarta, 1964.

Kolenda, Konstantin, *Cosmic Religion*, New York, 1991.

Koller, J. M., and Koller, P., *A Sourcebbok in Asian Philosophy*, New York, 1991.

Krieger, D., *The New Universalism: Foundations for a Theology of Religions*, Chicago, 1987.

Krishnamurti, *The Wholeness of Life*, New York, 1979.

Krissantono, (ed.), *Pandangan Presiden Soeharto tentang Pancasila* (President Soeharto's View on Pancasila), Jakarta, 1977.

Kumar, Ann, (ed.), *Surapati , Man and Legend: A Study of Three Babad Traditions*, Leiden, 1976.

Lebar, F.M., (ed.), *Ethic Groups of Insular Southeast Asia*, New Haven, 1972.

Legge, J.D., *Indonesia*, Sydney, 1980.

Legrand, L., *Unity and Plurality*, Maryknoll, 1990.

Leur, J.C. van, *Indonesian Trade and Society*, The Hague, 1955.

Lévi-Strauss, Claude, *The Structural Study of Myth*, in: Sebeok, T.A., (ed.), *Myth. A Symposium*, Philadelphia, 1955.

Levy, R., *The Social Structure of Islam*, Cambridge, 1969.

Loeb, E.M., *Sumatra: Its History and Peoples*, Wien, 1935.

Lohnizen, J.E. van, and Leeuw, de, "Indonesia", *Le Civiltà dell' oriente* 1 (1956).

LP3ES, "Indonesia: Unity in New Diversity", *Prisma* 41, 1986.

Lubis, Mochtar, *Manusia Indonesia* (Indonesian Man), Jakarta, 1979

Mahmud Yunus, H., *Sejarah Pendidikan Islam di Indonesia* (History of Islamic Education in Indonesia), Jakarta, 1979.

Nunuk Murniati, A., and Kuntara Wiryamartana, I., *An Indonesian Contribution to a Spirituality of Liberation: Two Perspectives. An approach from the Javanese World View*, in: Fabella, V., Lee P.K.H, Kwang-sun Suh, D., *Asian Spirituality Reclaiming Traditions*, Maryknoll, 1992.

Olthoff, W.L., (ed.), *The Babad Tanah Djawi* (The History of the Land of Java), The Hague, 1941.

Omoyajono, J.A., *Diversity in Unity*, Boston, 1984.

Panitia Lima, *Uraian Pancasila* (The Exposition of Pancasila), Jakarta, 1977.

Palmier, L., *Social Status and Power in Java*, London, 1969.

——————— *Indonesia*, London, 1965.

Pannikar, R., *The Invisible Harmony. A Universal Theory of Religion or Cosmic Confidence in Reality*, in: Swidler, L. (ed.), *Toward a Universal Theology of Religion*, Maryknoll, 1987, pp.118-153.

Parsudi Suparlan, *Keselarasan dan Keseimbangan: Strategi Kebudayaan dalam Masalah Lingkungan* (*Keselarasan and Balance: Strategy of Culture in the Ecological Problems*), Jakarta, 1987.

Pelzer, K.J., *The Agricultural Foundation*, in: Ruth T. McVey, (ed.), *Indonesia*, New Haven, 1967, pp. 118-154.

Pemberton, J., *On the Subject of "Java"*, Ithaca and London, 1993.

Pesink, G.J., *Indonesia History Between the Myth Essays in Legal History and Historical Theory*, The Hague, 1968.

Pickthall, Muhammed Marmaduke, *The Meaning of the Glorious Qur'ān*, Cairo-Beirut, 1972.

Pipitseputra, *Beberapa Aspek dari Sejarah Indonesia* (Some Aspects of Indonesian History), Ende, 1975.

Plato, *Plato: The Collected Dialogues*, (editedy by Edith Hamilnton and Huntington Cairns), Princeton, 1989.

Poerbathjaraka, R. Ng., *Riwayat Indonesia* (Story of Indonesia), Vol.I., Jakarta, 1962.

Porter, J.M., and Vernon, Richard, *Unity, Plurality & Politics: Essay in Honour of F.M. Barnard*, New York, 1986.

Pranarka, A.M.W., *Sejarah Pemikiran Pancasila* (History of Thought on Pancasila), Jakarta, 1985.

Pringgodigdo, A.K., *Sejarah Pergerakan Indonesia* (History of Indonesian Movements), Jakarta, 1978.

Prio Hartono, *Inner Wisdom. A Journey through Seen and Unseen Worlds*, New York, 1988.

Prior, W.J., *Unity and Development in Plato's Metaphysics*, Beckenham, 1985.

Pujasumarta, J., *Indonesia: Una Società Pluralistica* in: *La Spiritualità Secondo Il Detto del Concilio Vaticano II*, (Dissertation), Rome, 1987.

Radhakrishnan, Sarvepalli, *Bhagavad Gītā*, (translated by Icilio Vecchiotti), Rome, 1964.

Raffles, T.S., *The History of Java*, London, 1976.

Ralph, Th., *Hymns of the Ṛgveda*, Vol. II, Delhi, 1987.

Rasche, C.A., "Religious Experience and Modern Synthetic Religiosity", *Journal of Dharma* 11 (1986), pp. 131-138.

Rassers, W.H., *Siva and Buddha in the East Indian Archipelago*, in: Rasser W.H., *Panji , The Culture of Hero*, The Hague, 1959, pp. 63-91.

Reiser, O. L., *Cosmic Humanism*, Cambridge, Massachusetts, 1966.

Resink, G.J., *Indonesia's History Between the Myths*, The Hague, 1968.

229

Resink, T. A., *Modern Indonesian Project*, Ithaca, 1968.

Ricklefs, M.C., *Yogyakarta under Sultan Mangkubumi 1749-1792. History of the Division of Java*, London, 1974.

——————— *War, Culture and Economy in Java 1677-1726*, Sydney, 1993.

——————— *A History of Modern Indonesia c.1300 to the Present*, London, 1981.

——————— *Unity and Disunity in Javanese Political and Religious Thought of the Eighteenth Century*, in: Houben, V.J.H., Maier, H.M.J. and MOLEN, W. van der, *Looking in Odd Mirrors: the Java Sea*, Leiden, 1992, pp. 60-75.

Roest Crollius, A. A, "Harmony and Conflict", Pontificium Consilium pro Dialogo Inter Religiones, *Bulletin* 81 (1992), pp. 360-377.

——————— *Islam as Religious Experience*, in: Thomas Mampra, (ed.), *Religious Experience. Its Unity and Diversity*, Bangalore, 1981.

——————— *The Source of Life at the Meeting of the Two Oceans: Reflection on the Majma'-al-bahrayn of Dara Shukoh*, in: Troll, C.W., (ed.), *Islam in India, Studies & Commentaries*, Vol. 1, Delhi, 1982, pp. 46-51.

——————— *Prophets and Sages. Some Notes for a Typology of Approaches to Religious Pluralism*, in: D'Sa, F.X. and Mesquita,R.,(eds.), *Hermeneutics of Encounter. Essays in Honour of Gerhard Oberhammer on the Occasion of his 65th Birthday*, Vienna, 1994, pp. 191-202.

Ronggowarsita, R. Ng., *Serat Paramayoga*, Yogyakarta, 1992.

——————— *Serat Pustakaraja Purwa*, Vol.I, Surakarta & Yogyakarta, 1993.

——————— *Serat Pustakaraja Purwa*, Vol.II, Surakarta &Yogyakarta, 1993.

Ronggowarsita, R. Ng., *Serat Pustakaraja Purwa*, Vol.III, Surakarta & Yogyakarta, 1993.

Rosales, G.B., and Arévalo, G., *For All the People of Asia. Federation of Asian Bishops' Conferences Documents from 1970 to 1991*, Quezon City, 1992.

Roeslan Abdul Gani, *Pengembangan Pancasila di Indonesia* (The Improvement of Pancasila in Indonesia), Jakarta, 1976.

Rulland, V., *Eight Sacred Horizons. The Religious Imagination East and West*, New York/ London, 1985.

Russel, Bertrand, *History of Western Philosophy*, London, 1991.

Rusli Karim, M., *Perjalanan Partai Politik di Indonesia. Sebuah Potret Pasang Surut*, (The Journey of Political Party in Indonesia. A Portrait of its Raising and Down), Jakarta, 1983.

Sal Murgiyanto, *Moving between Unity and Diversity: Four Indonesian Choreographers*, (Dissertation), Ann Arbor, 1991.

Satyawati Suleiman, *Pictorial Introduction to the Ancient Monuments of Indonesia*, Jakarta, 1976.

—————— *Concise Ancient History of Indonesia*, Jakarta, 1977.

Sajid, R.M., *Serat bab Ungah-Unguh, Empan Papan sarta Tetembunganipun: Prayogi Kagem Tuntunan Dhateng Para Putra-Putra* (Letter on the form of Politeness, *Empan Papan* and its Words: Good Guideline for Children), Sala, 1987.

Sastrapratedja, M., *Culture and Religion: A Study of Ibn Khaldun's Philosophy of Culture as a Framework for a Critical Assessment of Contemporary Islamic Thought in Indonesia*, (Dissertation), Rome, 1979.

Scherer, Savitri Prastiti, *Keselarasan dan Kejanggalan Pemikiran Pemikiran Priayi Nasionalis Jawa Abad 20* (*Keselarasan* and Oddness of the Thoughts of Javanese Nationalist Priayi in 20th Century), Jakarta, 1985.

_____ *Harmony and Dissonance: Early Nationalist Thought in Java,* Ithaca, 1959.

Schrieke, B., *Indonesian Sociological Studies,* The Hague, 1955.

Scott-Kenball, J., *Javanese Shadow Puppets: The Raffles Collection in the British Museum,* London, 1970.

Sedgwick, J.P., Jr., *Harmonic of History,* New York , 1985.

Sherry, P.,(ed.), *Philosophers on Religion,* London, 1987.

Sidjabat, Walter Bonar, *Religious Tolerance and the Christian Faith: A Study concerning the Concept of Divine Omnipotence in Indonesian Constitution in the Light of Islam and Christianity,* Jakarta, 1982.

Sindhunata, *Hoffen auf den Ratu Adil. Das eschatologische Motiv des "Gerechten Königs" im Bauernprotest auf Java während des 19. und zu Beginn des 20. Jahrhunderts,* (Dissertation), Hamburg, 1992.

Slamet Muljana, *Runtuhnja Keradjaan Hindu-Djawa dan Timbulnja Negara-Negara Islam di Nusantara* (The collapse of the Javanese Hindu Kingdom and the Emergence of Islamic Countries in Nusantara), Djakarta, 1968.

Snelling, J., *The Buddhist Handbook,* London, 1989.

Snyder, L., *The Meaning of Nationalism,* New Jersey, 1954.

Soebadio, Haryati, and Sarvaas, Carine A. du Marchie, (eds.), *Dynamic of Indonesian History,* Amsterdam, 1978.

Soediman Kartohadiprodjo, *Pancasila dan/dalam Undang-undang Dasar 1945* (Pancasila and/in the 1945 Constitution), Jakarta, 1976.

Soekmono, *Chandi Borobudur. A Monument of Mankind*, Paris and Assen/Amsterdam, 1976.

_____ *Pengantar Sejarah Kebudayaan Indonesia* 3 (Introduction to Indonesian History of Culture 3), Yogyakarta, 1973.

Soejono, R.P., (ed.), *Sejarah National I. Jaman Prasejarah di Indonesia* (National History I. Prehistoric Age in Indonesia), Jakarta, 1975.

Soepomo Poedjosoedarmo, *Javanese Influence on Indonesia*, Canberra, 1982.

Solichin Salam, *Sekitar Wali Sanga* (Surrounding the Nine Walis), Kudus, 1970.

Spence, Lewis, *Introduction to Mythology*, Delhi, 1990.

Sri Swami Shivananda, *The Principal Upanishads. Isa, Kena, Katha, Prasna, Mundaka, Taittiriya, Aetareya and Svetasvatara Upanishads with Text, Meaning and Commentary*, Shivanandanagar, 1983.

Steenbrink, K.A., "The Study of Comparative Religion by Indonesian Muslims", *Numen* 37 (1990), pp. 141-167.

_____ "The Rehabilitation of the Indigenous. A Survey of Recent Research on the History of Christianity in Indonesia,*Exchange* 22/3 (1993), pp. 250-263.

Steinberg, Joel. D., et al., *In Search of Southeast Asia: A Modern History*, Honolulu, 1987.

Moorgan, Stephani and Sears, Laorie Joe, *Aesthetic Tradition and Cultural Transition in Java and Bali*, Madison, 1974.

Stott, P.A., *Nature and Man in South East Asia*, London, 1978.

Sudargo Gautama and Hornick, R.N., *An Introduction to Indonesian Law: Unity and Diversity*, Jakarta, 1972.

Sudershan Chawla, Melwin Gurtov, alain Gerard Marsot, *Southeast*

233

Sudershan Chawla, Melwin Gurtov, alain Gerard Marsot, *Southeast Asia Under the New Balance of Power*, London, 1974.

Sujamto, *Reorientasi dan Revitalisasi Pandangan Hidup Jawa* (Reorientation and Revitalization of the Javanese Way of Life), Semarang, 1992.

Supomo, *Indonesia Facing Problems of New Life and Reintegration*, Jogja, 1958.

Sutherland, Heather, *The Making of a Bureaucratic Elite: The Colonial Transformation of the Javanese Priyayi*, Singapore, 1979.

Sutjipto Wirjosuparto, R.M., *A Short Cultural History of Indonesia*, Djakarta, 1954.

Sutterheim, W.F., *Studies in Indonesian Archaeology*, The Hague, 1956.

Swidler, L., *Toward a Universal Theology of Religion, Faith Meets Faith Series*, Maryknoll, 1987.

Tachibana, S., *The Ethics of Buddhism*, London, 1975.

Takakusu., J., (ed.), *A Record of the Buddhist Religion as Practised in India and the Malay Archipelago (A.D. 671-695) by I-Tsing*, Oxford, 1896.

Talamanca, Figa, *A Harmonic Analysis on Free Groups*, Dekker, 1983.

Talbi, M., "Religious Liberty: A Muslim Perspective", *Islamochristiana* 11 (1985), pp. 99-113.

Thomas Aquinas, *Summa Theologiae*, Torino, 1988.

Uhlenbeck, E.M., *Critical Survey of Studies on the Languages of Borneo*, Leiden, 1958.

—————— *Studies in Javanese Morphology*, The Hague, 1978.

—————— *Javanese Linguistic. A Restrospect and Some Prospects*, Dordrecht, 1983.

Uka Tjandrasasmita, *The Sea Trade of the Eastern Countries and the Rise of Islam in Indonesia*, London, 1969.

——— (ed.), *Sejarah National III. Jaman Pertumbuhan dan Perkembangan Kerajaan-Kerajaan Islam di Indonesia* (National History. The Periods of Growth and Development of Islamic Kingdoms in Indonesia), Jakarta, 1976.

Verdu, A., *The Philosopphy of Buddhism. A "Totalistic" Syntesis*, The Hague, 1981.

Villiers, J., *L'Asia Sud-orientale*, Milano, 1968.

Vineeth, V.F., "Dialogue and Theology of Religious Pluralism: Theological Reflections", *Journal of Dharma* 13 (1989), pp. 376-396.

Vlekke, B.H.M., *Nusantara. A History of Indonesia*, Leiden, 1959.

Walz, H., *Islam und Abendland. Toleranz und Doktrin in der Reconquista am Beispiel Chrislicher Ependichtung des 12 Jahrhunderts*, in: *Stimmen der Zeit* 202 (1984), pp. 383-391.

Wanandi, J., *Socio Political Development in Indonesia*, in: Institute of Asian affairs, (ed.), *Indonesia Seminar, Hamburg November 22-23*, Hamburg, 1977, pp. 47-71.

Watson, G., *Greek Philosophy and the Christian Notion of God*, Dublin, 1994.

Watt, W. Montgomery, *Islamic Philosophy and Theology*, Edinburgh, 1962.

——— *Islamic Political Thought*, Edinburgh, 1968.

——— *Islamic Surveys*, Edinburgh, 1970.

——— *Muhammad at Mecca*, London, 1953.

——— *Muhammad at Medina*, London, 1956.

Watt, W. Montgomery, *Muhammad, Prophet and Stateman*, London, 1961.

——————— *The Formative Period of Islamic Thought*, Edinburgh, 1973.

Weatherbee, D. E., *Ancient Indonesia and its Influence in Modern Times*, New York, 1974.

Weinstein, M.A., *Unity and Variety in the Philosophy of Samuel Alexander*, W.Lafayette, 1984.

Weizsacher, Carl Friedrich von, *The Unity of Nature*, (translated by Zucher, F. J.), New York, 1980.

Westerman, C., *Genesis 1-11*, (translated by J.J. Scullion), London, 1984.

Whyte, Landlot L., *The Unitary Principle in Physics and Biology*, London, 1949.

Wilber Ken, *No Boundary: Eastern and Western Approaches to Personal Growth*, Boulder and London, 1981.

Wilczek, F., *Longing for Harmonies*, Norton, 1988.

Windyatmadja, J.P., *A Spirituality of Liberation: An Indonesian Contribution*, in: Fabella, V., Lee, P.K.H., Kang-sun Suh, D., *Asian Spirituality. Reclaiming Traditions*, Maryknoll, 1992.

Winternitz, M., A History of Indian Literature, Calcutta, 1927.

Wiratmo Soekito, "Pancasila as a Cultural Philosophy", *The Indonesian Quarterly* XV, No. 4 (1987), pp. 568-577.

Wolf, Charles, Jr., *The Indonesian Story - the Birth, Growth, and Structure of the Indonesian Republic*, New York, 1948.

Wolter, O.W., *Early Indonesian Commerce: A Study of the Origin of Srivijaya*, Ithaca, 1967.

Woodman, Dorothy, *The Republic of Indonesia*, New York, 1955.

236

Zaehner, R. C., *Hindu Scriptures*, London, 1992.

——————— *Hinduism*, Oxford, 1992.

——————— *The Bhagavad Gītā*, Oxford, 1973.

Zecca, Adriano, *Indonesia, Java Bali Sumatra Nias Siberut Sulawesi Lombok Sumbawa Komodo,* Milano, 1976.

Ziemek, Manfred , *Pesantren dalam Perubahan Sosial (Pesantren Islamische Bildung in Sozialem Wandel)*, Frankfurt, 1983.

III. DICTIONARIES AND ENCYCLOPEDIAS

AAVV, *Enciclopedia Filosofica*, 8 vols., Firenze, 1982.

Compagni, F., Piana, G., Privitera, S., *Nuovo Dizionario di Teologia Morale*, Milano, 1990.

Edwards, P., *The Encyclopedia of Philosophy*, 8 vols., New York, 1967.

Ernout, A. - Meillet, A., *Dictionnaire Etymologique de la Langue Latine*, Paris, Klinsick, 1954.

Glassé, Cyril, *The Concise Encyclopedia of Islam*, London, 1991.

Stutley, James and Stutley Margaret, *A Dictionary of Hinduism. Its Mythology, Folklore and Development 1500 B.C. - A.D. 1500*, London, 1985.

Sutarno, R., A.K., *Ensiklopedia Wayang* (Encyclopedia of *Wayang*), (3rd Edition), Semarang, 1992.

Wehr, H., *A Dictionary of Modern Written Arabic*, (edited by J. Milton Cowan), Wiesbaden, 1979.

Zoetmulder, P.J., *Old Javanese - English Dictionary*, 2 vols., s'-Gravenhage, 1982.

Riproduzione anastatica: 15 novembre 1996
Tipografia Poliglotta della Pontificia Università Gregoriana
Piazza della Pilotta, 4 – 00187 Roma

From the same publisher

AA.VV.: *Human Rights and Religions*. (Studia Missionalia, 39).
pp. VIII-460. Lit. 70.000

AA.VV.: *Women and Religions*. (Studia Missionalia, 40).
pp. VIII-368. Lit. 70.000

AA.VV.: *Religious sects and movements*. (Studia Missionalia, 41).
pp. VIII-392. Lit. 70.000

AA.VV.: *Theology of Religions*. (Studia Missionalia, 42).
pp. VIII-396. Lit. 70.000

AA.VV.: *Interfaith Dialogue*. (Studia Missionalia, 43).
pp. X-366. Lit. 70.000

AA.VV.: *Inculturation. Gospel and Culture*. (Studia Missionalia, 44).
pp. VI-390. Lit. 70.000

AA.VV.: *Local Theologies*. (Studia Missionalia, 45).
pp. VIII-400. Lit. 70.000

BRODEUR, Scott: *The Holy Spirit's Agency in the Resurrection of the Dead. An Exegetico-Theological Study of 1 Corinthians 15,44b-49 and Romans 8,9-13*. (Tesi Gregoriana, Serie Teologia, 14).
pp. 300. Lit. 30.000

CONN, James J.: *Catholic Universities in the United States and Ecclesiastical Authority*. (Analecta Gregoriana, 259).
pp. XVI-348. Lit. 45.000

D'SOUZA, Rudolf V.: *The Bhagavadgītā and St. John of the Cross. A Comparative Study of the Dynamism of Spiritual Growth in the Process of God-Realisation*. (Tesi Gregoriana, Serie Spiritualità, 1).
pp. 484. Lit. 46.000

GIBBS, Philip: *The Word in the Third World. Divine Revelation in the Theology of Jean-Marc Éla, Aloysius Pieris and Gustavo Gutiérrez.* (Tesi Gregoriana, Serie Teologia, 8).
pp. 448.   Lit. 42.000

GWYNNE, Paul: *Special Divine Action. Key Issues in the Contemporary Debate (1965-1995).* (Tesi Gregoriana, Serie Teologia, 12).
pp. 376.   Lit. 39.000

HARTEL, Joseph F.: *Femina ut Imago Dei. In the Integral Feminism of St. Thomas Aquinas.* (Analecta Gregoriana, 260).
pp. XVI-356.   Lit. 45.000

HENNESSY, Anne: *The Galilee of Jesus.*
pp. X-78.   Lit. 15.000

IMODA, Franco: *The Spiritual Exercises and Psychology. The breadth and lenght and height and depth (Eph. 3,18).*
pp. 88.   Lit. 11.000

KIZHAKKEPARAMPIL, Isaac: *The Invocation of the Holy Spirit as Constitutive of the Sacraments according to Cardinal Yves Congar.* (Tesi Gregoriana, Serie Teologia, 5).
pp. 200.   Lit. 21.000

MALPAN, Varghese: *A Comparative Study of the Bhagavad-Gītā and the Spiritual Exercises of Saint Ignatius of Loyola on the Process of Spiritual Liberation.* (Documenta Missionalia, 22).
pp. 444.   Lit. 48.500

MCDERMOTT, John M. (editor): *The thought of Pope John Paul II. A Collection of Essays and Studies.*
pp. XXIV-244.   Lit. 24.000

MONIZ, John: *"Liberated Society". Gandhian and Christian Vision. Comparative Study.* (Documenta Missionalia, 23).
pp. 544.   Lit. 56.000

MROSO, Agapit J.: *The Church in Africa and the New Evangelisation. A Theologico-Pastoral Study of the Orientations of John Paul II.* (Tesi Gregoriana, Serie Teologia, 6).
pp. 456.   Lit. 42.000

NANGELIMALIL, Jacob: *The Relationship between the Eucharistic Liturgy, the Interior Life and the Social Witness of the Church according to Joseph Cardinal Parecattil.* (Tesi Gregoriana, Serie Teologia, 7).
pp. 224.   Lit. 23.000

PALAKEEL, Joseph: *The Use of Analogy in Theological Discourse. An Investigation in Ecumenical Perspective.* (Tesi Gregoriana, Serie Teologia, 4).
pp. 392.   Lit. 39.000

PONNUMUTHAN, Selvister: *The Spirituality of Basic Ecclesial Communities in the Socio-Religious Context of Trivandrum/Keral, India.* (Tesi Gregoriana, Serie Spiritualità, 2).
pp. 358.   Lit. 35.000

RUESSMANN, Madeleine: *Exclaustration. Its nature and use according to current law.* (Tesi Gregoriana, Serie Diritto Canonico, 1).
pp. 550.   Lit. 52.000

RULLA, L. M. - IMODA, F. - RIDICK, J.: *Psychological structure and vocation.* Introductory overview by R. CHAMPOUX S.J. 3ª ristampa.
pp. XII-258.   Lit. 24.000

VAN ROO, William A.: *The Christian Sacrament.* (Analecta Gregoriana, 262).
pp. VIII-196.   Lit. 25.000

Orders and payments to:

AMMINISTRAZIONE PUBBLICAZIONI PUG/PIB

Piazza della Pilotta, 35 – 00187 Roma – Italia
Tel. 06/678.15.67 – Fax 06/678.05.88 – Conto Corrente Postale n. 34903005
Monte dei Paschi di Siena – Sede di Roma – c/c n. 54795.37